Medieval Empires and the Culture of Competition

Medieval Empires and the Culture of Competition

Literary Duels at Islamic and Christian Courts

Samuel England

EDINBURGH
University Press

For Rachel,
whose voice I missed while I wrote on my own,
and whose companionship makes everything worthwhile.

Edinburgh University Press is one of the leading university presses in the UK. We publish academic books and journals in our selected subject areas across the humanities and social sciences, combining cutting-edge scholarship with high editorial and production values to produce academic works of lasting importance. For more information visit our website: edinburghuniversitypress.com

Edinburgh University Press Ltd
The Tun – Holyrood Road
12 (2f) Jackson's Entry
Edinburgh EH8 8PJ

Typeset in 11/15 Adobe Garamond by
Servis Filmsetting Ltd, Stockport, Cheshire

A CIP record for this book is available from the British Library

ISBN 978 1 4744 2522 3 (hardback)
ISBN 978 1 4744 2524 7 (webready PDF)
ISBN 978 1 4744 2525 4 (epub)

Contents

Acknowledgements and Note on Arabic Transliterations vi

List of Abbreviations ix

Introduction: Courtly Gifts, Imperial Rewards 1

1 'Baghdad is to Cities What the Master is to Mankind': The Rise of Vizier Culture 24

2 The Sovereign and the Foreign: Creating Saladin in Arabic Literature of the Counter-Crusade 67

3 Alfonso X: Poetry of Miracles and Domination 105

4 *Saladino Rinato*: Spanish and Italian Courtly Fictions of Crusade 141

Conclusion: The Ministry of Culture 177

Bibliography 188

Index 225

Acknowledgements and Note on Arabic Transliterations

I hope that I am more collaboratively minded than competitive, even though my book's topic has seized my interest for years now. Perhaps I can do justice here to the debt I feel to my collaborators. Most of all, I am grateful to loved ones, whom I often roped in to playing the collaborative role, regardless of whether or not they were fellow scholars.

For their endless support, I thank several generations of Englands, and brother and sisters of many family names but one family. I especially appreciate my parents Liz, Terry, and Barbara. Whatever I may need or want – even as a sometimes-grouchy adult writing a book rather than the plaintive kid they'd shepherded along in past decades – they continually provided it. I have found in the Korniks a new family of deep generosity, a home full of impromptu music sessions and mind-boggling spreads of Middle Eastern food. Amy, Misha, Mitch, and Sarah, I'm looking forward to many more chances to say *l'chaim*, *ṣaḥtayn* and *na zdrovie* with you.

Wonderful friends and interlocutors helped me along the way, including Kareem Abu-Zeid, Michael Allan, Motaz Attalla, Rachel Bernard, Axel Berny, Tien Berny, Matt Borman, Paco Brito, Juan Caballero, Ryan Calder, Emily Drumsta, Rachel Friedman, Katherine Halls, Sharif Idris, Liz Idris, Seth Kimmel, Margaret Larkin, Robin Mittenthal, Daniella Molle, Donaldo Osorio, Jesús Rodríguez Velasco, Rania Salem, Anat Shenker-Osorio, Adam Talib, Levi Thompson, Laura Wagner, and Toby Warner. Nicholas Baer welcomed me twice to Berlin, where I came in search of manuscripts and good company. I find myself constantly wishing I would do a better job on the former, but he could not possibly have offered more of the latter.

Also deserving thanks for supporting that research travel in Germany, as well as in Spain, Italy, Egypt, and throughout North America, are the African Studies Program and the Graduate School of the University of Wisconsin–Madison, the Andrew W. Mellon Mediterranean Regional Research Fellowship provided by the Council of American Overseas Research Centers and the American Academic Research Institute in Iraq (TAARII).

When I was an undergraduate, I saw a documentary about one of the most fascinating Arab writers I have encountered, Emile Habibi. Its title was taken from Habibi's gravestone, which reads *Bāqin fī ḥayfā*: 'One who remains in Haifa', a city with which the author had an emotional, sometimes painful relationship. The documentary's Hebrew title changes the expression slightly, to 'I stayed in Haifa.' I doubt it sounds as meaningful to say, 'I came back to Madison,' but coming back was the best thing that could have happened to me, 34 years after I left the city as an infant. The University of Wisconsin–Madison has welcomed me from my first day teaching. At the same time, it has weathered incredible political and economic attacks, in sharp contrast to the thoughtful graciousness of the university community itself. Thanks to Lisa Cooper, Ivy Corfis, Dustin Cowell, Jim Delehanty, Jo Ellen Fair, Victor Goldgel Carballo, Chris Kleinhenz, Tejumola Olaniyan, Aliko Songolo, Katrina Daly Thompson, Sarah Wells, and many more colleagues on our campus who deserve acclaim. Edinburgh University Press is another organisation of the highest-calibre people. I owe special gratitude to Nicola Ramsey, who has been tremendously supportive in all phases of editing and production. The fabulous artwork of Wael Shawky on the book cover was another act of generosity. My thanks to him and Lisson Gallery.

Never mentioned in this study, but woven into it nonetheless, is a fond remembrance of Tom Dodd, one of my first writing teachers. For decades he published captivating oral histories of our home state of Michigan, and kept hundreds of us students and friends updated on contemporary life around Ypsilanti. Once, he inscribed a book to me, predicting that I'd be sending him my own volume soon. I'm sorry I was too late to get it to him. Tom's uniquely literary, witty friendship stays with me. So does the Great Lakes lore he wrote with extraordinary care for his subject. I hope I have lived up to that standard, but of course all errors in this book are mine.

Note on Arabic Transliterations

This book uses a modified system of the *International Journal of Middle Eastern Studies* transliteration style, except in cases of Arabic words and names commonly used in English, such as Basra, the Caliph Ali, jihad, the Prophet Muhammad, and Qur'an.

Abbreviations

AW = Al-Tawḥīdī, Abū Ḥayyān. *Akhlāq al-wazīrayn.* Ed. Muḥammad bin Tāwīt al-Ṭanjī.

CEM = the lyric poems *Cantigas d'escarnho e de mal dizer.* Citations of the original texts are from *Cantigas d'escarnho e de mal dizer dos cancioneiros medievais galego-portugueses.* Ed. Manuel Rodrigues Lapa. Individual *cantigas* cited by the number Lapa assigns them.

CSM = Alfonso X el Sabio's lyric poems *Cantigas de Santa María.* Citations of the original texts are from *Cantigas de Santa María.* Ed. Walter Mettmann. Individual *cantigas* cited by the letter or number Mettmann assigns them.

DSIA = Ibn ᶜAbbād al-Ṭālqānī, Abū l-Qāsim Ismāᶜīl ('Al-Ṣāḥib'). *Dīwān al-ṣāḥib ibn ᶜabbād.* Ed. Muḥammad Ḥasan Āl Yāsīn.

EAL = Meisami, Julie Scott and Paul Starkey, eds. *Encyclopedia of Arabic Literature.*

EI2 = Bearman, P. J., et al. eds. *Encyclopaedia of Islam, Second Edition.*

MU = Al-Rūmī, Yāqūt al-Ḥamawī ('Yāqūt'). *Muᶜjam al-udabā': irshād al-arīb.* Ed. Iḥsān ᶜAbbās.

OIM = Ibn Munqidh, Usāma. *Ousâma ibn Mounḳidh, un émir syrien au premier siècle des croisades (1095–1188).* Ed. Hartwig Derenbourg.

TU = Miskawayh, Abū ᶜAlī. *Tajārib al-umam wa-taᶜāqub al-himam.* Ed. Sayyid Kasrawī Ḥasan.

YDQ = al-Thaᶜālibī, Abū Manṣūr ᶜAbd al-Malik. *Yatīmat al-dahr.* Ed. Mufīd Muḥammad Qumayḥa.

Introduction: Courtly Gifts, Imperial Rewards

Contests at court were also tests of the court itself. In the thirteenth century, King Alfonso X of Spain (1221–84 CE, r. 1252–84) recognised this predicament, and his own responsibility as a ruler to provide a model for nobles' courts throughout the empire by carefully governing the competitions held before the throne. As his witty subjects faced off against one another, he legislated the poetic language that they used. His Spanish laws insist that a well-run empire needs to impose clear rules on the troubadours, comedians, and chroniclers vying with one another for patronage. Poets and other skilled noblemen exchanging jokes possess what he terms *grant bienestancia*, a 'great gift' that magnifies the kingdom's image. Eloquent troubadours represent the highest class of composers, those best equipped to win the distinction of *palanciano*: literally, those with access to the royal palace that, Alfonso's laws explain, is a distinction exclusive to knights. In medieval Spain, performing well in poetic games effectively meant to serve the empire against its enemies. But if poets were to allow their slanderous desires to overpower their sense of decorum, the wordplay would become injurious, signalling their insufficient fealty to their kingdom. The court would then need to identify the crime of *enfamar* (defamation) and execute its penal responsibilities; even in poetic form, slander could be the articulation of dissent, tearing at the court's cohesiveness.[1,2] Alfonso knew all too well the difficulties in holding together a troubled court. He was deeply frustrated, both by the Muslim empire of Granada and by his insubordinate knights who were supposed to be fighting for control of southern Iberia. Just as crucially, he also determined that he may profit by supporting poetic exchanges among his subjects, overseeing them, and in fact taking active part in the contentious games. Assembling the laws that would govern Spaniards' speech and behaviour for centuries, he simultaneously engaged his subjects as an intimidating poetic interlocutor. He strove to channel the energy of troubadours' contests towards the goal of glorifying his own imperial projects. Over his years of rule, Alfonso meditated at length on how to effectively govern his embattled kingdom with the aid of a vigorous poetic court. Despite all his efforts, however, his introspective writings from late in life suggest that this remained an open, nagging question for him. As a critical and historiographic concern, it animates the study that follows.

This book is about the social, material, and political role of court literature in the Middle East and Mediterranean. Wrestling with major political disruptions from 950 to 1350 CE, Islamic and Christian imperial courts sought to hold themselves together by stoking the competitive ethos among their poets, secretaries, and writers of didactic prose. Monarchs and high administrators cultivated an environment of charged but orderly literary contest, and also sponsored literature centred on themes of competition. They sought to reassure their empires' elite population that a stable court system continued to rule with authority. At the sites of great martial and diplomatic tension – ʿAbbāsid Iraq and its provinces; the Levant under Saladin; and Spain and Italy in the latter Crusades – literary contests became indispensable tools for royal governments. The Arabic, Spanish, Portuguese, and Italian texts produced at these courts suggested to imperial citizens that the high court had a lasting hold on power, that it was capable of enticing the most prestigious artists into duelling, and that the rewards that it offered still held high value. As a cumulative effect, the rituals insisted to the audience that their own polity was unquestionably superior to those it encountered in diplomacy, war, travel literature, and official correspondence. Politically elite patrons undertook such efforts precisely because the large-scale conflicts with which they struggled were chaotic, enervating, and oftentimes resistant to their control. Infighting among rival regimes and, at the geopolitical level, regional wars between empires destabilised courts, stimulating patrons to promote competition in a wide variety of forms: poetic contests encompassing praise and invective, contentious chancery writing between officials, and chivalric narrative works. Whereas tests of wit in previous centuries had chiefly magnified individual poets, their patrons, and tribes, during the tumultuous last four hundred years of the Middle Ages the competitive project shifted towards broader themes: political institutions and inter-imperial relationships.

Late medieval courts tended to produce self-congratulatory literature that confirmed the prestige of the court. This show of power sought to compensate for deep imperial anxieties. During those moments when they were acutely pressed to hold together a troubled empire, they reasoned that the performance of a competitive poetics would serve their political goals. And, I will argue, the strategy generally worked – not because of the soundness of their policies so much as the ideological efficacy of their literature. The vizierial court of Isfahan provides a telling example. During the tenth and eleventh centuries, it was contested by the Būyid princes and governors who, at that time, controlled the ᶜAbbāsid Empire. At the centre of courtly tensions was al-Ṣāḥib ibn ᶜAbbād (326–85 H, 938–95 CE), a secretary born near Isfahan who became the foremost vizier of his generation.[3] An accomplished poet as well as a highly regarded chancery prose writer, he dominated the court with his patronage, his reputation for deep linguistic knowledge, and his willingness to use aggressive defamatory verse with his courtiers. He had many adversaries, some of them powerful. To the peripatetic, cunning vizier, Isfahan was both a home city and the ideal base to which he consistently returned from his postings in other regions of Iran and around the imperial centre in Iraq. Ibn ᶜAbbād's rise to power coincided with a period of unprecedented fortification of the city, which was part of the Būyids' physical and military acknowledgement of the eastward direction in which they were moving major ᶜAbbāsid cultural centres. Isfahan provided him a safe haven when a fellow vizier planned to kill him in the city of Ray, and when Ibn ᶜAbbād gained the opportunity for revenge, he travelled back to Isfahan to take part in the counter-conspiracy (MU 4:267, AW 535). Over his career, he honoured Isfahan in the belles-lettres he wrote and commissioned. He also oversaw its robust fortification so that it may anchor the eastern ᶜAbbāsid provinces, and he built a grand mosque and palace in the city centre. Upon finishing the palace, he invited poets to celebrate his architectural legacy and his stewardship of the city. The event became anthologised as *Jary al-shuᶜarā' bi-ḥaḍrat al-Ṣāḥib fī maydān iqtirāḥih al-diyārāt* ('Poets competing at the Ṣāḥib's court, per his request for mansion-themed poems'). His long-time courtier Abū Bakr al-Khwārizmī hails the vizier's reputation as an intimidator.

بنيت الدار عالية كمثل بنائك الشّرفا
فلا زالت رؤوس عداك فى حيطانها شرفا

You have built the house tall to match your towering stature –
– May the heads of your enemies always top the walls around it!

Another poet, Abū ᶜAbbās al-Ḍabbī, strives to win his patron's approval by emphasising the cultural primacy of the house, where Ibn ᶜAbbād hosted Isfahan's major courtly gatherings:

دار الوزارة ممدود سرادقها ولا حق بذرى الجوزاء لاحقها...
فمن مجالس يخلفن الطواوس قد أبرزن في حلل شاقت شقائقها

The roof atop the vizierate truly soars! Not even the highest star of Gemini could hope to attain its height …
Trailing behind (the house's) courtly assembly are peacocks in gowns so brilliant, they're the envy of all their peers.[4]

The house and the city in which that house was built are politically contested spaces for Ibn ᶜAbbād. Having established a physical space with a grand interior where courtly activities are to take place, he makes the first such activity a convivial but nonetheless charged gathering of poets. Al-Khwārizmī offers the court a macabre embellishment on the house's fortified exterior, conceptually linking the house to the vizier's military authority in Isfahan – and, we may conjecture, positioning Ibn ᶜAbbād's rival vizier among the beheaded. Al-Ḍabbī's peacock imagery praises the court itself, its peacocks being the retinue of patron and courtier alike. The impaled enemies look out upon the militarised, putatively violent region that Ibn ᶜAbbād sought to master. His strutting courtiers engage in self-regard within their physical and cultural walls. Despite their shared implicit knowledge that their patron may reward one of them as superior, on this occasion al-Khwārizmī, al-Ḍabbī, and their assembled fellow poets were only nominally at odds with one another. Working in a poetic dialogue, they fashioned the vizier into the city's overseer of beauty, security, and violence for the cause of good.

Ibn ᶜAbbād's poets anticipate the unspoken goal of late medieval competition. By using contest as an organising principle for literature, courts developed the necessary conceptual tools to situate themselves and their kingdoms vis-à-vis those around them. Ultimately, that process would allow discrete Islamic and Christian empires to perceive each other as courtly interlocutors. In the Classical Arabic tradition, ʿAbbāsid idioms, rituals, and genres circulated throughout Muslim societies, as far away as Iberia. In the Levant during the Second and Third Crusades (1145–92), Saladin's court employed those ʿAbbāsid models as a means of strengthening itself during a period of extraordinary political challenge. While poets and scribes looked to Saladin as a unifying figure and a restorer of an era of the sultanate's high authority, they also sought out ʿAbbāsid instruments of courtly language in order to articulate their own place in the world. Poets' contests such as those we have seen in Isfahan, as well as ʿAbbāsid-style written debate and the confrontational discourse of chancery prose, served not just an ideological but also an orienting function for the literary counter-crusade. While one empire crumbled in Iraq, its neighbours to the west tapped its venerable authority and repurposed its rich set of traditions for both intellectual and strategic gains.

Competition gave a sense of order – both temporal and spatial – that enhanced the court's oftentimes coercive power over its subjects: temporal, in the numerous turns taken by poets or chancery correspondence seeking to outdo one another with each new composition; and spatial in the authors' (and sometimes reciters') physical postures, as well as their evocations of the courtly interior and the imperial exterior with poetic language. Finally, their work with space allowed the courtiers to conceive of the imperial landscape, in which their own empire claimed the highest position. '[T]he core ideology of any medieval corporate body,' Charles Burroughs argues, '… involved the restitution of unity and harmony when disturbed or damaged through actions often construed as unnatural because they seemed injurious to a divinely ordained state of the world' (Hanawalt and Kobialka eds 66). To hold together the court institution was to state and restate a much larger claim of the court, namely: its subjects belonged to the one desirable polity, whose success was guaranteed by God.

Alfonso recognised this structural aspect of competition in his own kingdom, and in fact marshalled it for the express purpose of asserting Spain's superiority over Islamic empires from the Levant to Gibraltar. In Spain and Italy, and especially in his own family line, kings had long hosted artistic bouts between troubadour knights, but Alfonso changed the image of the sovereign vis-à-vis the court's artistic contenders. Struggling to expand upon the territorial gains of his immediate predecessors against Muslim armies, he saw the utility of becoming an aggressive, humourous, and crusading troubadour himself. As a result, he created a dialectical image of the king at court, and used poetic language to advance his agenda for conquest. Stylistic, legal notions of *bienestancia* and *enfamar* were no longer separable from the sovereign's conduct of war and diplomacy with rival empires. In the case of thirteenth-century Spain, 'rival empires' primarily meant Muslim entities around Gibraltar and the Holy Land. At the end of his rule, Alfonso's courtiers seized upon his notion of crusading royal wordplay and used it to narrate Christian–Islamic imperial relations. I conclude this study by examining Alfonso's legacy as it was elaborated in the generation following him. His definition of the sovereign as a wit, debater, and imperial combatant enabled prose authors of his court to provide a new account of empire. Their fables of troubadours and knights incorporated Saladin, who challenged his European counterparts in courtly games, mapping out a new geopolitical space. What began as documented contests between the Spanish king and his troubadours became a fictionalised kind of wordplay, providing a long-term account of Mediterranean empires and how they related to one another. For Classical Arabic courts and their Spanish and Italian counterparts, competition went from being a mode of poetic practice to a hermeneutic, a means of understanding and narrating imperial history at the end of the Middle Ages.

The narration of history is also the modern methodological problem that this book seeks to address. Competition opens up new avenues for comparisons between empires, and this is what makes it such a useful central idea for the study of the premodern era. Its capacity and utility, however, also underscore our ongoing challenge as medievalists working to establish a suitable comparative language. From a modern critical perspective, the problem with courts is that they tended to represent themselves as singular, authoritative refineries of culture, even though their own membership was diverse and often recalcitrant. Comparative scholars working on Islamic and Christian empires have generally responded to this tension by either celebrating that diversity as multicultural or by focusing on the courts' representation of self and other. As a result, we have a critical corpus deeply interested in medieval identity categories, whether the goal is to show their plural coexistence in the formation of communities or to detail how each category was separated in courtly thought. One of the key disciplinary goals of this book is to shift away from identity as an ethnic or religious question, laden as it is with stubbornly modern notions of the self. While there is no doubt that medieval courtiers devoted much effort to dividing and labelling the constituents of their empires as well as foreign interlocutors, I argue that their most pressing concern was to stabilise the position of their respective courts. That political project framed their subsidiary efforts to categorise and represent people across empires.

As academic trends, multiculturalism and the study of othering have a contrapuntal relationship. They take political routes that could scarcely be more different from each other. The multicultural model is not fully comfortable with the court's hegemonic power, while the self/other approach is fixated on power relationships. What they have in common is that both emerge from theory and historiography dating from the latter half of the twentieth century: in many respects, their respective explorations of medieval history are academic responses to the political predicament of late modernity. In the case of multiculturalism, it is telling that two of its foundational thinkers, Shelomo Goitein and Américo Castro, wrote from positions of exile during the Second World War and its aftermath. They linked (even if inadvertently) plurality and nostalgia as the organising principles of their Mediterranean historiography. As people in the Middle East and Europe navigated postwar nationalism, postcolonial independence, and the durable legacy of fascism, multiculturalists looked for premodern examples of cultural diversity to research and ultimately valorise.

Castro's famous promulgation of the term '*convivencia*' to describe Iberian culture, often translated as 'coexistence' but literally meaning 'living-together', has provided the basis for subsequent waves of multiculturalist thinkers into the twenty-first century.[5] They now apply it far beyond al-Andalus or pre-Inquisition Spain. The term has become a means of understanding Mediterranean societies and a signifier of social relationships that could in theory occur anywhere political conditions allow for it. For historian Thomas Glick, 'Convivencia ... must encompass the ability of persons of different groups to step out of their ethnically-bound roles, in order to interact on a par with members of competing groups' (Mann, et al. eds, *Convivencia* 2). A decade later, in a book that openly acknowledges its painful coincidence with the events of 11 September 2001, Maria Rosa Menocal urgently attempted to reenergise multicultural thought, moving from Glick's role-changing model to cultural dialectic. '[M]edieval culture positively thrived on holding at least two, and often many more, contrary ideas at the same time' (*Ornament* 11). The thesis has come to represent a touchstone of Mediterranean Studies, since the book has broadly appealed to both academic readers and popular audiences. In Menocal's view, the lasting, concrete expression of this medieval capacity of thought is the court itself. Referring most notably to al-Andalus but simultaneously to a broader region that stretched from Iberia to southern France and much of Italy, Menocal uses the phrase 'a first-rate place' to denote an idealised zone where diverse, mostly urban courts anchored a more widespread cultural efflorescence. Multiculturalism in Medieval Studies, then, has come to privilege certain Mediterranean literary communities in which Muslim, Christian, and Jewish courtiers exchanged texts in a variety of languages. The image of a capacious, dialectical court has proven so compelling to this school of thought that its proponents call for expanding Menocal's reading across the entire Mediterranean region and the Middle East.[6]

The multicultural label of the courtly dialectic represents a crucial, if often unacknowledged, distinction from the binary structure of self/other discourse. When medievalists explore the possibility of othering in medieval thought, even if their intent is to establish distance from modern critical paradigms, they necessarily confront the legacy of Edward Said and the Subaltern Studies movement that followed his intervention in modern imperial knowledge. Insisting that 'the binary opposition of East and West, fundamental to Said's theory, cannot be projected back onto a Middle Ages which seldom conceived the world as bipartite',[7] Suzanne Conklin Akbari responds to a long series of studies that have attempted that very projection – including works that directly attack Said's political position as a critic of modern Orientalism. Said's binary, and for that matter the conceptual parts of alterity and especially the subaltern, requires a political scenario in which one subject seeks to master a foreign interlocutor. It is rigidly tied to colonialism and is, I would argue, resistant to critics' attempts to apply it to the Middle Ages. When the courts of Islamic- and Christian-ruled empires devoted effort to represent foreigners, they did so in a manner distinct from the mode assumed by late-modern readers. Akbari's point is not just accurate but necessary, for studies in recent decades have become ensnared in anachronistic references to a cultural dualism. Some do so more casually than others, and their views differ on Orientalism's history and politics, but they have in common a tacit acceptance of the East–West model of medieval identity and power relations.[8]

If critics of Orientalism focus on representation in modern empire, and the Subaltern Studies school questions how a postcolonial subject is represented, then we must ask how profitable it is to use them as entryways to the Middle Ages. These critical vocabularies of identity formation via self and other are, at their root, tied to modern notions of knowledge, subjectivity, and political power. The Foucauldian basis for Said's critique of Orientalism – largely intact through the decades of studies in dialogue with Said, including Subaltern Studies – not only theorises power, but also historicises how the self has been defined in discrete eras. Unless one wishes to reverse that historicist move, or separate contemporary discourse on power from Foucault's theory, then it is very difficult to see a firm basis for a premodern self/other binary, despite its popularity. For this reason, and due to the historical evidence suggesting that medieval binary discourse only began in the fourteenth century, the critical framework of representation will require much more calibration than it has thus far received in order to become more directly useful to medieval historicist research.[9] Sharon Kinoshita points out 'that to lose sight of the specificity of the Middle Ages is to lose sight of the specificity of Modernity as well. Delinking the study of medieval texts from the nineteenth-century obsession with nationalism and colonial expansion makes visible aspects of the premodern' (Wilson and Connery eds 89). At a more metacritical level, we may argue for the same delinking between medieval texts and twentieth-century accounts of the postcolonial modern era.

Although the courts examined in this book indeed produced images of foreigners, their primary concern was not the difference between a unitary version of their own ideal subject and the Other. They instead fixated on the ideal courtly subject and those of questionable credentials seeking admission to the court. Such interlocutors may be from far-off lands and may even subscribe to a non-hegemonic religion, but the more important question was whether they qualified for a position through their morals, comportment, and, most importantly here, their eloquence. The specific question of whether someone belonged to a particular empire was subordinate to the question of whether that person deserved to belong to a court. Usāma ibn Munqidh, one of Saladin's foremost knights and literary commentators, writes of an Arabic-speaking European crusader offering dinner to a Muslim warrior in Antioch:

مائدة حسنة وطعاماً في غاية النظافة والجودة

– that is, 'a very fine table, with food that was extremely clean and delicious,' cooked by an Egyptian servant and appetising enough for the Muslim knightly class. Above all, however, what astounds the unnamed Muslim, and Usāma as he relates the story, is that the crusader protects his guest from a European would-be attacker in the marketplace, using the Latinate word *burjāsī* (burgess, that is, merchant) to disguise the Muslim's identity.[10] It is unimportant whether this hospitable crusader knows the finer points of Islamic belief. Instead, what makes him compelling to Usāma is that he can move between the well-regulated courtliness of the meal to the dangerous unpredictability of the marketplace, and from the veracity of conversation between two peers to the deceptive language he employs to calm the potentially violent scene. His understanding of language allows him to figuratively move his Muslim interlocutor, placing him for a moment in a civilian position outside the world of courts and cavalry. By mastering those divisions, he shuttles freely around empires in conflict. Although it may be tempting to amplify a Muslim/Christian binary here, according to Usāma it is the crusader's multiplicity of roles that demand attention, as well as his ability to cross over from courtly hospitality and discourse to foreign, deceptive speech in a public setting. He is not simply the Other but instead several kinds of individuals, both one who is familiar to courtly Muslims and one who mediates between a Muslim and the violent world of Christian Antioch.

It is not my intention to cast off every element of the two dominant approaches to comparative Medieval Studies. Using competition as the organising principle of reading is a means by which to draw from the remarkable critical energy of post-Said discourse around Orientalism, while providing a new frame for the dialectic so prized by multiculturalists. As this book turns from ᶜAbbāsid poetics and chancery to Saladin's counter-crusade, then to the struggle for courtly authority in Castile, and finally to Spanish and Italian narratives of contention, I will insist that the most important imperial literature derived its power from the same dialectical structures that *produced* policy. Similarly to the intellectual work of legislation and administration, the poetic and narrative arts took shape in the words of courtly speakers, that is, in discourses between leaders, bureaucrats, and courtiers. Medievalists by and large agree that it is anachronistic to try to neatly divide the medieval scriptorium according to our modern distinctions between fiction and non-fiction, or between aesthetic composition and utilitarian text-making. We must also acknowledge that imaginative literature and legislation similarly resist such a division. To compose literature for a court was to conceptually align the past with the present, to provide useful explanations for the moment in which courtiers were living. In many cases, too, a poetic or prose-narrative account of past events meant leading the audience to adopt the court's perspective on history. In that view, the court maintained control of its subjects even through the vagaries of long-term imperial change (Ali, *Arabic Literary Salons* 57–65; Stanesco, *Jeux d'errance* 5–15). A common epistemological and political feature unites distinctly different courts from Islamic societies to Mediterranean Christendom: the literature of contest drew attention to the binding nature of decisions made at court. By recruiting authors to perform or compose the competitive ethos, a patron could attempt to secure the machinery of legislation and administration.

Paradigms in Literary History

Critical to Arabic language arts from their beginnings, the competition ritual became explicitly tied to empire as the caliphate settled in Damascus during the first century Hijra, seventh century CE. Throughout the transition from a pagan, largely Bedouin society to the establishment of urban Islamic leadership in Arabia and then the Umayyad Empire in Syria, the major poetic standard in which premier artists contended was the *qaṣīda*, or long-form ode. What had been the format for self-praise and promotion of one's tribe evolved into a dependable means of promoting individual officials in the caliphate. More importantly, it confirmed the caliphate's legitimacy in a larger Islamic political narrative. The *qaṣīda*'s distinguishing feature under the Umayyads in Syria was its panegyric type, which the ᶜAbbāsids in Iraq later adopted and expanded. Agonistic art – the versification of insults between poets that could appear in *qaṣīdas* or in compositions as short as one line – was secondary but still of unquestionable import. Like the panegyric, invective's usefulness in pre-Islamic artistic rituals was clear to the courtly population of the emerging empires. It blossomed both as a mode of poetic speech and as a social spectacle. Not only could it provide stimulating contrasts in a *qaṣīda* dedicated to praise – the patron rose in stature as the poem ridiculed or scorned his putative adversaries – it also anchored entire works and elicited extraordinary protracted exchanges between two people. Major Umayyad poets specialised in invective, known as *hijā'*. Indeed, in some cases they seem to have depended upon each other to stoke the rivalry and excite audiences. The officials convening courts had mixed views of *hijā'*. Its popularity was obvious, but it was frequently turned against the patron himself, especially during disputes over payment. It is for that reason that we find accounts of patrons keeping famous satirists on their payroll prophylactically, the better to keep them content and therefore incentivised not to attack. And although Umayyad poets attacked patrons, their best-known *hijā'* focused on each other.[11]

In the first century of Islamic life, this set a precedent from which subsequent courts seem to have derived a crucial lesson. Because patrons had more to lose from embarrassing characterisations in verse than poets did, they inevitably benefited when *hijā'* became a battle among literary peers. The agonistics, eloquence, humour, and social interaction of such performances promoted the courts from which they issued, and of course also boosted the renown of the poets and patrons themselves. Umayyads followed the ancient Arabian tradition of staging slanging matches at a prominent way-station for Bedouins and traders. Whereas the marketplace of ᶜUkāẓ near Mecca had been the focal point of pre-Islamic poets' gatherings, the Umayyads centred their poetic efforts on Mirbad, a trading site outside Basra. Mirbad's historical role as a space for resting caravans and drying dates made it ideal for all manner of Arabic linguistic pursuits, since tribes mingled there and exchanged poetic composition as well as the distinct dialects that enriched the poetic lexicon as a whole. It was there that the masters of *hijā'* took the defamatory art to what many critics consider its peak. Acerbic and self-referential, the poetics acknowledge the spectacle that they create, at that relatively early point in the Classical tradition.

When the Umayyads were overwhelmed and supplanted by the ᶜAbbāsids in the second/eighth century, Basra ascended in cultural, political, and economic importance. Mirbad continued to host performances, competitive and otherwise. Thanks to ᶜAbbāsid prose, the marketplace maintained its position of importance and its paradigmatic status achieved a new dimension: as the empire expanded, so did the discipline of lexicography. Supported by urban patrons, language scholars documented the language of a wide swath of the Arab population, including far-flung Bedouin communities. Mirbad thus became the site at which changing tribal dialects, as well as Arabic of 'pure' pre-Islamic origin, could be recorded. For language scholars in that era, Mirbad's role was dual. It was a station for diverse peoples, and therefore a place in which many varieties of Arabic were spoken. At the same time, lexicographers considered the Arab nomads passing through to be all-important links to an older, more prestigious version of the language. The ᶜAbbāsid prose master Abū ᶜUthmān al-Jāḥiẓ, who collected *bons mots* in the Basran marketplaces, reports that Mirbad was where 'true reciters of poetry' were distinguished from their mediocre colleagues.[12] Not coincidentally, it was in the fourth/tenth century – when Mirbad had fallen slightly from its supreme position – that poetic duels became explicitly concerned with foreignness. The contestants' ethnic and geographic identities were now at the centre of self-praise and derision of the other; we also find that the texts themselves deeply explore cultural distinctions. By that time, vizierial courts were the proving ground upon which authors traded *hijā'* and practised other confrontational literary forms. In the late ᶜAbbāsid era, the competitive facet of the literary tradition noticeably merged with ethnography and political administration.

This is a moment at which imperial tumult and ethnic reorganisation shifted the literary tradition's course. It is therefore the point of analysis and intervention for the present study. Throughout its history, Mirbad had showcased competitive rituals as a means by which individuals and tribes sought distinction. The ritual continued during the ᶜAbbāsid twilight, but now it defined the increasingly diverse imperial elite. The ᶜAbbāsids were keenly aware of Islamic history predating them and their own departures from previous models. They dominated the Middle East for some five hundred years, from circa 130 to 650 H (750–1250 CE). ᶜAbbāsid supremacy was most emphatic in the first two centuries of their rule. Following that initial era of geographic expansion and courtly textual production, what had been one of the keys to the ᶜAbbāsids' political success also led to a period of intense doubt within the empire. The rulers' eventual response – to embrace new literary genres as their upper social classes diversified – would set a key precedent for subsequent Islamic regimes. In the history of medieval Arab Islamic governments, the ᶜAbbāsids distinguished themselves by the complexity of their views on Middle Eastern ethnic and religious plurality. Arab political leaders, including the Prophet Muhammad himself, had been keenly attuned to the region's rich variety of peoples living under Islamic rule, but the highest governmental positions were occupied by Arabs. That status quo held until certain crucial developments in ᶜAbbāsid history forced the court to expand its criteria for evaluating both politicians and authors. Non-Arabs, especially Persians, began integrating into the bureaucracy from the first decades of Baghdad's rise as a capital, and in 334/945 a cabal of Persian military officers who came to be known as the Būyids parlayed their success in lands east of Iraq, achieving bona fide administrative power in Baghdad. Taking over the major positions of authority, they preserved the Sunni caliph as a symbolic leader and marshalled ᶜAbbāsid legitimacy for themselves. For the first time, the paradigmatic empire was dominated by non-Arab royals and administrators: all ᶜAbbāsid princes and many viziers were Būyid.

The result was that the court, after centuries of balancing its own cosmopolitanism with Arabocentrism, increased the opportunities for its new masters by expanding the generic field of competition. Prior to the Būyids, artists of a variety of disciplines recognised poetry as the surest means by which courtiers such as themselves would ascend in cultural standing. And while no form of expression would displace poetry, the latter part of the ᶜAbbāsid era saw the new leaders recalibrate the literary field in which authors proved their worth. The tradition of poetry 'continued to champion a disappearing ideal of Arab glory and ethnic chauvinism' but we see the inherent tension between that fact and the spectacle of the Būyids at the helm of court activities, as they 'fashioned themselves and their reign as a reappearance of the lost Iranian monarchy'.[13] Drawing from their own multiplicity of cultures, the Būyids promoted genres that had been more highly valued in the Persian tradition than in the Arabic one – especially epigrams and chancery prose, two courtly products that I examine throughout this study. By incorporating practices from well east of the imperial centre, they inadvertently helped prepare subsequent Islamic court systems to promote themselves when major political shifts arrived from far west, in the form of the Crusades.

I argue that the synthesis of Persian and Arabic models of high culture was just as vital to the medieval world as were the ᶜAbbāsid literary products that are best remembered now, namely panegyric production and the translation of ancient Greek texts. As the empire fell, its literature continued to circulate from South Asia to West Africa and around the Mediterranean, fixing ᶜAbbāsid ideals of art and politics in the minds of subsequent courtly communities. The specific accomplishments of Būyid litterateurs – their synthesis of proud Persian identity with old Arab cultural ideals, as well as their interest in spoken 'non-courtly' languages in formal, recorded events – played a key role in the building of a durable ᶜAbbāsid legacy, well beyond the historic reaches of that empire.[14] This capacious generic vocabulary is among the empire's most important contributions to Arabic literary culture, a legacy less often cited than other portable elements of ᶜAbbāsid identity. When the Kurdish Ayyūbids led the next large Arabophone empire two hundred years later, they recognised that signature ᶜAbbāsid means of striving for cultural distinction would be indispensable to their courts as they prosecuted a lengthy set of wars against European occupiers. These cultural norms were so useful and popular that their resonances are still noticeable in modernity, as will be shown in the concluding chapter.

The Crusades of the twelfth and thirteenth centuries occupy the historical centre-point of this book, and constitute the critical transition from Arabic to Romance-language analysis. Whereas the poetics of contest in Classical Arabic served to prepare Muslim courtiers to promote their new Ayyūbid leadership through the long campaign for the Levant, in Spanish and Italian courts that same struggle became a lens through which poets, fabulists, and patrons understood their own evolving courtly game. In other words, Arabic competitions progressively developed an ideology and a set of orienteering tools leading up to the historical event of the Crusades, and in vernacular Romance traditions the contest helped members of the court to narrate the same events. Alfonso's many depictions of quarrelling nobles at his court led him to publicly satirise them in his lyrics, blaming them for cowardice in the face of Muslim forces. The prominent troubadour Pae Gómez answered those complaints from the Galician courts. His poem suggests that the king is more skilled at disproportionate taxation than at conquest, asking,

> por que viestes jantares comer,
> que ome nunca de vosso logar
> comeu? (CEM 305)
>
> Why have you been coming to dine
> on meals in which no one of your stature
> has even once partaken?

In his troubadour persona, Alfonso answers that no leader can match his appetite. Pae Gómez playfully chided Alfonso for underfunding the Crusade in this dialogic poetry, but we will see that the model of king–knight dialogue played a completely different role in Spanish prose, despite the many points of overlap between lyrical and narrative traditions. Alfonso's courtier and nephew Juan Manuel composed didactic narrative in which the king engages his wisest knight in challenging conversation on a range of topics, including Holy War. In Juan Manuel's crucial intervention, the nobleman effects a different understanding of the Crusades and internal courtly politics. His idealised courtier uses the legend of Saladin to explicate Spain's position in the world, the lessons of past conflict, and the need for the court to deliver those lessons to the empire. It was through Saladin, I argue, that Spanish and subsequently Tuscan courts expanded the idea of the contentious literary nobleman, moving from crusading troubadours to a more complex dialogue between Christian and Moorish knights. At what is now thought of as the transition from the Middle Ages to the Renaissance, courtly contest became an examination of imperial history.

These late medieval authors worked with an array of formal tools designed to fuse imperial politics, pious morality, and eloquence. Their antecedent generations had synthesised epic traditions into uniquely medieval forms, most notably the *chanson de geste* and the romance, which gained political purchase as statements of a long-term Christian imperial mission. Lyric poets and raconteurs of heroic stories tapped the venerable, singular authority of the epic as they had in prior centuries, but now the very undertaking of heroism required a chivalric crusading figure. It was not just the strength of courage that was required of the epic adventurer, but also courtly speech and, in some cases, the erotic impulse so essential to late-medieval poetics. We see the early traces of that move in the Cid epic of Spain. The Christian hero returns from his land conquests to correct his own fellow courtiers' violations of the social code. Later, the Arthurian cycles test the court's coherence: in those stories, courtiers' divergent and even opposing interests drive them to contend with one another in language and the joust. In the span of the first three Crusades, solo heroism still had an important mythopoeic role to play, but the inherently social structure of the knighthood stationed epic figures more and more in courtly conversation with one another.

Although protracted war proved destabilising for Mediterranean empires in this era, crusader politics were largely a boon to authors. This situation provided them with captivated audiences – which included patrons – and a sense of historical mission as they used courtly discourse (Hodgson, *Women* 4–5). In turn, those authors, especially the lyric poets among them, voiced the call to pilgrimage and war in troubadour genres such as the *canson de crozada* and the *Minnesang*. The prominence and increasing sophistication of European chivalry meant that composers of literature, whose professional identity was tied up in the knighthood during the late Middle Ages, assumed positions in the martial court alongside prose chroniclers. Their poetry serviced the larger effort to represent, comment on, and incite broad interest in the crusade as a pilgrimage and military campaign. Exploiting the inherent contentiousness of courtly exchange, they evoked a bracing sense of danger in Christendom: threats from Muslim forces and dissenting European factions. In the poetry's logic, crusading individuals, congregations, armies, and courts could then be identified and privileged as forces holding together the embattled holy institution. It followed that some such individuals and groups were superior to others, just as certain poets were superior to other poets. To poeticise the Crusade was to engage the mimesis between the ideal knight and the ideal litterateur, since in both categories individuals vied with each other using many of the same courtly techniques.

European thinkers understood chivalry as a sometimes-permeable category. Therefore, its literature could imagine Muslim knights equipped to converse and be recognised at Christian courts. In literary discourse on knights, chivalric qualities were not inherent to individuals but were instead learned through social and moral training (Rodríguez Velasco, *Order and Chivalry* 8). The result was that some fables portrayed even putative enemies of the Cross as illustrious knights. Seemingly unaware of the irony, composers in this vein of literature and oral tradition used one of the most effective tools of Crusades ideology for the purposes of valorising certain Muslims and naturalising them, in the same legendary courts where that ideology had emerged. The hyperbolically anti-Muslim lyric of *La Chanson de Roland* expresses admiration for the enemy's most powerful knights. Even as it constantly reminds the audience of Saracen idolatry and bloodlust, the epic song allows itself to imagine the very best of their mounted warriors perfected by Christianity (l.1,358, 3,164, 3,297). In the Middle High German tradition, Wolfram von Eschenbach goes further, depicting a Muslim Easterner as the font of ethical knowledge. Von Eschenbach's character of the elder Persian knight, Arofel, 'hât si dicke … / vil rîterlîche gelêret' ('Many times did he … teach you rigorous chivalry').[15] These examples of popular, widely circulated, and adapted poetic texts give us a sense of broad trends in thought regarding the portability of knighthood. Fabulists and lyric poets were at pains to depict certain illustrious Muslims as part of the chivalric order. The specific European production of Saladin, which is explored in depth in this book's last chapter, folded into the evolving discourse of courtly foreigners during the twilight of the Crusades. Flexible boundaries of chivalric identity served to permit a transcendent figure in the narrative tradition, someone who would contend not just with his fellow knights but with the very institution of the crusading court.

A historical paradox of the Crusades is that they built up certain classes of authors and patrons even as those wars badly disrupted some of the same literary communities that had sustained them. The emergence of the troubadour in the twelfth century provided a lyrical interlocutor to Crusades politics and a highly effective ideological tool for holding together the court. Then, as Pope Innocent III coordinated armies in and around France to attack Cathar 'heretics' in 1209, the troubadours' Occitan homeland was besieged by fellow Christians. Fleeing what has since become known as the Albigensian Crusade, they sought out the royal courts in Spain and Italy, where troubadours had for more than half a century found receptive patrons. With that move, they deepened their involvement in the troubadour cultures that were quickly evolving, in a variety of Romance languages, throughout the western Mediterranean. As with so many violent disruptions to a people's life in their homeland, the Albigensian Crusade highlighted and accelerated cultural synthesis as peacetime voluntary migratory patterns became forced migration.

Because the troubadour model of poetic voice was inherently contrapuntal and competitive, its effect on Mediterranean literary culture went beyond form. Its marks were visible throughout Iberia and Italy in the shifting idea of a court. The conceit of the lyric persona pining over the beloved was just one of several modes of speech, albeit the most famous one, popularised by Provençal troubadours and integrated into many languages. The mark of Mediterranean Romance-language lyric in the wake of the Albigensian Crusade is its articulation of sociopolitical relationships between discrete members of the nobility (who comprised the archetypal class of troubadours) and between nobleman and king. Such classes of people took up lyric positions and vied with one another, addressing one another in verse and struggling for material gains in an imagined sphere of crusading courts and diplomacy. The royal estate in Spain, famous for supporting its Occitan arrivals, joined its own noble literate class in composing lyric in troubadour idioms of desire and politics. As Alfonso X's kingdom lurched into economic crisis in its imperial and diplomatic ambitions throughout the western Mediterranean and central Europe, it merged the ideology of Crusade with the courtly linguistic prowess of the lyricist. Wielding the poetic language to maintain his jeopardised court, the king crafted a monarchical troubadour. His persona addressed the beloved while also lampooning fellow leaders in Christendom and his recalcitrant Spanish knights, some of whom were themselves poets. They responded in kind. Against this backdrop of poetics, courts established themselves and, over time, empires established their positions relative to one another.

Courtly and Critical Structures

This book traces a historical route from the twilight of ᶜAbbāsid power in western Asia to the rise of aristocratic court networks in fourteenth-century Italy. Chapter 1 focuses on the Būyids' notions of Arabic excellence as they exerted control over Baghdad and its provinces. The ᶜAbbāsid empire's crisis was initiated by the very patrons and authors responsible for combative literary exchange. As Persians who had taken control of an Arab caliphate, the Būyids deepened ᶜAbbāsid insecurities about the Arab ethnic hegemony that was supposed to prevail in the empire. Chapter 2 addresses Egypt and Syria during the Crusades, and in particular the struggle among writers there to attach themselves to a new sovereign and political saviour. To promote Saladin, they combined certain Būyid-era forms of contentious literature with their innovations unique to the counter-crusade project. Chapter 3 initiates the shift from Arabic to Romance-language literature, turning from conflicts over the Holy Land to the Gibraltar Crusade. The focus is the royal literary work of Alfonso X, specifically his insertion of his own persona into the contentious field of Iberian troubadours during difficult military and diplomatic campaigns. Chapter 4 investigates the literature of competition and Crusade, especially the Spanish and Italian writing that represented Saladin's last incarnation before modernity. The moment of literary retrospect of Mediterranean politics places the sultan in a new version of the court, in which Christendom's putative enemy now challenges his crusading interlocutors ethically rather than militarily. I conclude the book by probing modern historiography on the Middle Ages and the unique case of Iraq during the twentieth and twenty-first centuries, when Baath Party officials organised a medieval revival encompassing ᶜAbbāsid-style poetic contest and Iberian lyric traditions.

A court's position at the centre of its empire was by no means guaranteed. Nor could the success of the empire itself be taken for granted. Medieval writers were well aware of these political realities. With their patrons, they searched for new ways to inscribe and reinscribe the idea of their own stability in the consciousness of fellow imperial subjects. When we turn our view towards the pugilistic literary techniques by which courts made their power seem inevitable and their incentives to courtiers undeniable, the cultural politics of the Middle Ages come into sharper focus. We also gain a better understanding of what comparative study may accomplish. At first glance, court competitions may seem to be inherently conservative strategies of an upper class under duress, as court members generally took pains to demonstrate their adherence to the official rituals of a single authoritative institution. But these attempts at conservation produced remarkable generic changes to medieval concepts of literature. Just as importantly, competitors developed views of many empires – both their own kingdom and the dynamic, if inferior, communities all around it. To speak of the late Middle Ages is to imply that a phase of thought was ending. But in certain crucial respects, the events of that era set in motion new comparative discussions of culture, geographic space, and politics.

Notes

1. See Alfonso's comprehensive legal code, *Las siete partidas* (Seven Divisions), at 2.9.30, for discussion of wit's *grant bienestancia* and the designation of *palanciano*; see 7.9.3 for the definition of and punishments for *enfamar*.
2. All translations in this book are mine unless otherwise noted.
3. In discussions of medieval Islamic societies, individuals, literature, and events that are central to this book, all centuries and years are given both in Hijra (H) and Common/Current Era (CE).
4. For the heading of *Jary al-shuʿarāʾ* ... given by the anthologist Abū Manṣūr al-Thaʿālibī, see YDQ 3:240. The two poems cited appear in YDQ 3:253 and 3:241. Pomerantz notes Ibn ʿAbbād's reputation for grand building projects and the vizier's poets' efforts to advertise the Eastern power base by praising Ibn ʿAbbād's architectural works ('Licit Magic and Divine Grace' 108).
5. Castro recast *convivencia* after his colleague and historiographic adversary Ramón Menéndez Pidal used it to suggest an inherent competition between the strains of Spanish language usage. For a detailed analysis of that debate and its continuation in the twenty-first century, see Szpiech in Akbari and Mallette eds 135–8.
6. Thanks in part to Goitein's research, contemporary multiculturalists can add Tunisia, northern Egypt, and Saladin's Damascus to Menocal's map of the Mediterranean centres of tolerant plurality (Goitein, *Mediterranean Society* 1:70–3). Importantly, though, Goitein distinguishes Muslim-ruled regions of the medieval Mediterranean from Europe in the late Middle Ages (1:72), whereas Menocal sees in Europe a multicultural legacy surviving in 'shards' throughout modernity (*Ornament* 271–3). Also, it must be noted that Goitein's groundbreaking work in the Cairo Geniza (alternatively spelled Genizah), the medieval synagogue's repository of documents, illuminates much more than court culture per se. The collection encompasses mid-level merchants' correspondence, trade documents, and family records, in addition to documents of more central interest to royal courts: high-level diplomacy and Arabic poetry (*Mediterranean Society* 2:172, 5:425). For a call to increase the scope of medieval

multiculturalism in the twenty-first century, with special attention to Menocal's legacy, see Balbale, 'Cacophony' 127.

7. Kabir and Williams eds 105. Akbari's solution to the problem is to chart the prehistory of Orientalism as an East/West discourse, persuasively arguing that European Christian scholars, poets, and fabulists of the late Middle Ages thought of the world as tri- and quadripartite, and thought of the peoples of interest to Christian courts as being divided into yet more complex categories before starker taxonomies developed in modernity (*Idols in the East* 28–40, 284).
8. Examples of scholars imposing a modern East/West binary upon medieval empires include ᶜAwaḍ, *Al-Ḥurūb al-Ṣalībiyya* 9–34; Goody, *The East in the West* 82–112; Gregg, *Devils, Women, and Jews* 19–20; Landes, *Wealth and Poverty* 31–40; and Lewis, *Islam and the West* 99–118.
9. Foucault's writings on the self are numerous, but his most detailed consideration of the question is *The Care of the Self* and lectures collected in *The Hermeneutics of the Subject*. For a probing analysis of fourteenth-century binary thought in European courts, ranging from geographic texts to poetry and legend, see Akbari, *Idols in the East* 47–50 and 156. In Middle East studies, see Cemal Kafadar, 'A Rome of One's Own' 15, which seeks to correct historians' assumptions that early modern courts inherited a set of Arab/Turk binaries from their medieval forebears. It should be noted that an effort to reframe subjectivity vis-à-vis the European Middle Ages is underway, although it has yet to gain major traction. Peter Haidu presses at the accepted definitions of subjectivity (medieval subjects as defined by their subordination to royal power, modern subjects as gaining limited autonomy as discrete thinking individuals). In so doing, he questions the historical category of the premodern in *The Subject Medieval/Modern* 341–8.
10. OIM 2:104; *Book of Contemplation* 153–4.
11. Competitive exchanges of *hijā'*, known as *naqā'iḍ* (sing. *naqīḍa*), were one of the main rituals by which Arab tribes asserted themselves in the Middle Ages. As with *hijā'* generally, the *naqā'iḍ* were repurposed in the age of Islamic empire. Tribal affiliations receded in importance – some adversaries in *naqā'iḍ* were in fact of the same tribe – as poets glorified their city of origin, religious school of thought, knowledge of Arabic, individual masculine traits, etc. The most famous Umayyad poets to face off in *naqā'iḍ*, Jarīr and al-Farazdaq, seem to have shared respect for each other and perhaps even an intimate friendship. When al-Farazdaq died, Jarīr composed a moving elegy for his rival. Cory Jorgensen provides a detailed analysis of the poets' relationship and contrapuntal texts (see 'Jarīr and al-Farazdaq's *Naqā'iḍ* Performance as Social Commentary').

12. *Al-Bayān wa-l-tabyīn* 4:23. Mirbad's key role as the site of invective poetry and ᶜAbbāsid conceptions of race and class is memorably explained by Houari Touati (*Islam and Travel in the Middle Ages* 49–50). Even now, the area remains a potent symbol of Arabs' oldest and most venerated art form, and of the rhapsodies unique to its competitive exchanges. The Baath Party of Iraq named its major arts festival Mirbad, a years-long tradition whose competitions once served to glorify Saddam Hussein and now praise the more abstract idea of the Iraqi people. Mirbad's modern revival is the focus of this book's conclusion.
13. Margaret Larkin in Behnam Sadeghi, et al., eds, *Islamic Cultures, Islamic Contexts* 388–9. In the first quotation, Larkin refers to the most famous poet of the Būyid-era ᶜAbbāsid empire, Abū l-Ṭayyib al-Mutanabbī (303–54 H, 915–65 CE), a proud Arab. Along with Larkin's reading of the ambivalent, multicultural discourse of Arab triumphalism in an increasingly Persian hegemonic system, see Brookshaw, 'Mytho-Political Remakings' 476. The Būyids' project should be viewed largely as making explicit the Persian cultural historiography that had been an implicit part of the ᶜAbbāsid court as early as second/eighth century (Gutas, *Greek Thought, Arabic Culture* 28–9).
14. Hillenbrand in Lange and Mecit eds, *Seljuqs* 22; Irwin, 'Mamluk Literature' 9–11.
15. *Willehalm* 7.345.18–19.

1

'Baghdad is to Cities What the Master is to Mankind': The Rise of Vizier Culture

The Būyids: New Claims on the Islamic Court

The political volatility of the late ᶜAbbāsid empire was matched by its cultural dynamism. Together, those two factors presented a wealth of artistic and material opportunities to courtiers of the era, who conspicuously benefited from their ᶜAbbāsid predecessors' history of poetic experimentation, rhetorical argument, and debates over ethnic and religious identity. In the fourth century Hijra (that is, approaching the third century of ᶜAbbāsid rule, approximately 940–1040 CE), authors and politicians engaged one another with literary techniques that prior generations could not have fully anticipated. As the Būyid regime advanced from Iran to Iraq, establishing power in Baghdad, key changes had been well underway in courtly arts. Principalities replaced the caliphate as the political institutions of real authority. In turn, viziers were tasked with executing much of the quotidian work of running each prince's government. They strengthened the position of the vizierate itself, especially in the empire's eastern segment, the Būyid stronghold. The most ambitious litterateurs recognised and took advantage of the process by promoting whichever prince they may serve. In the case of peripatetic viziers, their service in the provinces allowed them relative autonomy. Even in such a field of high ambition, Abū l-Faḍl ibn al-ᶜAmīd (ca 290–360H, 900–70 CE) and al-Ṣāḥib Ibn ᶜAbbād (326–85 H, 938–95 CE) stood out. Their vizierates, their stewardship of Būyid political matters, the manuscript production that they cultivated, and their marshalling of literary forms have left enduring marks upon the Arabic court. In a splintered, contentious world of textual production, now overseen by these non-Arabs, the ᶜAbbāsids' imperial self-concept shifted. The hierarchy of literary genres adjusted with it. The praise *qaṣīda* (long-form ode), while still the centrepiece of ᶜAbbāsid arts, shared more and more space with short poetry and a wide variety of prose forms. As Abū l-Faḍl and Ibn ᶜAbbād acquired status as government officials, they wrote and patronised works in ascendant genres and, in so doing, presided over two of the most prolific and fiercely contested courts in Islamic history.

Modern criticism tends to view artistic and administrative skills as separate, but that bias deserves scrutiny. The development of courtly arts in Islamic empire was at no point divorced from politics. Grouping together people for poetic recital, as a social ritual, necessarily overlapped with official political negotiation in the court. Furthermore, organising an ᶜAbbāsid court of any renown entailed inviting poets, essayists, mathematicians, geographers, physicians, and official secretaries to the same space. Many individual courtiers held more than one of these professional titles. Poetry retained its historically superior position among the forms of courtly expression, but the spectrum of intricately related disciplines worked to the advantage of polymaths such as Abū l-Faḍl and Ibn ᶜAbbād. This is especially true in the case of the secretarial arts, whose impact on poetry was acutely felt for generations thereafter. Abū l-Faḍl's fame for his chancery composition was, as we will see, crucial to his literary career. The same applies to his pupil Ibn ᶜAbbād. The Būyids of Abū l-Faḍl's generation inherited an ᶜAbbāsid system that had both shaped their intellectual ambition and was well-suited for their project of diversifying court literature. ᶜAbbāsid political and literary hierarchies, already more flexible than the Umayyads' prior imperial system, became their most dynamic under Būyid rule. So, when Abū l-Faḍl explores the poetics of chancery prose, his document recalls the swift evolution of late ᶜAbbāsid culture. From the time of Baghdad's construction as an Islamic capital two hundred years before, ᶜAbbāsid rulers had absorbed Iranian models of kingship, social class, and high culture. Now, with Iranians in command, the court issued Persian-language declarations of authority while Arabic remained the main currency of literary expression and administration. It was a potent mix of official discourse.[1]

This medieval period of synthesis reminds us that, in our own modern moment, our approach to Classical Arabic is itself changing. Late ᶜAbbāsid courtly arts serve as a pivot-point for our shifting critical debates on literary form, because of its chronological position immediately following the period that modern scholars had uncritically accepted to be the cultural Golden Age. Through the end of the twentieth century, Arabists tended to privilege earlier periods of literary development, in which the *qaṣīda* was putatively dominant in official culture and the most important patrons were caliphs and kings who did not, in most cases, compose texts themselves. While that understanding of Arabic poetry's performance and reception is useful in reading late ᶜAbbāsid literature, its clear limits present a challenge to scholars of the twenty-first century. We are beginning to make the adjustments necessary to read the literary field as a diverse generic field. Just as importantly, recent work shows the vital links between our manuscript record of courtly arts and the social interactions that enabled them.[2] Here I wish to contribute to an encouraging movement in the discipline by explicating the competitive functions of epistle, poetry, and the courtly social rituals inherent in those texts. I furthermore consider the long-term effects of such competition. Abū l-Faḍl and Ibn ᶜAbbād used their expansive cultural competency to promote the political office of the vizierate. At times, they did so in tense confrontations with fellow members of the literary class. Although we cannot know if they appreciated the historical significance of their projects, they largely merged the political notion of the striving vizier with the long-term cultural work of achieving expansive, even intimidating literary ability.

Central Ideas and Ideals of the ᶜAbbāsid Vizierate

These literature-minded viziers were elaborating upon a model well known to their fellow members of the courtly class. Two centuries before, the Barmakids had set the standard for ᶜAbbāsid administration, scientific patronage, and artistic projects shortly before the reign of the caliph Hārūn al-Rashīd (148–93 H, 766–809 CE). They were Khorasanians who identified closely with their ancestral role as governors and mediators among the religious and ethnic communities of Central Asia, even as they made a name for themselves as Baghdadi operators. During that first ᶜAbbāsid century, it was Barmakid officials who could take credit for commanding substantial portions of the army; for satisfying both sovereign and populace in matters of tax policy east of Baghdad; for sponsoring much of the construction of the capital and its environs; and for tutoring Hārūn during his ascent to supremacy, a caliphal reign capping the era that modern historians have called the empire's Golden Age. The Būyid-era belletrist al-Muḥassin al-Tanūkhī (329–84 H, 941–94 CE) describes the Barmakids as the pinnacle of vizierial prestige. When his *Nishwār al-muḥādara* narrates a patron – whether a vizier or a royal figure – making a public show of his generosity and erudition, al-Tanūkhī repeatedly asks his reader to consider the Barmakid vizierate. This rhetorical move suggests that Abū l-Faḍl's generation declared fealty to the caliphal legacy of Hārūn but more actively emulated the empire's first great viziers.[3]

The parallels between the ambitious Barmakid and Būyid vizierates were not subtle, but nor were the risks faced by any generation of ᶜAbbāsid social climbers. Just as the Barmakids signified the height to which administrators may ascend in ᶜAbbāsid high courts, they also offered a historical note of caution. Hārūn was famously vindictive, eventually sequestering his Barmakid administrators and executing the vizier Jaᶜfar al-Barmakī, son of Hārūn's own tutor, Yaḥyā. The great poet Abū Nuwās (ca 139–98 H, 756–814 CE) is said to have composed his elegy for the Barmakid vizierate when passing by the house of al-Faḍl ibn al-Rabīᶜ. For Abū Nuwās, as well as Arab historians who would later chronicle the era, Ibn al-Rabīᶜ was essentially a bureaucrat at heart. He stood to benefit from the famous Persian family's misfortunes even as he paled in comparison to their cultural greatness. Ibn al-Rabīᶜ provided a vizierial sort of counter-example to Jaᶜfar. The Barmakids' active involvement in producing *adab*, and their nonpareil competence in government, made the family's fall from grace all the more painful to Abū Nuwās. He had enjoyed the playful dialectics of performing as their poet, as his *dīwān* attests. The poet chafed at al-Rabīᶜ during the rise of this new vizier-patron, whom Abū Nuwās found uncreative and loyal to a fault to the caliph.[4] We note some of the poetic resentment here:

ما رعى الدهر آل برمك لما أن رمى ملكهم بأمر فظيع
إنّ دهرا لم يرعَ حقا ليحيى غير راعٍ ذمام آل الربيعِ

This age has hardly been kind to the Barmakid family, striking that regime a terrible blow.
Any age that won't give Yaḥyā his due will be no kinder to al-Rabīᶜ. (*Dīwān* 1:344)

Abū Nuwās's haunting two-line poem speaks both pessimism and praise, and reminds us of viziers' mercurial fortunes throughout ᶜAbbāsid history. In the Būyid era 150 years later, viziers were aware of the dangers that their ascent may bring. Although the Barmakids' ultimate failure to please a potent, vengeful caliph would never have been a concern for Abū l-Faḍl and Ibn ᶜAbbād, the secondary quality of the vizier's political position consistently held. The great prince ᶜAḍud al-Dawla (324–72 H, 936–83 CE) is said to have had elephants trample a vizier and suspected intriguer, Abū Ṭāhir ibn Baqiyya (dates of birth unknown, died ca 366 H, 977 CE). Ibn Baqiyya was known for his political savvy and felicitous use of language, but also for ambitions that irked his superiors (EI2, 'Ibn Baḳiyya'). We may imagine the message that the elephant spectacle sent around the Būyid power structure, as Ibn Baqiyya's crushed body was then crucified for display. Viziers were free to exploit the opportunities that their relative autonomy offered them, but their superiors took any hint of insurrection seriously.

Beyond these matters of rank and physical violence, we find the two viziers in a rhetorical battle. It was lopsided, occurring when Ibn ᶜAbbād had neared the end of his life and Abū l-Faḍl had died. The prose virtuoso Abū Ḥayyān al-Tawḥīdī (ca 320–414 H, 932–1023 CE) offers an eloquent commentary on these viziers, a back-handed kind of praise that will punctuate the present chapter in key respects. His acerbic prose book *Akhlāq al-wazīrayn* (The Moral Qualities of the Two Viziers) means to excoriate Abū l-Faḍl and Ibn ᶜAbbād, but it becomes a metapoetical treatise on the very enterprise of insult. Al-Tawḥīdī seems to have honed that skill, despite his insistence that the viziers themselves were paragons of slander. Of all the ᶜAbbāsid writers to contemplate the new order governing the empire, as patrons' roles changed vis-à-vis the official chancery and the poetic court, al-Tawḥīdī is the fiercest in his response. There can be little doubt that the power wielded by Abū l-Faḍl and Ibn ᶜAbbād outraged al-Tawḥīdī at a visceral level. Al-Tawḥīdī saw them as unworthy of the Barmakid standard established in the courts. In the book he characterises both men as foul-tempered, boastful rather than truly eloquent, and stingy facsimiles of their great forebears.

As with so many cases examined in the present study, the acrimony began as a problem of patronage. After unsuccessful stints as an essayist for Abū l-Faḍl and court scribe for Ibn ᶜAbbād in Ray, al-Tawḥīdī parted from their company embittered. It seems that he was also determined to exact his literary revenge. Ruminating on his experiences, he wrote a condemnation of both officials. *Akhlāq al-wazīrayn* is a tour de force of intellectual biography and slander. His work stands alone in Classical Arabic extant prose as the only book-length character assassination of individuals. Ibn ᶜAbbād receives the harshest treatment. Al-Tawḥīdī reflects upon his brief employment as a scribe in the vizier's house, astonished that a high official would sully the prestige of the office:

> الوصف لا يأتي على كنه هذه الحال لأن الحقائق لا تدرك إلا بلحظ ولا يؤتى عليها باللفظ. أفهذا كله من شمائل الرؤساء وكلام الكبراء وسيرة أهل العقل والرزانة؟ لا، والله! وتربا لمن يقول غير هذا

> It's impossible to do justice to the way he is. You have to see it (in person), rather than just hearing a description, to appreciate how out-of-line he is. Are these the qualities of leaders? Is this the kind of speech that great men use? Is this the approach taken by the wise, by the intelligent? No, by God! Anyone who says otherwise is not to be believed. (AW 141)

Spite was surely a primary motive for al-Tawḥīdī, and he probably sought to justify his failure to stay in Ibn ᶜAbbād's employ, explaining through such anecdotes that the vizier was impossibly crude and arrogant. More importantly, however, the author was responding to large-scale political developments of his era. To judge from surviving manuscripts, al-Tawḥīdī joined a chorus of writers in examining viziers and their ascension.[5] The effort he exerted to malign Abū l-Faḍl and Ibn ᶜAbbād provides insights beyond a personal feud, as it taps into philosophical and aesthetic arguments reflecting the ᶜAbbāsid courtly ethos. It furthermore compels its readers – at least those sympathetic to al-Tawḥīdī – to consider whether the vizierial office may be redeemed. Al-Tawḥīdī's language of taste, courtly protocol, and morality explicates the reasoning behind his composition: if literary erudition had been these viziers' formula for success, then in al-Tawḥīdī's hands it could become their biographical undoing.

Cultural History, Appropriation and Intervention

In the middle of the fourth/tenth century, the greater ᶜAbbāsid Empire was contracting geographically, while its ideology was expanding in important ways. The Būyid princes, initially uninterested in mastering Arabic, founded in Baghdad a dynasty that fully adopted ᶜAbbāsid notions of high Arabic culture after a few decades of convening courts with official translators, who then became redundant. By the time ᶜAḍud al-Dawla established control over the largest swath of land under Būyid sovereignty, becoming the prince of all princes in ᶜAbbāsid territory, he oversaw an empire whose hegemony was compromised in central Asia while the Byzantines remained a threat to the west. The era of caliphal supremacy and the steady growth of land holdings had passed a century before. Further, the upheaval in central government would not have instilled ready confidence among subjects throughout the empire. As Shīᶜī Muslims, the Būyids would have been controversial figures during the height of ᶜAbbāsid power, and indeed theological polemics continued, but by this era Sunni triumphalism seemed belaboured. The military prowess and administrative capabilities of the new regime were more important, both to the long-time ᶜAbbāsid court population and to the Būyids themselves. What endured, and motivated cultural development, was the variegated definition of ᶜAbbāsid identity. The notion of who was culturally ᶜAbbāsid, and how one could serve the empire while benefiting from it, expanded once more in this era. Its privileged linguistic currency of Classical Arabic appealed to the second Būyid generation, who saw in it an opportunity to establish lasting legitimacy in Baghdad by cultivating its literary usage. Ideology – the relationship between language, belief systems, and sociopolitical power – required literature, and late ᶜAbbāsid texts leave little doubt of the politics conducted in Arabic poetry and ornate prose. Even while the empire was tested militarily and economically throughout its provinces, it produced a literature of triumphal acquisition. In his position atop the hierarchy of Būyid princes, ᶜAḍud al-Dawla founded a large and prestigious literary court. Eventually, Ibn ᶜAbbād's provincial court would trump that of the prince, emerging as the premier destination for Arabophone intellectuals. The pressure to contend with these viziers was felt in Baghdad, by ᶜAḍud's son Ṣamṣām al-Dawla and his literature-minded administrative corps (Al-Shaar,

Ethics in Islam 37–8). The tension between Baghdad's customary supremacy and the rise of great ᶜAbbāsid courts in Iran animates much of the cultural activity explored in this chapter.

As Persian and Arab ideologies cointegrated more and more thoroughly, the idea of competing at court broadened. Poets not only vied with one another for position vis-à-vis patrons, they also found themselves in artistic matches with the patrons themselves. Furthermore, the administrative competencies to which viziers aspired – chancery eloquence, ingratiating oneself to princes and the caliph, economic knowledge, familiarity with the material sciences, deep understanding of ᶜAbbāsid geography and demography – engaged the ideals of poetic ability. Abū Manṣūr ᶜAbd al-Malik al-Thaᶜālibī (350–429 H, 961–1038 CE), whose anthology *Yatīmat al-dahr* is the main source of Būyid-era poetry and epistles, tells of his surprise at hearing that Ibn ᶜAbbād had written a treatise on medicine. After searching for and finding a manuscript of it, he realises that the vizier's medical understanding is of a piece with his linguistic ability and general powers of perception.

وجدتها تجمع إلى ملاحة البلاغة ورشاقة العبارة حسن التصرف في لطائف الطب وخصائصه
وتدل على التبحر في علمه وقوة المعرفة بدقائقه

> I discovered that it (the treatise) consisted of rhetorical eloquence, felicitous expression, beautifully navigating the fine points of medicine. It showed the extent of his knowledge and his precise grasp of the details. (YDQ 3:238)

Especially for polymaths like Abū l-Faḍl and Ibn ᶜAbbād, demonstrating skill in a multitude of disciplines often meant blurring the boundaries between the bodies of formal knowledge that each one entailed.[6]

In epistolary exchanges, politicians and their scribes tended to portray their courts as practising a master discourse, a versatile form of prose conveying information like medical description, all the while constantly calling attention to its own high artistic style. Al-Thaᶜālibī's story of surprise seems disingenuous, given his intimate knowledge of the capacious prose in which the viziers trained. *Kitāba* (the art of secretarial writing, the practitioner of which is a *kātib*) emerged as an important form of Classical Arabic discourse in the second/eight century with the solidification of ᶜAbbāsid power. By the time Abū l-Faḍl trained as an official secretary in Khorasan, *kitāba* had achieved great sophistication, encompassing poetic ability, keenness of diplomatic perception, geographic knowledge, and of course soundness of prose composition.[7] The opportunities for administrators to acquire cultural legitimacy were great, and the textual record shows that viziers plotted their rise by elaborating upon the literary register. Būyid-era poetry moves steadily away from the language of subordination and exculpation employed in prior eras of Islamic cultural life. With vizierial poetics, literature instead takes on the complex discourse of political competence, the basis of which is *kitāba*. The office of *kātib* skewed towards the performance of political discourse, making it indispensable to Abū l-Faḍl and Ibn ᶜAbbād.

To produce their vocabulary of power, the Būyids worked across two distinct elements of Classical Arabic court history: the long-term tradition of patronage and the discrete cultural work of prior ᶜAbbāsid viziers, especially the Barmakids. The model by which poets gained patronage was well established over centuries. Traditionally, authors had contended with one another for the favour of political elites and, although their compensation could include the granting of governmental appointments, the poet's chief means of protection was precisely his lack of official political authority. Whether composing praise works or taking part in poetic slander contests, he could rely upon the ritualistic nature of poetic performance to grant himself an excuse or escape route should his patron become displeased with him. That model, a popular topic for contemporary studies of Classical Arabic, had undergone a subtle adjustment as part of the Barmakid legacy. As formidable, literature-minded viziers, the Barmakids made explicit what many courts had understood implicitly: the caliph had no permanently guaranteed monopoly on the top level of patronage. Through sponsorship of cultural projects and especially the strategic distribution of wealth, Barmakids challenged the caliph's hegemony over the courtly ideal. The caliph in turn jealously sought to affirm his position, as we have seen in Abū Nuwās's rueful poem. A political limit to their social and cultural dynamism had been established (Hanne, *Putting the Caliph in his Place* 109). Without the pressure of a supreme caliph looming above them, the Būyids recognised the broader possibilities of princely and vizierial patronage. Where the Barmakids had funded a variety of art and architecture, Būyid administrators focused their efforts on literature and, more importantly, took on positions as both patrons and poets. Caliphs and kings were no longer presumed to represent the peak of patronage, which meant that even second-tier administrators could concern themselves with the immediacy of courtly manoeuvres. The viziers' authority derived less from any hereditary position of leadership (although some of them did indeed inherit their posts from their fathers, and Abū l-Faḍl's son followed him into the vizierate) than from their expansive knowledge of written Arabic forms, and their ability to compose poetry at their own courts.

Būyid vizierial projects were doubly instrumental. First, the patron-poets astounded their contemporaries, including career authors, with the range of literary expression they commanded. Second, they mapped out a distinct position for an administrator at the apex of courtly status. Great poets and great patrons had generally been separate categories, but that structure had come under challenge in ᶜAbbāsid Baghdad. These Būyid officials then promulgated the idea of a savant and court master, creating poetry, offering both rewards and chastisement, and composing responses in kind to the poets in attendance. The viziers complicated the social endgame of courtly exchange, given how difficult it would have been for anyone but themselves to achieve the extraordinary status of the multifaceted politician-poet. Whereas the foremost practitioners of courtly arts had generally vied with one another, and their works were geared to solicit material payment and social relationships with patrons, at vizierial courts they now had to adjust to a more dialectical environment than that which their predecessors had navigated. Arab societies had held gatherings of poets and political leaders as far back as the historical record allows us to trace; defining and practising high culture were among the most important functions performed at these sessions. Without drawing great attention to their move, ᶜAbbāsids came to utilise Classical Arabic literature to valorise the vizierial disciplines of chancery correspondence, argumentation at court, ambassadorial missions, and records-keeping. The rituals that the elite had in the past viewed more as mundane court functions than high literature were now fully integrated in *adab*, an overarching term for written forms of worldly knowledge, including entertainment literature.[8] In previous dynasties, Arab viziers had patronised literary sessions – the extant textual record suggests that they only rarely contributed their own works. Now, the authority of patronage remained intact, but the court's definition of the patron himself now could include versification. This opened up new possibilities for contest in the formal structure of poetic performance. In the space of two generations, viziers made their secondary/tertiary position into one of outright cultural primacy.

Conflicting ʿAbbāsid Positions: Al-Mutanabbī and Abū l-Faḍl's Shifts through the Courts

Viewed in the historical context of his century, Abū l-Faḍl's work seems prescient. In one piece of poetry he announces the renewal of the vizierate to its position at the forefront of ʿAbbāsid literary production, while in another moment he provides telling evidence of the resistance to viziers' high authority in culture. The most famous poet he employed, albeit briefly, was Abū l-Ṭayyib al-Mutanabbī (303–54 H, 915–65 CE). Perhaps more than any other poet in Arab history, al-Mutanabbī has enjoyed readers' admiration from the late Middle Ages to this day. In his own lifetime, he was a polarising figure. An Iraqi, he achieved great fame in royal and vizierial courts of Syria and Egypt before moving back to the Fertile Crescent and then to the eastern provinces late in his career. His employment with Abū l-Faḍl and ʿAḍud al-Dawla were the high points of his tenure in Iranian regions – he praised both patrons in spectacular style, maintaining a hint of his trademark self-promotion, as we will see subsequently in a panegyric for Abū l-Faḍl.

As far as we know, al-Mutanabbī and Abū l-Faḍl each admired the other, or at least saw the mutual benefits in their brief relationship at court. But the poet was also known to deride viziers for their rank. During the gradual eastward shift that he made, he sojourned in the Mesopotamian area where he had been raised, and anecdotes report his stirring controversy in Baghdad. The vizier and accomplished poet Abū Muḥammad al-Muhallabī (291–352 H, 903–63 CE) was at the centre of Baghdadi literary culture, hosting salons and offering his own acclaimed compositions. When al-Mutanabbī received al-Muhallabī's request to deliver praise to the vizier, he demurred, saying that only rulers merited his panegyrics. Al-Mutanabbī was not known for modesty nor, perhaps, a keen sense of irony: his previous career phase in Egypt included writing anguished, faint praise for the vizier Abū l-Misk Kāfūr and unsuccessfully seeking the employ of a general, Abū Shujāʿ Fātik. One of al-Muhallabī's many talents as a cultural figurehead, which Ibn ʿAbbād would try to emulate in his own career, was an understanding of how to seek retribution in the rarefied field of courtly discourse rather than through rude gesticulations or physical punishment. Al-Muhallabī urged his courtiers to make the poet's life difficult by interrupting his performances and penning rhetorical attacks on him to be distributed in the manuscript market. Al-Mutanabbī shrugged off initial such attempts as trifling but al-Muhallabī's efforts seem to have been successful, to judge from the volume of surviving texts attacking the poet's style.[9] So even while al-Mutanabbī in one instance would like to demote the vizierate as culturally second-tier, over the course of his life he confirms its preeminence. His conceit is as much anachronistic as it is egotistical – he subconsciously gestures towards a vague, different era, when caliphs and other royal figures would have unquestioned dominion over the main salons. This is the kind of nostalgic projection that helped construct such legendary personas as Hārūn al-Rashīd: the idea that political and cultural hierarchies mirrored one another provides a foundation for 'Golden Age' models of imperial history.

Abū l-Faḍl demonstrates that he too was aware of this ambivalent attitude towards his office. In a companionship-themed poem to a friend of his, he makes a poetic game out of the discrepancy between monarch and administrator.

وزعمت أنك لست تفكر بعدما علقت يداك بذمة الأمراء
هيهات لم تصدقك فكرتك التي قد أوهمتك غنى عن الوزراء
لم تغن عن أحدٍ سماء لم تجد أرضاً ولا أرض بغير سماء

> You act as if you think little (of me), now that you've been granted power from princes,
> But look! The very thoughts that deluded you, made you neglect the vizierate, now betray you.
> A sky that finds no earth (below it) can hardly claim to be fine on its own, no more than the earth can do without the sky. (YDQ 3:204)

We will see the canny use of self-debasement throughout confrontational poems, coercive even as it is deliberately playful. No known historical data document the royal favour that the addressee, one Abū l-Ḥasan al-ᶜAbbāsī, seems to have enjoyed. But Abū l-Faḍl takes sufficient pains to point out his lower status, then presses it into service and makes it the basis for his complaint. (The last quoted line uses the *samāʾ/arḍ* – that is, sky/earth – antithesis twice over.) At a time when al-Muhallabī vigorously defended his customary position atop the Baghdadi poetic scene, Abū l-Faḍl displays a much more complex awareness of the criteria by which superiority was assessed by his society. If al-Mutanabbī could plausibly claim to believe in the prince-only policy, even while violating that rule throughout his career, then that would suggest that a limited but substantial portion of the courtly population gave it credence. Abū l-Faḍl exploits the court's ambivalence. He has a basis for complaint insofar as the prince is nominally supreme; he enjoys power of poetic speech because no one can confidently state that such supremacy holds.

In prose, however, Abū l-Faḍl adhered to protocols of royalty-above-all, largely because of the epistolary genres in which he made a name for himself. Of the many changes in tastes exhibited by late ᶜAbbāsid literati, the increased emphasis on *kitāba* provides us a window through which to observe the vizier in court culture. The secretarial art integrated, by design, multiple Arabic genres, promoting both the patron's authoritative voice and the scribe's command of discourse. In other words, *kitāba* was simultaneously utilitarian and aesthetic. It could be wielded as a blunt instrument of bureaucratic power but it was almost always self-consciously literary. Abū l-Faḍl seems to have written few book-length works, and none are extant. There are few remaining manuscripts of his chancery letters, such that we as readers must rely upon anthologists' quotations of his work. He is known to have been unfailingly loyal to his master, the prince Rukn al-Dawla (ca 300–66 H, 912–76), whose court he both represented and promoted as a centre of culture, based primarily in the eastern city of Ray.[10] Although the limited textual record leaves open many questions about the vizier's life and career, the available sources make clear that his impact on literature was major.

In Abū l-Faḍl's time and indeed now, a great many scholarly debates on Arabic hinge on prose's dual role as an empirical tool and a signature, emotive register of Arab culture. *Kitāba*'s evolution did not end with the ultimate fall of the ᶜAbbāsid Empire but instead took on new ideological directions in Crusades-era Egypt and Syria, as we will see in the next chapter. What remained constant in *kitāba* was its tendency to grant secretaries and viziers substantial control over written language and, by extension, over taste. Although the chief function of the *kātib* was of course to represent his patron in an effective manner, the Ayyūbid courts in particular will show us how deceptively powerful he was in his secondary position. And now in the late modern period, the questions of prose ability, authority, and formal categories again prove crucial to Arabs seeking to assign literary excellence. During the last year of his life, Edward Said meditated upon written genres of Arabic from the position of a self-described outsider, educated mainly in English. His article, as it attacks an Egyptian scholar's statement that the formal written language should be deemphasised in favour of spoken dialects, recounts Said's determination

> that the finest, leanest, most steely Arabic prose that I have either read or heard is produced by novelists (not critics) like Elias Khoury or Gamal El-Ghitany, or by two of our greatest living poets, Adonis and Mahmoud Darwish, each of whom in his odes soars to such lofty rhapsodic heights as to drive huge audiences into frenzies of enthusiastic rapture, but for whom each of which prose is a razor-sharp Aristotelian instrument. ('Living in Arabic' para. 34, parentheses original)

Said's interest in the relationship between poetry performance and the inductive/deductive powers of written prose echoes almost perfectly the rationale given by Classical rhetoricians for Abū l-Faḍl's prominence. By the time of the Būyid takeover, writers of Arabic had spent three centuries integrating poetic techniques into prose compositions such as administrative documents and especially sermons, seeking to produce the 'enthusiastic rapture' that Said sees in poetic performance (Irfan Shahîd, 'Review' 531). Abū l-Faḍl was a beneficiary of this stylistic work. To Said, aesthetic judgements take precedence over more technical concerns, such as the question of which disciplines a writer chooses to practice. The most essential link for our purposes, however, is the Aristotelian one. The centrality of translated Greek philosophy to ᶜAbbāsid readers and writers is well known: by Abū l-Faḍl's time it was both an operative part of court culture and a productive cliché. Courts were populated with avid readers of Aristotle (EI2, 'Arisṭūṭālīs' paras 4–5) and with intellectuals familiar only with the Arabic pseudo-Aristotelian tradition – it seems probable that some of the literary audience was entirely unfamiliar with Greek philosophy. ᶜAbbāsids associated Aristotle, more than any other writer of the Hellenic world, with both depth of thought and eloquence of prose. They translated him as an aphoristic source – long, flowing

Classical Arabic courtly prose includes pithy Aristotelian references even as its overall style contrasts with Greek philosophical and rhetorical writing. Aristotle was an authoritative symbol, and Abū l-Faḍl inspired comparisons to the philosopher. The vizier greatly benefited from such rhetoric. Abū l-Ṭayyib al-Mutanabbī (303–54 H, 915–65 CE), during a brief period as Abū l-Faḍl's court poet, composed a panegyric likening the vizier to both Aristotle and Alexander. In the space of one hemistich the poem marks the historical apogees of both eloquence and political mastery, while giving al-Mutanabbī himself credit for discerning the greatness of a patron-litterateur (*Dīwān al-mutanabbī* 525). For al-Tawḥīdī, the comparisons between the vizier and ancient philosopher are exactly the problem, distracting people from what he sees as a pattern of greed and abuse. He combines sarcastic direct address with third-person commentary:

> تزعم أنك من شيعة أفلاطون وسُقراط وأرسطوطاليس، أوَ كان هؤلاء يضعون الدّرهم على الدرهم، والدينار على الدينار، أو أشاروا في كتبهم بالجمع والمنْع، ومطالبة الضعيف والأرملة بالعسف والظلم
>
> ...
>
> وهو يزعم مع هذا أن أرسطاطاليس لو رآه لرجع عن آراء كثيرة ببيانه
>
> (AW 324–7)

> [Abū l-Faḍl,] you claim to belong to the school of Plato, Socrates, and Aristotle – oh, did they stack dirham on top of dirham, dinar on dinar? Did they write in their books of hoarding and withholding (wealth), taxing sick and widowed people under the threat of force?
>
> ... Despite all this (that is, Abū l-Faḍl's depravity), he contends that Aristotle himself would reconsider many of his views if the two were to meet!

In the binaries that al-Tawḥīdī diligently constructs, the majesty of Greek philosophy is incompatible with the vizier's administrative policies, which are of course a function of his offensive personality. The author is just as diligent, however, in avoiding the question of eloquence and worldly knowledge, the basis of al-Mutanabbī's praise. For everyone but al-Tawḥīdī, policy and moral fibre were secondary criteria by which to judge the vizier. Al-Thaʿālibī calls Abū l-Faḍl 'the latter-day al-Jāḥiẓ', and there is evidence to support his claim that educated people knew the vizier by that title in the tenth century (YDQ 3:183; Ibn Khallikān, ʿAbbās ed. 2:405 and 3:256).

The Aristotle and al-Jāḥiẓ comparisons are closely related, marking two of the cultural standards to which Arabs looked when assessing high prose: ancient and contemporary, foreign and domestic. Whereas Aristotle's writings were curricular – artefacts of another era and culture, only discrete parts of which did ᶜAbbāsids adopt in their new Arabic works – Abū ᶜUthmān al-Jāḥiẓ (ca 160–255 H, 776–869 CE) was the author of arguments still current and important in the Būyid era. To inherit al-Jāḥiẓ's prose distinctions in the century after his death meant a reputation for erudition, persuasive power, and the shapely composition of prose. The hyperbole of such comparisons is a hallmark of Classical anthologising, but this particular one necessitates a stylistic note. The *risāla* (epistle) genre that helped make al-Jāḥiẓ so famous overlaps with, but is crucially different from, official *kitāba* such as that which Abū l-Faḍl practised. In the world of *adab*, a *risāla* by a career writer could function as entertainment, meditation, edification, or argumentation. Oftentimes, a *risāla* played all of these roles at the same time. For the vizier functioning as secretary, an official letter tends to do little arguing as we currently understand the term: 'Cogently convincing the addressee of one's argument seemed less important than demonstrating the power of one's position through the parameters of the relationship between writer and addressee' (Gully, *Culture of Letter-Writing* 10). In other words, Abū l-Faḍl and his vizierial colleagues were taking part in performance first and foremost, and the aesthetic goals of their *kitāba* were those of power rather than persuasion. Here Abū l-Faḍl exemplifies his use of the bully pulpit, writing on behalf of Rukn al-Dawla to Ibn Bullakā Wandād-Khūrshīd,[11] an army officer involved in a military revolt:

> وأنا مترجح بين طمع فيك ويأس منك، وإقبال عليك وإعراض عنك، فإنك تدل بسابق حرمة
> وتمتّ بسالف خدمة، أيسرهما يوجب رعاية، ويقتضي محافظة وعناية. ثم تشفعها بحادث
> غُلول وخيانة، بآنف خِلاف ومعصية، وأدنى ذلك يحبط أعمالك ويسحق كل ما يرعى لك.
> لا جرم أني وقفت بين ميل إليك وميل عليك، أُقدم رجلاً لصدك وأُؤخر أخرى عن قصدك،
> وأبسط يداً لاصطلامك واجتياحك وأثني ثانية لاستبقائك واستصلاحك
> (YDQ 3:193)

I waver between my (feelings of) attachment to you and despairing of you, between turning towards you and turning away from you. You make a show of being an enthusiastic servant, the first to give reverence. To truly

> offer such fealty, one needs to be scrupulous, bringing it to full fruition, but instead you have been contemptuous and disloyal, and you follow that up with arrogance and hubris. It ruins the work that you do, crushes everything that had been cultivated for you, to say the least. It is certainly understandable that I would be caught in this position, between taking your side and taking sides against you. I've put one foot forward to ram into you and the other foot backward, to divert you. I've reached out one hand so as to attack and cut you down, and the other I've held back so as to steady you, to serve your best interests.

This passage, especially its use of *sajʿ* (rhymed prose), is a reminder both of the challenges presented by sophisticated prose and the groundswell of excitement surrounding *kitāba* in the fourth/tenth century. Multisyllabic rhyme by itself adds a note of distinction to the highly self-conscious style: we note it in *riʿāya … ʿināya*, here used as synonyms, and in the near-lyrical admonishment *adnā dhālika yuḥbiṭu aʿmālaka wa-yasḥaqu kulla mā yurʿā laka*, in which he recruits the final two words to conform to the rhyme scheme.[12] In a *kitāba* text so unsubtle in its threats and sketch of power, its musical qualities call constant attention to aesthetics along with politics. While certainly not in the same register of 'rhapsodic heights' Said identifies in modern poetic performance, the genius of *sajʿ* usage is that it suggests Classical poetry in its emotive capacities, while reserving for itself the unique empirical authority of descriptive prose.

As a performed text, Abū l-Faḍl's letter depends upon two political moves, elision and separation. *Kitāba* identifies its own individual author but, more importantly, issues from an institution: Abū l-Faḍl writes this letter from his chancery office that, as a node of the court itself, is a mobile and largely conceptual place. It also renders him simultaneously vizier and prince, in certain respects, or a vizier wielding royal authority in the space of the letter. Such elision means that, when the *sajʿ* speaker chides, cajoles, and menaces Ibn Bullakā, he wields Abū l-Faḍl's famous command of language and Rukn al-Dawla's famous command of armies.[13] Doing his secretarial duty by composing this letter on behalf of his prince, Abū l-Faḍl assumes – even if only within the space of the discrete letters he penned for Rukn al-Dawla – the prince's authority. He uses the voice of 'Abū l-Faḍl', the chancery persona, but the threat of aggression mentioned in this letter gives a clear sign that he also speaks as the ruler who punishes by mandate.

The separation of power at the conceptual level is, as Gully has argued, inherent to the *kitāba* genre. After quoting the letter at length, al-Thaᶜālibī reports that Ibn Bullakā responded to the letter, 'By God, reading that section, it was as if the Master were directly addressing my own self! The letter took the place of entire armies of men, scrubbing my skin (manners), setting me straight, and restoring my loyal service to its author' (3:195).[14] The language of discovery in this response suggests the 'razor-sharp Aristotelian instrument' Said privileges as he describes his recalibrated notion of Arabic prose: 'scrubbing my skin' is *ᶜark adīmī*, literally 'to scrape my tanned hide'. Tempting though it may be to liken razor to tanner's blade, the letter does not construct a proof but instead demonstrates power, as Gully avers. That power, because it has already been acquired before the moments of composition and delivery, has a fixed or even banal aspect in most individual works of *kitāba*. The letter means not to discern truth from falsehood, or even good from bad, but rather master from servant, obeisance from insubordination.

To be able to conjoin and separate status in the provinces of one's empire is the essential criterion for an administrative writer. For that reason, *kitāba* is the literary and administrative format in which secondary- and tertiary-level officials began to enjoy the empire's highest political authority, albeit limited to the temporal confines of individual texts' composition, delivery, and recitation. *Kitāba*, as an art practised episodically, pays more dividends in the subsequent phases of textual industry. One such phase is the actions of addressees to acknowledge the text, in writing and other notable moves. However, even Abū l-Faḍl's own letters are mostly lost, and very rarely are written responses collected. Documentation of imperial subjects' interactions with Abū l-Faḍl, oral and written, is scant. What is clear and attested in detail is the fact of his great body of correspondence, the place his letters took in the secretarial curriculum, and a now-lost instructional book he authored on eloquence, *Al-Madhhab fī l-balāghāt*. Beyond bibliography and canonisation, his long-term effect on Arab written culture is largely owed to the tutorial role he played for Ibn ᶜAbbād, and for Rukn's son ᶜAḍud al-Dawla, who would become the foremost Būyid prince. Abū l-Faḍl's lasting cultural primacy was therefore as much a campaign waged by his protégés as by the vizier himself. Most of all it was Ibn ᶜAbbād, the focus of the analysis to follow, championing his mentor as he entered the contentious arena of literature.

Learning Patronage, *Kitāba* and Poetic Self-conceit in the Vizierate

In the year 347/958, Abū l-Faḍl dispatched his twenty-year-old pupil Ibn ᶜAbbād from the Ray court in which they both served to Baghdad, where Rukn al-Dawla's son was to be married. Ibn ᶜAbbād composed letters on the event and his overall experience in the capital, a formative moment for him. His letters sent back to Ray, collected in a book entitled *al-Rūznāmāja*, depict an early awareness of social dynamics, the workings of courts, and literary sensibility. So much of the document focuses upon one *majlis* ('assembly', literally 'a sitting') or another, it is easy to forget the wedding itself and fixate upon the informal performances and interactions that Ibn ᶜAbbād prized.[15] He practises the multiplicity of performances folded into the epistolary format: the chronicle of poetic recitations in gatherings by Baghdad luminaries and Ibn ᶜAbbād himself, the presumed subsequent recitation of the text upon its arrival in serial form to Ray, and of course the performance of power dynamics that make *kitāba* cohere. In this document we see the junction of several key elements of the vizierial formation and identity. Geography, ethnicity, and family name inform virtually every cultural movement in this era of the empire: to read *al-Rūznāmāja* is to see a politically ambitious intellectual contemplating his origins and trajectory at court.

Ibn ᶜAbbād relates to his addressee with techniques dialogic but, significantly, not contrapuntal. He shows his ability to praise his teacher so that he responds to Abū l-Faḍl's directives – stated and unstated – while gradually asserting his own literary identity. In an oft-repeated anecdote, Abū l-Faḍl asks Ibn ᶜAbbād about the visit upon his return to Ray and the vizier-in-training responds, '*Baghdādu fī l-bilādi ka-l-ustādhi fī l-ᶜibādi*' (YDQ 3:183) ('Baghdad is to cities what the Master is to humankind'). The 'Master' reference is of course Abū l-Faḍl's honorific cited above; what is less obvious is the way that this quip responds to the elder vizier's own quoted speech. As al-Thaᶜālibī notes, Abū l-Faḍl declared that the simplest way to reliably judge a man's erudition is by that man's appreciation for the capital (*Laṭā'if al-maᶜārif* 170–1). Therefore, the honour that Ibn ᶜAbbād confers to city and teacher is also self-praise, employing the logic of Abū l-Faḍl's own formula. Ibn ᶜAbbād's *sajᶜ* quotation is illustrative of the praise offered upward from student to mentor, but it contains one suggestion that we, from our historical perspective, may deem misleading. It is clear that both Abū l-Faḍl and Baghdad carried enormous symbolic weight for Ibn ᶜAbbād throughout his career. Whereas Ibn ᶜAbbād indeed surpassed his mentor in literary fame and political power (Ibn Khallikān, *Kitāb wafayāt al-aᶜyān* 1:216), he never established himself in the capital, where his father had trained. Even in that century of decentralisation, to identify a person or a cultural project as Baghdadi invariably meant prestige. *Al-Rūznāmāja* attests to Ibn ᶜAbbād's unfulfilled desire, intimately tied to ᶜAbbāsid history, for a vizierate in the capital.[16]

As Ibn ᶜAbbād details the invitations he receives and accepts around Baghdad, his physical movements act out the social, artistic, and ethical concerns with which *al-Rūznāmāja* is so intensely preoccupied. The text serves as a reminder that courts both followed their patrons but could have deep conceptual ties to cities of empire. Most illustrious of this dual nature is the vizier al-Muhallabī, Ibn ᶜAbbād's docent in Baghdadi salon culture. Originally from Basra, al-Muhallabī cultivated and built upon the reputation of his family line, established in Islamic politics during the Umayyad era more than two centuries prior. Ibn ᶜAbbād's exclamations at al-Muhallabī's hospitality have a dual purpose. They provide Abū l-Faḍl with the information he would desire about his peer's cultural activities, while affirming that Ibn ᶜAbbād himself understands the rules of propriety: how to accept an invitation, how to stand and sit depending on the host's prompts, when to speak, when to stay silent, and how to offer his own poetic speech to serve the interests of the court. *Al-Rūznāmāja* is phrased so as to emphasise the young visitor's gracious acceptance of his host's requests, while detailing a series of peregrinations around central Baghdad and the bucolic outskirts where al-Muhallabī preferred to entertain. Ibn ᶜAbbād's techniques for recording and framing his own contributions to the *majlis* consistently portray him as learning to master performances that would please those around him, even in this unfamiliar setting. In ᶜUkbarā, a small, verdant city approximately 70 kilometres up the Tigris from Baghdad, al-Muhallabī is said to have hosted drinking parties such as this one:

فاستدعى دنا للوقت، وخماراً من الدير، وريحاناً من الحانة، واقترح غناء من الماخور، وأخذنا في فن من الانخلاع عجيب، بطريق من الاسترسال رحيب، ورسم أن يقول من حضر شيئاً في اليوم، فاستنظروا وركبت فرسي، فاتفقت أبيات لم تكن عندي مستحقة لأن تكتب أو تسمع، لكن رضاء القوم جمل لدي صورتها، ولو لا حذري من توبيخ مولانا لطويتها:

تركت لسافي الريح بانة عرعرا وزرت لصافي الراح حانة عكبرا
وقلت لعلج يعبد الخمر زفّها مشعشعة قد شاهدت عصر قيصرا
فناولنيها لو تفرّق نورها على الدهر نال الليل منها تحيّرا
وأوسعني آساً ووردا ونرجساً وأحضرني ناياً وطبلاً ومزهرا
هنالك أعطيت البطالة حقّها وألقيت هتك الستر مجداً ومفخرا
كأنّي الصبا جرياً إلى حومة الصبا أناغي صبياً من جلندا
مزنّرا فعانقته والراح قد عقرت بنا فكررت تقبيلاً وقد أقبل الكرى
وصدّ عن المعنى النعاس وصادني إلى أن تصدى الصبح يلمع مسفرا
وهبت شمال نظّمت شمل بغيتي فطارت بها عني الشمول تطيّرا
فكان الذي لو لا الحياء أذعته ولا خير في عيش الفتى إن تسترا

(Āl Yāsīn ed., *Nafā'is* 4:104–5; DSIA 227–8)

(Al-Muhallabī) called for wine, for a wine-server from the monastery, and for fragrant greens from the shop. He cued a song from the group of drinkers and we began to lose ourselves in the enchanting art, relaxing us deeply. Then, as I mounted my horse (to leave) they were waiting in expectation, so some lines of poetry came forth from me that I hardly consider worthy of writing or hearing. But the audience's encouragement made them seem more beautiful to me than they truly were. If not for my fear of disappointing our Good Sir al-Muhallabī, I would have folded them away!

1 I left a cypress's palm tree to the lofting breeze and visited the tavern in ᶜUkbarā for pure wine.
2 Calling out to the hardy young man serving it, 'Bring it out, that glimmering one that has seen the Age of Caesar!'
3 And he gave it to me – if its light had shone on our age, the night itself would have given in, bedazzled.
4 He regaled me with myrtle, roses, and narcissus; he brought before me a flute, drum, and tambourine.
5 (Dizzied,) I called falsehood the truth, and I found the great glory in disgrace!
6 Full of party spirit, I whispered sweet nothings to the young

man, as if I were a light breeze wafting over the very best parts of youth.
7 I embraced him, kissing him again and again, the wine taking hold of us, drowsiness setting in,
8 My speech sleepily slurring, tilting me off-kilter, until the glitter of dawn came.
9 A north wind blew, a good omen, rekindling my desire when the wine had drifted off.
10 He's the one whom, if it weren't for discretion, I'd tell everyone about – ah, there's no point in living the high life of youth if it's kept secret!

Ibn ᶜAbbād's junior status in the gathering disappears in the poem itself, which uses the rules of genre to make him more senior, and therefore dominant. In part, this is what distinguishes the *khamriyya* (wine poem) from the event's prose description: throughout *al-Rūznāmāja*, prose anecdotes signify his vizierial education in process and, by extension, the symbolic benefits accruing both to student and master(s). The *khamriyya*, whose sociopolitical meanings are contested issues in modern criticism, typically invokes love and sex. In odes to wine-drinking, amorous motifs rely almost always upon the master–servant relationship.[17] To dominate and/or seduce the wine-server (poets and rhetorician most frequently call him *sāqī*, 'pourer'), the archetypal *khamriyya* poetic speaker exploits the boy's liminal age and position (Wright and Rowson eds, *Homoeroticism in Classical Arabic Literature* 7). No longer a small boy but not yet a bearded man, the *sāqī* occupies the only role for which the poem may present him as off-limits, tantalising in his young beauty, and at the same time licit according to the libertine poetic world. Line 6's 'light breeze wafting over the very best parts of youth' (*al-ṣabā jaryan ilā ḥawmati l-ṣibā*) celebrates both pleasure and the exploratory, knowledgeable hand of age. By adopting the voice of experience before an audience of elders, the twenty-year-old poet and emissary depicts his own graduation from studious novice to educated adult. He also engages the ephebe-loving aesthetics reportedly preferred by the highest Būyid rulers, Muᶜizz al-Dawla (303–56 H, 915–67 CE) and ᶜAḍud al-Dawla, the former of whom had provided the auspices for Ibn ᶜAbbād's Baghdad junket in the first place.[18]

The poem relies on the authority of its genre to perform its author's prowess, while balancing between societal licence and its stated self-censorship. From latter ᶜAbbāsid centuries to the present, that has meant specifically engaging the wine-song's generic avatar, Abū Nuwās. The poem's final line emphasises the necessity of keeping secrets – expressed with the verb *tasattara*, literally, to take on the protection of a veil or curtain – and clinches its acknowledgement of the genre's master. Ibn ᶜAbbād's *wa-lā khayra fī ᶜayshi l-fatā in tasattarā* ('Ah, there's no point in living the high life of youth if it's kept secret!'), unambiguously refers to Abū Nuwās, not just in theme but nomenclature as well. Litterateurs of Abū l-Faḍl and al-Muhallabī's erudition would have had little trouble detecting the presence of two phrases from an Abū Nuwās tavern celebration: *fa-ᶜayshu l-fatā fī sakratin baᶜda sakratin* ('the high life of a young man is in drunkenness after drunkenness') and *lā khayra fī-l-ladhdhāti min dūnihā sitrū* ('there's no point in pleasures kept secret').

The vizier's characteristic mix of bravado and obsequy served him well as he developed a body of work and parlayed it into his own distinguished legacy. There was very little doubt among the literati of the fourth/tenth century that Abū l-Faḍl's primacy in *kitāba* would prove lasting, and Ibn ᶜAbbād offered tributes to 'the Master' and to the profession of *kātib* for producing the finest literary scholars (*Al-Kashf* 31–2). At the same time as he identified with the secretarial class and especially with his mentor's achievements therein, Ibn ᶜAbbād looked to another recent precedent to see how forcefully he may intervene. Abū l-Faḍl and al-Muhallabī were of course skilled, renowned poets, and both held literary gatherings of great fame. Ibn ᶜAbbād recognised that he could achieve their rank in the poetic field, but he also aimed to push further what they had begun: establishing new norms of a politician's artistic speech in a court context. He had seen Abū l-Faḍl speak the political authority of the emirate, writing letters that forcefully imposed upon subjects the courtly power of Rukn al-Dawla.

Just as importantly, he would have known the anecdote of al-Muhallabī satirising a royal – gently but pointedly. Rukn's brother, the prince-of-princes Muᶜizz al-Dawla, was said to have become enamoured of a young male servant, whom he foolishly placed as an officer in the imperial cavalry. Al-Muhallabī composed a short poem teasing his prince for the move, portraying the gentle servant as burdened by 'a belt and sword, weighing him down' and inadvertently losing a major battle for his regiment (YDQ 2:267). With his emphasis upon the man-child's slender body and swaying hips, al-Muhallabī destabilises the whole cavalry as it would be imagined by his poem's audience. Relying upon one of his predecessors in anthologising the incident, al-Thaᶜālibī notes that al-Muhallabī's poem was prophetic: Muᶜizz's forces indeed fell in battle not long after the servant episode (2:268). What had begun as a court joke evolved into a political, military embarrassment for the monarch – at least if we are to believe the chroniclers. That sequence of events ultimately lends credit to al-Muhallabī for judging his sovereign's matters more clearly than Muᶜizz himself, for not allowing physical beauty to confuse his political mind.

In the course of Ibn ᶜAbbād's literary education, he saw and seized upon opportunities to shed the armature of princely employ. At times, he chose merely to may make a show of such an emergence, while maintaining the prince–vizier relationship. Both kinds of gesture – his claim to autonomy and his respect for certain facets of the established hierarchy – he seems to have learned from the two great viziers of the generation before him. Ultimately, he achieved a synthesis of literary, vizierial techniques that amounted to more than the sum of its parts. Another way of saying this is that he surpassed the already-ambitious models that Abū l-Faḍl and al-Muhallabī had provided. Al-Tawḥīdī is correct that Ibn ᶜAbbād was power-hungry and capable of scathing language, but the anti-vizier polemic fails to note precisely what the goals were of his courtly outbursts. On that count, Ibn ᶜAbbād's career opens up an enquiry into cultural politics during the latter centuries of Arab empire, reaching far beyond the moral and rhetorical frames upon which his biographers fixate.

Making Ethics from Poetics: Ibn ᶜAbbād's Humour and Slander

Ibn ᶜAbbād was known for *mujūn* and *hijā'* among the highest political elites, willing to use a degree of profane speech beyond that which his colleagues uttered. His brazenness, combined with his political position, granted him unique power at court. It also helped make him the target of al-Tawḥīdī's extraordinary slanderous writing. Ibn ᶜAbbād has the rare distinction of prompting the most extended of literary attacks in Classical Arabic – the book AW purports to demean both viziers, but as we have seen, Ibn ᶜAbbād receives much more attention than Abū Faḍl. In a certain sense, Ibn ᶜAbbād confirms the charges against him: his revelry in 'low' poetry left him open to moralising critique but also proved one of his assets as a power broker. Al-Tawḥīdī, a disgruntled ex-courtier, devotes special attention to Ibn ᶜAbbād's penchant for obscene speech and poetry. The book uses the terms '*sukhf*', '*khalāᶜa*', and '*mujūn*' (150), all of which are closely related and take idiomatic literary meanings having to do with impetuosity and libertinism, although their levels of emphasis vary.[19] The focus here will be on *mujūn*, which the vizier was well-known for enjoying and that he employed for the express purpose of slander. The most common and probably most capacious word used for risqué poetry, '*mujūn*', is often used by rhetoricians and anthologists with appreciation rather than al-Tawḥīdī's scorn, and it is furthermore anthologists' preferred term to apply to Ibn ᶜAbbād. Whereas al-Tawḥīdī portrays the courtly sessions in which such words are exchanged as a decadent show of Ibn ᶜAbbād's poor taste and moral depravity, in fact the vizier keenly understood how he may take the reins of that entertaining spectacle of language. Al-Tawḥīdī's accusation, mirthful in spite of itself for the colourful literature it indignantly quotes, ignores or misunderstands patrons' techniques for controlling courts. A brief review of poetic trends at that historical moment places into relief the matter of *mujūn*.

Just as viziers were a supposedly secondary or tertiary rank of officials who reformed the existing order, poetry itself was rearranging its priorities. The Barmakids' paradigm of the cultured administrator, still very much a part of Būyid life, required knowledge of not only long-form poetry but also short poetic quips, and of quotations to punctuate speech and commemorate occasions. Abū l-Faḍl's famously comprehensive memory for poems included the shortest of verses along with pre-Islamic, Umayyad, and ᶜAbbāsid poems of more than a hundred lines each. In the fourth/tenth century, the long-form *qaṣīda* continued to hold a symbolic place atop all of the arts but for two centuries the *qiṭᶜa*, the occasional poem, had acquired greater stylistic sophistication, and its versatility was obvious. For the polymath Ibn ᶜAbbād, this process allowed the occasional poem not only to punctuate spoken exchanges but also to serve as the centrepiece of artistic performances.

Ibn ᶜAbbād's composition and performance of *mujūn* uses power as adroitly as Abū l-Faḍl's chancery writing. Using poetry to engage the rhetorical and theological polemics current in his day, the younger vizier exerted the force of *hijā'* (invective) while reserving for himself the flexibility and exculpability of jest.[20] Al-Thaᶜālibī fondly presents them as *bons mots* fitting particular occasions, distilling the courtly moment to its essence. Whereas al-Tawḥīdī fixates on the question of taste – quoting the speech of poets and courtiers he insists pleased the venal Ibn ᶜAbbād – al-Thaᶜālibī celebrates the vizier's ability to string words together in felicitous ways. Both of these commentators prefer to respond to the moral and aesthetic qualities that they detect in Ibn ᶜAbbād's speech. Likewise, they both leave open the question of its ideological use value in the vizierate and its empire, an interpretive task that now falls to us.

At a broader critical level, it is crucial to explore the ideology of *mujūn* in Arabic for the precise reason that neither medieval nor modern scholars have done so. The interrelated stylistic ideas of *mujūn* and *hijā'*, and the poetic convention of the occasional or impromptu *qiṭᶜa*, all enjoyed great popularity as the ritualistic and oftentimes contentious games played by courtiers. What they also have in common is their anxious treatment at the hands of modern critics. Commentaries of the past two centuries range from morally dismissive to apologetic. Rarely do they approach the works as 'proper' compositions, nor do they ask why the poetry conspicuously refrains from trying to excuse its own indiscretions of language. When it was performed, apology generally appeared in separate works, following a poet's offending recitation. The telos of humourous, scandalous, and most of all slanderous poetry was to eschew the very idea of regret; a subsequent work could apologise if necessary, expedient, or ritually fitting. Similarly, modern readers' apparent preference for poems longer than a few lines has led to dubious interpretations of Arabic cultural history. A much-needed redress of *mujūn* and *hijā'* is underway in critical literature, although it has been slow to reach the later Classical tradition.[21] Just as important is our evolving conversation on the *qiṭᶜa* and its place in the poetic field. To Geert van Gelder, the long *qaṣīda* in fact risks overemphasis: *qiṭᶜa* methods 'are, on the whole, more important. More important, at least, it would seem, to traditional Arabic literary critics, while it is not improbable that most present-day readers derive far more joy from a felicitous line, an ingenious conceit, a euphonious choice of words than from recurrent or other patterns of composition' ('Al-Mutanabbī's Encumbering Trifles' 6). Van Gelder's call to readers becomes all the more insistent when applied to the vizierial court, where the *qiṭᶜa* became a site of political contest.

Ibn ᶜAbbād's short *hijā'* is both dialogic and powerfully normative. The technique that he employs most frequently to denigrate in poetry is to station the *mahjuww* (the target of *hijā'*, the ritual enemy) in the territory of taboo. Most frequently, the norm is behavioural, and specifically sexual, providing an index of masculine virtues. The poem calls out to a man in order to place his manhood in question. All of this of course requires the substrate of gender logic and, most importantly, of sex as a discipline: both a practice that is learned in the acquisition of manhood and a means of marking one's place in the boy-to-man formative process. Al-Thaᶜālibī provides a brief introduction before each quotation of Ibn ᶜAbbād's repertoire of short poetry:

وقال في رجل يتعصب للعجم على العرب ويعيب العرب بأكل الحيات:
يا عائب الأعراب من جهله لأكلها الحيات في الطعمِ فالعجم طول الليل حياتهم تنساب في الأخت وفي الأمِ
وقال فيمن زوج أمه:
زوجت أمك يا فتى وكسوتني ثوب القلقِ
والحرُّ لا يهدي الحَرامَ إلى الرجال على طبقِ
(YDQ 3:316)

He said about a man who sided with the Persians against the Arabs and who disparaged them (the Arabs) for eating snakes:

Out of ignorance, you fault the Bedouin Arabs for eating snakes,
But the Persians' snakes spend all night slithering into their sisters and mothers!

He said about a man who married his own mother:

You married your mother, young fellow, giving me the creeps all over
– a free man doesn't serve up sin to men on a platter!

Both of the above poems offer the opportunity to understand the paradigms of *hijā'* consistently reworked in Ibn ᶜAbbād's poetry. The first problematic to address is that of family, whose popularity in *hijā'* is matched by modern theorists' level of interest. Among social and cultural researchers it has been taken more or less for granted since the nineteenth century that incest is one of the most important taboos in the individual psyche and in the organisation of social groups. Both of these compositions use the social to engage deeper problems of authority in the empire, a literary operation that asserts the speaker's intellectual, artistic, and political dominance over his interlocutor(s). The second *qiṭᶜa* of the two above is the one more directly concerned with taboo per se, and its basis for condemning the oedipal transgression is social.[22] The implication of *ḥurr* ('a free man', with which *ḥar* in *al-ḥarāma* achieves consonance three words later) is that he should exercise his choice in the question of whom to marry. Although the poem has referred to him as *fatā* ('young fellow'), its double entendre includes 'slave', a secondary but still common signification that may not otherwise have complicated the verse were it not for the free/enslaved tension established in the second line. The act of creating illicit union is therefore a surrender of one's masculine agency: to 'serve up sin to mankind on a platter' emphasises less the sin than the servant status. By violating the societal norms of marriage, the young man loses the social privilege of freeman and also reverses, or at least arrests, the maturation process that would deliver him from *fatā* to man (the figurative platter of sin is delivered to *rijāl*, full-fledged men).

The first *qiṭᶜa* indicates the deep ethnic anxieties with which Ibn ᶜAbbād contended via literature. Although he hardly shied away from his familial identity, enjoying Persian performances and inviting discourse with fellow native speakers at court (ᶜAwfī, *Lubāb al-albāb* 255; AW 142–4, 306, 466; MU 2:699), he followed his era's convention: Arabic was the exclusive language of his written literature. His polemic engages with the ᶜAbbāsid literary and historiographic convention of Shuᶜūbiyya, the ideology of extra-Arab ethnic identity over Arabness. As Ibn ᶜAbbād and his foremost court savants well knew, viziers from diverse familial backgrounds were expected to energetically champion Arabic discourse, affirming their commitment to existing ᶜAbbāsid standards of high culture. Even more than Abū l-Faḍl, Ibn ᶜAbbād promoted his superiority in Arabic in such a way as to ritually guard against perceived threats to the existing order. In the case of Shuᶜūbiyya rhetoric, the perceived threat is largely an imagined one, because outside of Classical poetry and certain modern Orientalist accounts, there is scant evidence to suggest a substantive movement to demean Arabness and realise non-Arab cultural hegemony in ᶜAbbāsid culture.[23] The poem above attests to that: an unnamed Persian iconoclast merits ridicule, intellectual punishment, and a half-serious form of correction, all because he has proposed an errant historiography. The opening line '*Yā ᶜāʾiba l-aᶜrābi min jahlihi*' plays on the term '*jahl*' to produce a disingenuous and overtly jocular marker of cultural history. In addition to 'ignorance', '*jahl*' has an older meaning, 'rashness', one half of the binary with *ḥilm* (equanimity) essential to Arabic ethical discourse. The period of Arab history prior to Islam is *jāhiliyya*, whose heavy Bedouin significations colour the poem. Whereas the unnamed enemy here would like to play on the hackneyed version of Arab history told in Islamic accounts – before revelation of the Qur'an, they lived in ignorance and tribes perennially fought among themselves – the poem calls him by the very name he would wish to employ. He has left himself vulnerable by championing a vile ethnography.

Ibn ᶜAbbād's aim in the poem is to show his mastery of history along with his fealty to Arabic as the hegemonic cultural system. He performs his own education, the ideology it produces, and the sometimes-violent language necessary to support it. Bearing in mind the formal mastery of texts that the empire's preeminent viziers were expected to acquire in their training, as both readers and authors, it is logical then that even jocular poetry should fixate on history and the telling of history. Shuᶜūbiyya was, essentially, an opportunity to compose poetry in an extravagantly retrospective mode. To take some of the most prominent literary examples, the Sasanian kings Kisrā (Chosroes) are invoked in the great pro-Persian Arabic poems but also in contrastive *qaṣīda* poetry of fealty to the Arab caliph, and in the originary anecdotes of Arabian politics that inform Shuᶜūbiyya literature. That such texts, including propagandist prose, were written down was the key to Shuᶜūbiyya's portability among litterateurs, as Ibn ᶜAbbād was acutely aware.[24] When *Al-ᶜIqd al-farīd*, a major work from al-Andalus that included Shuᶜūbī arguments and counterarguments, arrived in eastern ᶜAbbāsid courts, the vizier is said to have declared, 'These are our goods returned to us' (al-Ṭāhir Makkī, *Dirāsa fī maṣādir al-adab* 287). To take part in a debate over ethnic superiority, whether the opponent is a courtier or an imagined polemicist, is a kind of credential. This moment echoes larger trends in poetry and identity. 'In general, the Persian pride movement in Baghdad contributed to a change in the concept of virtue, and the use of praise poetry to express it, from an emphasis on noble lineage to an emphasis on a person's actions' (Sharlet, *Patronage and Poetry* 188). The poet links himself to the intellectual history in which he himself claims expertise, through his training in the Arabic language arts. When Ibn ᶜAbbād engages a poetic opponent with pointed jokes, he insists that the interlocutor is both ethically and mentally inferior, prone to take refuge in a family name or obscure genetic history.

In the instances in which the poem names its *mahjuww*, the dialogic qualities of slander forcefully emerge. A telling anecdote quotes both Ibn ᶜAbbād's *qiṭᶜa* and the response that he prompted: the vizier takes the predictable route of impugning the manliness of his interlocutor, the Daylamī prince and accomplished writer Qābūs ibn Wushmagīr (ca 338–403 H, 950–1012 CE).[25] The poem makes light of the syllable *būs* that, taken by itself, is a Persian-derived word for 'kiss'. Not to be outdone, Qābūs replies,

من رام أن يهجو أبا قاسم فقد هجا كلّ بني آدم
لأنه صوّر من مضغة تجمعت من نطف العالم
(MU 5:2187)

> He who wants to make *hijā'* on Abū Qāsim[26] actually makes *hijā'* on all mankind,
> Because (by saying the name) he gets the sensation of a mouthful of all men's sperm in the world!

Ibn ᶜAbbād here has invited the exchange of insults, almost always more hyperbolic than virulent, turning the office of vizier into an institution of poetic challenge of all kinds – not merely praise and descriptive versifications but also the choicest quips, bawdy and oftentimes decidedly pointed. Both poet-politicians employ popular *hijā'* conventions, Ibn ᶜAbbād punning on the *mahjuww*'s name, Qābūs hyperbolising sexual promiscuity and submission. Those two techniques run through Classical *hijā'*, especially in this era of wordplay introduced by *badīᶜ* (mannerist poetry), popular since the second/eighth century. Then, in a sustained attack, Ibn ᶜAbbād takes on a certain Ibn Mattawayh, complicating the invective language we have already seen in his poetry:

قال ابن متويه لأصحابه وقد حشوه بأيور العبيد
لئن شكرتم لأزيدنكم وإن كفرتم فعذابي شديد
...
أبصرت في كفّ ابن متوي عصاً فسألته عنها ليوضح عذرا
فأجانبي إني بها متشايخ هذا ولي فيها مآرب أخرى
...
سبط متوي رقيع سفله أبداً يبذل فينا أسفله
اعتزلنا نيكه في دبره فلهذا يلعن المعتزلة
(YDQ 3:314–15)

> 1. Ibn Mattawayh said to his companions after they had stuffed him with penises,
> 'If you show gratitude, I'll give you more, but if you're ungrateful, my punishment will be terrible!'
> . . .
> 2. I saw a staff in Ibn Mattawayh's hand. I asked him about it so that he could offer up an excuse.
> He said, 'I'm using it to act like an old man. That, plus I have other uses for it!'
> . . .
> 3. Mattawayh's grandson has a ragged bottom; he's always showing us his lower end.
> We cut ourselves off (*iᶜtazalnā*) from anal sex with him – that's why he curses Muᶜtazila![27]

It is not known who this Mattawayh was, or indeed if the references to Ibn Mattawayh and 'Mattawayh's grandson' (*sibṭ mattawayh*) truly aim for a father–son duo or if the family name is a catchall, as al-Thaᶜālibī assumes (YDQ 314–15). The flexible conventions for names and the attribution of *ibn* (son) and *sibṭ* (grandchild) allow for either possibility. Historical records of Ibn ᶜAbbād's court are equally inconclusive as to whether this poetic Ibn Mattawayh is the famous Abū Muḥammad ibn Mattawayh, a prominent theologian. Although it is tempting to presume such a connection, there is insufficient evidence to do so, and the analysis here will treat him as a historical unknown.[28]

The poems take up that popular topos of invective – the inability of the *mahjuww* to master desire and sexual politics – and insert it into a religious discourse that would like to purport itself as transcending poetry. To the onomastics and sex of the Qābūs exchange, Ibn ᶜAbbād now adds a theological wrinkle, making his poetry a historicist footnote to a long intellectual debate. *Qiṭᶜa* 1 and 2 quote Ibn Mattawayh, amidst his promiscuities, as reciting the Qur'an. 'If you show gratitude, I'll give you more, but if you're ungrateful, my punishment will be terrible!' is a line describing the covenant at Sinai between God and the Jews led by Moses: *la'in shakartum la'azīdannakum wa-la'in kafartum inna ᶜadhābī la-shadīdun* (14.7).[29] Ibn Mattawayh uses God's admonishment to humanity in order to increase the bounty of sodomy. Likewise, 'That, plus I have other uses for it!' is what the Qur'an attributes to Moses, describing the staff in his right hand, which serves him to tend and feed his flocks. *Wa-lī fīhā ma'āribu ukhrā* (20.18) presages the miracles that God effects via the staff, turning into a snake and curing disease. In *qiṭ*ᶜ*a* 2 the multipurpose, shape-shifting penis transmits the power of the pathetic, the spectre of Moses's snake tying it to the Persians' phallic snakes in our first example of *hijā'* above: animals that slither willy-nilly, abundant and also threatening.

These poems' statement of power issues from their brazenness in the midst of religious awe. To utter God's own words in the context of sodomy, a mortal sin, could be grounds for severe punishment according to a strict view of licit speech. Even the formulations of the vizier's contemporary, al-Mutanabbī, straddling sacred and profane in verse, exposed the poet to charges of apostasy (Larkin, *Al-Mutanabbi* 103). Those charges, levelled by a literary commentator after the poet's death, do not seem to have dogged him in life, and here we have reason to ask why Ibn ᶜAbbād was similarly untroubled in the wake of his apparently blasphemous poems. The conventional historical answer has been that social attitudes had relaxed, especially among political elites, towards risqué poetic speech. Sinan Antoon correctly revises this conclusion by showing the late ᶜAbbāsid rhetorical emphasis upon craftsmanship rather than a vague, modern-inflected notion of cleanliness.[30] To that it must be added that *mujūn* poetry provided its authors with political flexibility. The *mājin* (practitioner of *mujūn*) poet perennially takes refuge in his own facetiousness, and Ibn ᶜAbbād could likewise count on his status as the semiautonomous master of his court. The Būyids' decentralised authority meant not just the dilution of particular powers (most notably the caliph's), but also a more widely dispersed community of poetic authorities. While these individuals competed with one another to attract authors and outshine one another with the texts they themselves produced, they also had ample reason to impose their own tastes on to the courtly class as a whole. The figure of Ibn Mattawayh quoting Qur'an while being sodomised marks not one but two outer points of the ethical world: the extent of the *mahjuww*'s humiliation and the poet's own licence to create the picture of blasphemy.

What connects the first *qiṭ*ᶜ*a* to the second – beyond the sacred quotation, the hint of Qur'anic Moses, and the shared *mahjuww* – is the Islamic text's prophecy and promise of abundance. Through that promise, the poems speak a language of domination and submission not only politically expedient to its author but also seemingly guaranteed by the stability of the quoted Qur'an. The persona of Ibn Mattawayh uses God and Moses's speech in order to plead for more sodomy (*qiṭᶜa* 1) and advertise his exposed penis (*qiṭᶜa* 2). His passive sodomy in the first example, and general fascination with his organ in the second, collapse several Qur'anic ideas into a set of sexual practices. The *ᶜadhāb shadīd* of which Ibn Mattawayh warns his companions (*aṣḥāb*, translatable even as 'lovers' in this context) is God's promise for life and afterlife: He holds out the wrath he would mete out on the world of mortal beings and, potentially, on the Day of Judgement. Suzanne Stetkevych articulates these fraught relations between the Qur'an and poetry, and the hermeneutical role that *adab* can play in medieval readers' understanding of the sacred. In a study of Abū l-ᶜAlā' al-Maᶜarrī's (363–449 H, 973–1058 CE) literary arguments, she shows how the adoption of Qur'anic conceits allows al-Maᶜarrī to draw a useful binary between mortality and immortality, then between pagan pre-Islamic poetry and the monotheistic world in which *adab* was being produced. The Qur'an offers al-Maᶜarrī – and, as we will see, Ibn ᶜAbbād – a poetic opportunity: God's word proscribes wine and certain kinds of sex on earth, while also promising ample wine and sex for pious souls in the afterlife. Noting the Greek mythic hero Ganymede's sexualisation as the object of Zeus's desire, Stetkevych points out that a

> parallel development occurs in Arabic poetry when in the Islamic period – particularly in Abū Nuwās – the discreet *sāqī* of pre-Islamic poetry is sometimes depicted in explicitly erotic terms. What the example of Ganymede tells us is that the reason for the attendance of the immortal ephebes upon the paradisiac carousers – and here both the snickerers and the prudes have missed the point – is that they are symbols of immortality. (Wright and Rowson eds, *Homoeroticism in Classical Arabic Literature* 224)

It is crucial to understand that love for the *sāqī*, especially in Nuwāsid poetry, can move a step past the chaste language of early Arabic amorous poetry, into vivid descriptions of sodomy. It is not just his boy-man liminality and his serving of wine that offer immortal pleasures. Sex with him is itself a way of crossing from one world to the other. Connections, then, emerge between Ibn ᶜAbbād's *hijā'* and his love poetics in ᶜUkbarā. By managing life and after-life via sodomy, *qiṭᶜa* 1 extends the *sāqī* to metaphysical extremes. It seizes the wine genre – already a poetics of licentiousness – and twists it upon itself. Ibn Mattawayh as a would-be *sāqī* is also a would-be God: he not only offers a bridge between mortal and immortal worlds, he claims ownership and total control of them. In each of the three poems translated above, Ibn Mattawayh attempts to change his boy-man status, whether towards the ephebe (*qiṭᶜa* 1 and 3) or the elderly man (*qiṭᶜa* 2). In a poetic field concerned with stages of maturation and the possibility of the immortal, he shifts between them all, moving forward and backward depending upon the position he seeks in sexual exchange. Offering up his organs and sacred speech, he also offers an index of masculine love poetry.

Finally, the third *qiṭᶜa* caps the poetry of sexualised religion by sexualising the very act of debating religion. Muᶜtazila proved one of the most divisive and long-lasting issues in ᶜAbbāsid courtly life, a driving force in theological polemics and, as Ibn ᶜAbbād demonstrates, poetics as well.[31] At the core of Muᶜtazila were the questions of (1) if the Qur'an could be said to have been created and (2) whether God endowed humans with free will. Muᶜtazilī scholars' insistence on seriously pursuing such controversial ideas, and their tendency to allow for affirmative answers to both questions, earned them the respect of ᶜAbbāsid caliphs initially. By the time of the Būyid takeover, however, a trend was evident: with occasional exceptions, the highest authorities in Baghdad had tended to disapprove of its doctrines for a century already. Būyid reign meant a new patronage system for Muᶜtazila among Shīᶜī princes and viziers. Muᶜtazila had proven to be a liability at the highest political levels but it nonetheless attracted and retained adherents throughout ᶜAbbāsid cities. The arguments that Muᶜtazilī theologians issued in the fourth/tenth century resonated throughout the empire: by itself the issue of free will could divide courts and stigmatise prominent individuals. One of Ibn ᶜAbbād's courtiers chides him in a poem for denying predestination, an apparent response to the vizier's expansive theological writing, including poems of Muᶜtazilī bent (YDQ 3:320, 327). Ibn ᶜAbbād's work of versification pairs with his court's abundant formal prose on Muᶜtazila. His argumentative writings both advocate Muᶜtazilī positions and attempt to educate readers on its principles, complementing the work of his chief religious judge, Abū l-Ḥasan ᶜAbd al-Jabbār (320–414 H, 932–1024 CE), one of the most prominent legal commentators on the movement.

As an invective topic, Muᶜtazila proved at least popular as Shuᶜūbiyya, and much more consequential. It motivated some of the most vital, impassioned, and eloquent arguments in the Islamic Middle Ages. The poem makes the putative anti-Muᶜtazilī position seem both pathetic (Sibṭ Mattawayh is passive in his sodomy) and ridiculous (he is insatiable and desperate). The verb '*iᶜtazalnā*' noted in the translation above means not just 'we cut ourselves off from' but also, in a theological context, 'we took up Muᶜtazila'.[32] The submissive party – an ironic position for Sibṭ Mattawayh, given the typical Muᶜtazilī complaint of being outnumbered among the politically powerful classes – resorts to petulant speech. His curses aim towards his own overwhelming urges and his sexless fate, fate itself being a main locus of Muᶜtazilī controversies. It would be convenient but mistaken to conclude that Ibn ᶜAbbād's intent was simply to dominate Ibn Mattawayh, although that may well have been among the goals of the *hijā'*. He sought to dominate poetry in its self-reflexive capacities, as his *hijā'* performs a key exegesis of wine poetry – and the dialogic format of joke- and insult-exchange. Further, he bound his court's poetics to the ethnic arguments and religious science crucial to late ᶜAbbāsid life, exercising control over those expansive fields of discourse. In this poem he asserts ownership, not only of the textual promotion of Muᶜtazila but also, in an abstract sense, of his courtiers' pejorative responses to it. Because short-form *hijā'* constantly anticipates rejoinders in kind, and because his court was the empire's preeminent site of poetic contests and theological argumentation, to enter into insult exchange with him was to also submit to the power of his oversight. He defined the parameters of speech one could use. Even al-Tawḥīdī, doing his utmost to portray the vizier's exchange of witticisms and poems as aberrant, affirms that Ibn ᶜAbbād's poetic taste was insidiously normative in his court (AW 374).

Al-Tawḥīdī's attack compels us to rethink the politics of insult, so conspicuous in his prose and, up to now, neglected in our studies of the vizierial poetry he disparaged. Since he wrote his screed, scholars have continued to wonder at and try to explain the questions of taste and humour, and how the vizier's bawdy speech at court relates to his intellect. Among modern commentators, a general conclusion prevails: Ibn ᶜAbbād embodied the openness of his cultural moment. Where readers disagree is whether his humour can truly be said to be of poor taste or if it is simply a sign of his lightheartedness and linguistic curiosity.[33] Aside from the anachronism inherent in qualitatively judging a medieval thinker's tastes, the problem highlighted in this debate is that it fails to historicise jocular poetry, even though our critical field has actively undertaken such work in the case of panegyric and martial poetry. The act of defending Ibn ᶜAbbād from moralistic charges against him has, in the past, attempted a moral language transcending eras. Kraemer insists on distinguishing between members of the vizierial court, lamenting some of its more libertine members but insisting that, in the case of Ibn ᶜAbbād, '[h]is humor is playful, not sardonic or aggressive. He was fascinated by language. Much of his wit has the flavor of the irrepressible punster and compulsive rhymester. He was competitive with his wit but not overly so, for while he loved to display his brilliance, he also appreciated cleverness in others' (271). Kraemer joins many literary historians in presuming that the vizier's humourous poetry was politically unmoored, despite the clear sensitivity of the court to biting jokes and their effect on one's standing among peers. The competitive spirit that he detects in Ibn ᶜAbbād's literature and court conversation could not have limited itself to stylistic play.[34] Matching poetic wits with the vizier was a game whose outcome was in many respects decided before it began. Ibn ᶜAbbād enjoyed his courtiers' clever speech because it served the interests of his court: even when they ridiculed his behaviour or theology, the exchange of insults ensured that superior thinkers and writers would be attracted to his vizierate, where the cultural stakes were highest in the empire. Al-Tawḥīdī was correct in a way that he probably did not foresee. Ibn ᶜAbbād's delight in *mujūn* and insults did indeed change the relationship between language, ethics, and politics: what al-Tawḥīdī calls perverting the court was in fact reforming it.

A Poetics of Combat

In this chapter I have tried to answer the question of how ᶜAbbāsid identity changed during a period of caliphal weakness and Persians' cultural ascent in the empire. A great many modern scholars have noted the Būyid regime's enthusiasm for Arabic literature – princes and viziers alike – and the formal innovations that came out of their period in power. But the office of the vizier is in no way coincidental to any of this, nor are the administrative skills that viziers flaunted as they commissioned and produced extraordinary *adab*. They revised the rules of courtly exchange and poets' ritual jousts. With their literary statements of self-praise, intimidating epistolary prose, religious dogma, and satire, viziers altered the relationship between patron and author, each of whom was now able to slander the other in rhyme. In effect, they had begun to legislate with literature. Their exchanges of inflammatory compositions were some of the most closely followed events among the courtly classes, not only in the Būyid era but also in the resurgence of ᶜAbbāsid authority in Syria and Egypt, two centuries later.

As our focus shifts here from the waning years of Arabic courts in the eastern Islamic world to the Crusades-era Levant in the next chapter, politics and key literary concerns change, but the most immediate critical question remains very similar: how does literary contention at court serve the political interests of the regime that presides over the match? Ibn ᶜAbbād traded lines of *hijā'* and *mujūn* with his poets and scholars in order to engage the entire courtly sphere. His message to the ᶜAbbāsid literary classes was that vizierial power had taken on a new dimension with his jokes and intimidation. He sharpened the language of power that his instructor Abū l-Faḍl had modelled. Now that we have seen the politics of literary confrontation and jest, the next chapter will examine a well-studied political world whose literature has been neglected: Saladin's vizierate and sultanate in the eastern Mediterranean. Abū l-Faḍl and Ibn ᶜAbbād inserted themselves into the contentious, volatile field of literary exchanges at court, shaping the ᶜAbbāsid ideal during the empire's last phase as a prominent world power. In turn, the authors around Saladin looked back to the ᶜAbbāsid model as a means of stabilising their sultan's court amidst the wars and diplomatic challenges presented by the Crusades. As Levantine writers composed literature to ascend in the court, they tapped ᶜAbbāsid theology, etiquette, panegyric, *hijā'*, and ethnic debates to form their own discourse of power.

Notes

1. Hanne, *Putting the Caliph in His Place* 43; Madelung, 'Assumption' 96–100; Naaman, *Literature* 5, 86, 131–2.

2. For major works that press the critical conversation in new directions and consider recent movements in the field of Classical Arabic studies, see Ali, *Arabic Literary Salons*; Antoon, *Poetics of the Obscene*; and Ḥajjār, *Madīḥ al-nabī*.
3. Al-Tanūkhī's praise for the Barmakids appears at various points in his collection of courtly anecdotes, *Nishwār al-muḥādara*. For a liberal sampling of his reflections upon the early vizierate, see ᶜAbbūd al-Shālji's edition of the work, especially 8:195–6 and 245–8. For interpretations of al-Tanūkhī's attitudes toward the Barmakids, see Margoliouth's more economic edition and translation of *Nishwār*, especially 1:12–13. The questionable 'Golden Age' model of ᶜAbbāsid history tends not to account for the acute administrative, economic, and political problems marking Hārūn's caliphate. Some historians go so far as to associate the Hārūn–Barmakid conflict, resulting in the liquidation of their vizierate, with the ᶜAbbāsids' initial decline as a dominant world power (EI2, 'Hārūn al-Rashid').
4. For a discussion of that changing relationship in Abū Nuwās's career, see Kennedy, *Abu Nuwas* 9–11. The Barmakids, Hārūn, and Abū Nuwās achieved proverbial fame outside the Classical tradition, in Arabic imaginative prose, World Literature, and Orientalist performing arts. Most notable are their roles in the Arabian Nights, translated and still fancifully adapted in drama, film, and cartoons. See *Arabian Nights Encyclopedia*, especially 1:167, 1:202–6, 1:235–6, 1:316–17, 2:585.
5. In al-Tawḥīdī's time, the production of long epistles, handbooks, and histories of the vizierial institution reached what appears to have been its peak. The best-known such works to have survived (albeit piecemeal, typical of Classical prose sources) are Hilāl al-Ṣābī, *Tuḥfat al-umarā' fī ta'rīkh al-wuzarā'* ('The Elites among Princes in Viziers' History') (better known by its more accurate descriptive title *Kitāb al-wuzarā'*, 'The Book of Viziers') and Abū l-Ḥasan al-Māwardī, *Al-Wizāra* ('The Vizierate'). One major precedent from which al-Ṣābī (himself a *kātib*, or chancery secretary) and al-Māwardī seem to have worked is Muḥammad ibn ᶜAbdūs al-Jahshiyārī's *Kitāb al-wuzarā' wa-l-kuttāb* ('Book of Viziers and Secretaries'), written under the Barmakid vizierate. All three authors make use of the intense positive and negative attention paid to viziers in order to produce histories of the Islamic vizierate as a long-term Islamic institution transcending the ᶜAbbāsid period.
6. In al-Tawḥīdī's other famous book, *Kitāb al-imtāᶜ wa-l-mu'ānasa* (its text consistent with its title, 'Delight and Friendly Companionship'), takes a moment to criticise Ibn ᶜAbbād for being poorly trained in court disciplines. Tellingly,

the harsh critique runs down a litany of the individual fields of knowledge in which the vizier is supposedly deficient, as if their careful separation in the text facilitates the degradation of Ibn ᶜAbbād's character. Even al-Tawḥīdī, though, grants that his nemesis is a good poet (61).

7. *Kitāba* overlaps in definition with the equally capacious term *inshā'*, which took stylistic definitions distinct from *kitāba* in rhetorical manuals especially in late centuries of Arab empire and Ottoman-era Arabic production: see Gully, *Culture of Letter-Writing* vii, ix, 15–23. Although *inshā'* was used by ᶜAbbāsids by the time of Būyid rule (EI2, 'Inshā'' para. 6), the writers of interest here tend to use *kitāba* for chancery composition. For discussion of the importance of *kitāba* in the Būyid poetic field – and a critical conclusion that the poetry emerging from the secretarial class was of greater quantity than quality – see Naaman, *Literature* 144–6.
8. Our modern understanding of medieval *adab* has evolved in recent decades. 'Humanistic knowledge' is Samer Ali's translation (*Arabic Literary Salons* 14), the most accurate and capacious English definition of *adab*'s role in Classical Arabic manuscript culture. Before Ali's study, the predominant translation had been 'belles-lettres'. Although *adab* is a field of learning most commonly associated with prose, metred poetry is also a key component. For an overview of the belles-lettres idea and the poetics of *adab*, see Bonebakker in Ashtiany, et al. eds, *ᶜAbbasid Belles-Lettres* 16–30.
9. For a detailed account of this episode and its fallout, see Bonebakker, *Ḥātimī and his Encounter with al-Mutanabbī*, especially 17–18. Ibn ᶜAbbād himself seems to have participated, writing the treatise *Al-Kashf ᶜan masāwi' al-mutanabbī* ('The Revelation of al-Mutanabbī's Shortcomings') that, although we may call it an ad hominem attack, restricts itself to manufacturing criticisms of the great poet's works rather than debasing his entire moral being, as al-Tawḥīdī does to his vizierial adversaries.
10. Abū l-Faḍl of course performed the duties of *kātib* but chronicles tend not to dwell on that title, referring to his vizierate instead. This is also true of Ibn ᶜAbbād. Abū l-Faḍl was known both professionally and affectionately as *al-ustādh al-ra'īs* ('the High Master', or simply 'the vizier of Ray'). On Ray's status as a crucial and contested site of vigorous intellectual, theological, and belletristic arguments, see Busse, *Chalif und Grosskönig* 410. On the administrative meaning of the title *al-ustādh al-ra'īs*, see Donohue, *Buwayhid Dynasty* 137n36.
11. On the revolt in which Ibn Bullakā was implicated, see TU 5:317–19 and Donohue, *Buwayhid Dynasty* 40–2.

12. *Riʿāya* means 'watching over' or 'cultivating', as in watching over animals or cultivating crops, thus Abū l-Faḍl's idea of giving careful attention; *ʿināya* is, idiomatically, a synonym; *adnā dhālika yuḥbiṭu aʿmālaka wa-yasḥaqu kulla mā yurʿā laka* is translated here as, 'The worst (of your actions) ruins the work that you do, crushes everything that had been cultivated for you.' This translation, in its appeal to precision, omits the sounds and stylistics of Arabic rhymed prose, which are salient aesthetic features of the original composition.
13. This combination of powers is strictly confined to the imaginary of the letter exchange. Organising chancery and organising soldiers were generally kept separate in ᶜAbbāsid politics (Mottahedeh, *Loyalty and Leadership* 170). Miskawayh, ever the extoller of Abū l-Faḍl's virtues after his service as the vizier's librarian, maintains that Rukn al-Dawla had only limited vision when it came to military strategy, in contrast to Abū l-Faḍl's broad political expertise (TU 5: 376–7). With regard to the letter's taxonomy, it bears note that the divisions between official political letters (*sulṭāniyyāt*) and 'letters of friendship' (*ikhwāniyyāt*) had become flexible by this period of Islamic empire and seem to have been becoming all the more so as centuries passed (Gully, *Culture of Letter-Writing* 8, 177).
14. The Arabic phrase is 'وردي إلى طاعة صاحبه' ('and restoring my loyal service to its author'). The multivalence of 'صاحبه' should be noted: I have chosen to translate it as 'its (i.e., the letter's) author' over the other possibilities: 'his companion' or 'his master', i.e., Abū l-Faḍl or even Rukn al-Dawla.
15. *Rūznāmāja* means 'journal', a Persian term used in that era of ᶜAbbāsid Arabic, which eventually became *rūznāma*, meaning an almanac or Ottoman-era governmental bureau. The readerly response could, however, be a function of the text's paleographic history more than of its author's mindset. *Al-Rūznāmāja* in its complete form may well have prioritised the prince's wedding and its political significance. The document survives only in al-Thaᶜālibī's selections of the text throughout *Yatīmat al-dahr*, and his primary interest is of course literary content. Because YDQ and all editions of the anthology are plagued by lacunae and errors, Muḥammad Āl Yāsīn's more exacting edition in his fourth volume of *Nafāʾis* is used here.
16. 'Baghdadi scholars were so numerous and so eminent that reference to them could continue to support the "center-of-the-world" thesis even when the material prosperity and political importance of the city had receded' (Cooperson, 'Baghdad' 100). On Ibn ᶜAbbād's long-term designs on Baghdad, see TU 6:100; Donohue outlines al-Muhallabī's precise vizierial authority in *Buwayhid Dynasty* 140.

17. For arguments on the politics of libertine poetry, including wine verse, see Halasā, *Al-ᶜĀlam* 96 and Kennedy, *Wine Song* 214.
18. The anecdote is permeated with the sexual reputations of Būyid officials and the political concerns of royal marriage. Muᶜizz al-Dawla is said to have become so infatuated with a 'Turkish young man' (*ghulām turkī*) that al-Muhallabī was moved to chide him for it in a poem (YDQ 2:267). ᶜAḍud al-Dawla, whose Arabic knowledge far outstripped Muᶜizz al-Dawla's, wrote his own amorous verse admiring a young man (YDQ 2:260). The official reason for Ibn ᶜAbbād's visit to Baghdad, where Muᶜizz al-Dawla presided, was the wedding of Mu'ayyid al-Dawla to Muᶜizz al-Dawla's daughter.
19. Al-Tawḥīdī's diatribe on Ibn ᶜAbbād's taste in language and literature appears in AW 142–94. Of the three terms given above, *sukhf* is the strongest and perhaps the most difficult to translate. Antoon meditates upon the word's complexities in Classical Arabic, including al-Tawḥīdī's own multiple polemical uses for the term (*Poetics of the Obscene* 7–12). Al-Tawḥīdī does not acknowledge the irony in his own celebration of *mujūn* (via another vizierial patron, Abū ᶜAbd Allāh ibn Saᶜdān) in another of his books, *Kitāb al-imtāᶜ wa-l-mu'ānasa* (191).
20. *Hijā'*, as one of the five to seven *aghrāḍ* (literally 'goals', idiomatically 'genres') delineated by Classical rhetoricians, appears in Arabic poems of all lengths and periods. Its popularity in the Būyid-era *qiṭᶜa* seems to be a product of long-evolving social practices in which *hijā'* took centre stage.
21. The ritual of poetic apology is detailed in Stetkevych, *Poetics of Islamic Legitimacy* 16–47 and touched upon by van Gelder in Peters ed., *Proceedings* 82, where he also notes Classical rhetoricians' difference of opinion on whether the *qiṭᶜa* or the *qaṣīda* is a better format for *hijā'*. For examples of major modern critics' discomfort with *mujūn* and the behavioural norms they see it reflecting, see Bouhdiba, *Sexuality in Islam* 116–17; Ḥusayn, *Maᶜa al-mutanabbī* 255; and Nicholson, *Literary History* 295–6. Szombathy responds in comprehensive fashion in *Mujūn* (see especially 284–310). See also Hämeen-Anttila's critical overview in Talib, et al. eds 13–23.
22. 'Oedipal' is used here merely to indicate the taboo on marrying one's mother. The term here should not be taken to suggest that ᶜAbbāsid literati had knowledge of Oedipus; they seem to have had none (van Gelder, *Close Relationships* 143).
23. For a historical perspective on the Būyids' position on ᶜAbbāsid cultural primacy, see Sourdel, *Le vizirat ʿabbāside* 2:576–7. A brief critique of the Orientalist ten-

dency to exaggerate the reach of Shuᶜūbiyya is offered by Savant, *New Muslims* 27–8.

24. For historical documentation of the political trends informing the literature of Arab and Persian history, see Ashtiany, et al. eds, *ᶜAbbasid Belles-Lettres* 34–5, 160, 181, 279; and Khalidi, *Arabic Historical Thought* 103.
25. The Daylam region, whose kings and princes enjoyed varying degrees of sovereignty vis-à-vis ᶜAbbāsid rulers, occupied the southern Caspian Sea coast and parts of the Alborz mountain range in northern Iran.
26. The text reads 'Abā Qāsim' rather than the proper 'Abā l-Qāsim'. This may be a copyist's error or a subtle private joke made by Qābūs, perhaps belittling Ibn ᶜAbbād by getting his name slightly wrong.
27. Al-Thaᶜālibī includes occasional comments and intervening *qiṭᶜa* poems between those numbered 2 and 3.
28. Abū Muḥammad ibn Mattawayh's dates of birth and death are unknown but likely straddle the fourth/fifth centuries H, tenth/eleventh centuries CE (*Encyclopædia Iranica*, 'Ebn Mattawayh' para. 1; EI2, 'Ibn Mattawayh' para. 1; Heemskerk, *Suffering* 62). Several scholars believe him to have studied with Abū l-Ḥasan ᶜAbd al-Jabbār (320–414 H, 932–1024 CE), a high distinction among Muᶜtazilī theologians. Ibn ᶜAbbād appointed ᶜAbd al-Jabbār chief judge of Ray (Heemskerk, *Suffering* 65–6, 41). For discussion of Ibn Mattawayh's poorly documented origins and the open questions of his involvement with ᶜAbd al-Jabbār and Ibn ᶜAbbād, see EI2, 'Ibn Mattawayh'.
29. Ibn ᶜAbbād removes a few particles and energetics appearing in the original Qur'an verse, so that he may fit the poem's *sarīᶜ* metre.
30. *Poetics of the Obscene* 19–24. The relaxation-of-tastes thesis is summed up in Kraemer, *Humanism* 28–9, 58.
31. The two words used for Muᶜtazila in Arabic, '*iᶜtizāl*' (isolation or separation) and '*muᶜtazila*' (separatist), give a hint of the iconoclast reputation its practitioners oftentimes carried, although the precise usage of those terms as the movement began are not definitively known (EI2, 'Muᶜtazila' para. 2). For Ibn ᶜAbbād's primary Muᶜtazilī writings, see Āl Yāsīn ed., *Nafāʾis* 1:11–30 and 2:87–95.
32. Grammatically, the poem's speaker may be understood as individual or plural; the third-person-common subject of this verb is often used as a formal way of voicing the first-person singular.
33. Following AW, dismissive and derisive treatments of Ibn ᶜAbbād's tastes began with poetry written shortly after his death (YDQ 5:119). Among modern commentaries, the extraordinary charges about the vizier become moralistic (Āl Yāsīn

in DSIA 306; Bosworth, *Mediaeval Islamic Underworld* 1:63). More recently, Lagrange ('Obscenity' 170–2), Naaman (*Literature* 184–208), and al-Tawātī (*Al-Muthaqqafūn* 2:176) attempt to counter the moralising approach to Ibn ᶜAbbād's poetic attitudes.

34. Naaman sees the main function of Ibn ᶜAbbād's jocular poetry as entertainment rather than intimidation, but delineates *hijā'* as a marker of power relationships (*Literature* 136–7, 159n51).

2

The Sovereign and the Foreign: Creating Saladin in Arabic Literature of the Counter-Crusade

During the late ᶜAbbāsid era, the vizierate had become its own industry of cultural contention. As the dynasty of Ṣalāḥ al-Dīn Yūsuf ibn Ayyūb (532–89 H, 1137–93 CE; hereafter Saladin) consciously adopted ᶜAbbāsid models of authority and literary means of courtly ascent, the new sultanate fashioned a new such industry. Ayyūbid intellectuals around Saladin saw that emphasising administrative prowess – his and their own – in literature had paid dividends for both the ᶜAbbāsids to whom Saladin cannily pledged fealty and for the Fatimids, whose Egyptian caliphate he would supplant. What was starkly different was the existential threat of the Crusades in many of the cities and fortresses where Islamic rule was supposed to be most powerful. In the centre of the military campaign, courtiers consolidated their ideological efforts around the vital figure of the ruler. Viziers, knights, legal officials, and secretaries engaged one another in order to articulate an effective counter-crusade. Through their ongoing work to win advantage in the court system, they compunctiously maintained some of the rituals of the outgoing Fatimid caliphate in Egypt, while appealing to the more hegemonic ᶜAbbāsid notion of *adab*. Composing *adab* texts allowed Crusades-era authors to claim the kinds of authority enjoyed by Būyid administrators generations earlier in Iraq and Iran. It also gave Ṣalāḥ al-Dīn's court key intellectual credentials as it marshalled support for the Levantine military campaign. The discourse of repelling and dominating the Crusaders required authors to contribute not just martial poetics but also a narrative of progressively mastering the enemy. Their texts meant to comprehend dangerous foreigners by using the material knowledge Muslim elites developed at court.

For authors, the social, political, and economic ravages of war seem to have been more of a boon to their livelihood than a threat. The games in which they were engaged for recognition logically fit into the larger struggle for control of the Levant. Framed by the counter-crusade, they acquired a sense of motivation, immediacy, and urgency as courtiers explored well-established rituals of literary contention. Along with the reassuringly unitary image of an invader, they also sought benefit from the presence of a dynamic, literarily minded sultan at the centre of the production. Saladin provided the court with an actively fighting object of praise and a type of organising principle that the courts had not had for several generations. The Ayyūbid sultanate, a dynasty of great importance to Islamic cultural development and political history despite its relatively short period of sovereignty, enjoyed a particular form of success unknown to those regimes preceding and succeeding it in the Levant. Faced with a unique cosmopolitan experience of Crusader war, poets constructed an image of the Ayyūbid ruler that I term 'panegyric concordance': they tapped the hyperbole of their own tradition to make Saladin necessarily world-conquering and just beyond their own powers of description. The sense of an unfinished portrait of glory helped to make the literary craftsman indispensable, the potential challenges from his peers ever-present but also involved in a collaborative effort to form the *mot juste* for Saladin.

At the same time, the less glamorous but equally contentious exchanges of literature instrumentalised war in multiple genres. Their results in text were highly evocative, and continue to play a paradigmatic role in literature. Fascinating, alien *ifranj* ('Franks', Arabic writers' catchall to describe Western European enemies) lent invective poetry a special telos, as we will see in the last moments of official Fatimid rule, when Muslim armies were just beginning to gain momentum against the Crusaders in the Levant.[1] It is well documented in scholarship that Ayyūbid poets consciously reproduced previous stylistic idioms, many of them from ᶜAbbāsid war poetry. We find the residues of Byzantine and Persian stereotypes in counter-Crusades literature, the familiar enemies providing fodder for new ones (Hermes, *European* 158–62). But that observation does not take into account the unprecedented events occasioned by the Crusades, nor their effect upon the production of court texts. For the first time, Islamic sovereignty over one of its three holiest cities had been overpowered by non-Muslims who were furthermore uncontrolled desecrators in Arabic descriptions. Poets and chancery scribes practised their respective arts in places bearing the signs of both Crusader-inflicted damage and collaboration between the enemy and coopted Muslim officials. Because the threat was multiple, and revealed the conflicted loyalties of Muslim subjects, elites in the empire needed to imagine a reassuring singular figure presiding over the court. In the course of two generations, the elite intellectual sphere would come to group around Saladin. As political and military leader, successful antagonist to Crusade forces, courtly conspirator, and of course patron, he provided a logical centre-point for literary creation. His literary persona synthesised the major thematic 'objectives' (*aghrāḍ*) of the era's poetry: through him, the court exalted in panegyric, tapped the imagery of amorous verse, ridiculed enemies, and called the populace to arms. In official prose documents, too, scribes wrote the language of political authority into his pronouncements and their own descriptions of his sultanate. Then, in Europe, Saladin would become a versatile and potent caricature in Western literature during the eight centuries following his death, a phenomenon addressed in this book's final chapter.

The scenario of politically minded belles-lettres centring around an extraordinary individual anticipates modern academic treatments of Saladin. He presents us with a major challenge as we undertake a sociopolitical, historicist critique of the court – not because of any inherent features of his reign but because modern writers still contend with the fantastic elements of his European portrayals from the Middle Ages onward. While he is among the most studied figures in Islamic history, the copious poetry produced for and about him is largely terra incognita for philologists and critics. The trend has attracted notice in recent decades, even as little work has been produced to reverse it. 'The Sultan loved poetry,' Robert Irwin notes.

> He was saturated in it. He knew by heart the *Hamasa* of Abu Tammam.[2] Saladin even composed poetry himself. Besides Arabic, he seems to have some Persian ... We won't fully understand Saladin ... until we come to grips with the role of poetry in shaping [his] ideals and sensibilities. (Jensen, et al. eds, *Cultural Encounters during the Crusades* 287)

Saladin's well-documented poetic attachments and sophistication are, as Irwin contends, ample reason to begin studying him as a major figure in

Arabic literary history. His Persian knowledge and his reputation as an author – bringing to mind Ibn ʿAbbād – are not proven in documents of his own court. If it is true that Saladin composed literature, such texts have not been discovered. What survives, however, is the work of his courtiers, the focus of this chapter.

Judged from a Formalist remove, there is little that is exceptional about the texts of Saladin's court. Much as his political role was distinct but not revolutionary, literary norms were by no means upended during his tenure. The sultan's politics themselves were very much a logical function of his predicament first in Syria, where he became a military officer, and in Egypt during the twilight of Fatimid rule, where he achieved supremacy. There can be no doubt, however, that his reign created distinct paradigms for his Ayyūbid successors and the much longer-lived Mamluk regime that would go on to dominate the region (Humphreys, *From Saladin* 1–4, 18–19; Petry, *Protectors* 32). What distinguishes his reign, so far as literary culture is concerned, is the unique role that Classical Arabic writers assigned him over two centuries of textual production. During his ascendancy and reign, but even more so in retrospective work of historical *adab*, Saladin became an uncommonly potent symbol of ideology and individual monarchical rule.

The sultan was, as befitted any logocentric ruler, an arbiter of taste. But what will compel our critical attention is his extraordinary status as a literary fiction, a figure invented for the many ideological purposes that literature served in his time. To articulate the name Saladin in the context of studying medieval Islamic life is to invoke multiple historic and artistic identities – this was true during his lifetime and is perhaps even more the case now. This chapter will attempt to understand the first such identity formation, the process by which poets and prose writers strove to make the sultan an icon, and the consequences that process had for the Middle Ages. I will examine two distinct but deeply interdependent forms of competition in literature, one in the service of the other. The poetic contests of the kind we have seen in the ʿAbbāsid empire continued under Saladin and, for the most part, set the same priorities as antecedent courts had done. But they also set the terms for a larger conflict. Throughout Saladin's vizierate and then his sultanate, his courtiers designed a literary Saladin who held the promise of success against the Crusades. He relieved the trauma of the Franks' presence in Islamic territory and the radical difference that they represented to the Muslim administrative class of society.

Preoccupations with the Crusades: Finding a New Approach

This chapter's historicist analysis of literature will question how modern scholars have used the historical record to portray Arab Muslims' conceptions of medieval Europeans. In the middle and latter half of the twentieth century, Middle Eastern Studies developed a refrain, still repeated after many decades: the Crusades produced in Muslims no breadth or depth of interest in who the enemies were, what their cultural origins were like, or what could be learned from them about the rest of the world.[3] Despite the essentialist declarations to be found in such works, they are still prominent required reading in Middle Eastern Studies: Claude Cahen's Crusades article in the *Encyclopaedia of Islam*, the standard reference text for the field, finds 'the Muslim mind' incapable of determining the Franks' inner motives (par. 4). Most spectacular and consequential, however, has been the synthesis of Orientalist claims presented by the historian Bernard Lewis. As his writing became increasingly political approaching the twenty-first century, Lewis repurposed the Crusades-as-quagmire idea to underpin a broad theory of world history, controversial in academia but enthusiastically received by Western governments and the popular press. What at first had been a statement about the Middle Ages – his finding of 'a complete lack of interest and curiosity among Muslim scholars about what went on beyond the Muslim frontiers in Europe' (*Muslim Discovery* 142) – became, in a subsequent and more widely read work, a thesis of Arabs' modern cultural decadence. The semi-rhetorical question chosen for the book's title, *What Went Wrong?*, found its answer in Lewis's previous writings: indifference and suspicion towards the West had held back the societies of the Middle East since a medieval Golden Age, finally resulting in a late-modern malaise that includes dictatorships and violent forms of Islamic politics. There is no doubt that historians and scholars of literary history have rebutted such claims but, as Nizar Hermes points out, the interest-deficit thesis remains popular among twenty-first-century academicians, some of them prominent in political discourse (*European* 4).

By approaching the Middle Ages in this way, Cahen and Lewis (as well as their historiographic adherents) would like to illuminate Islamic thought, but in certain respects they tell us more about modern epistemology. The last generations to identify as Orientalists have felt compelled to view the late Middle Ages as an age that would explain such events as the European Renaissance and the colonial enterprise of early modernity, even – in Lewis's case – geopolitical developments in the twentieth century onward. The theory depicts Islamic societies in the Middle East as sabotaging themselves with their own intellectual complacency once their European neighbours, who had proved vulnerable in the Crusades, eventually developed superior technologies and, stemming from the Renaissance, a superior cultural attitude. Lewis's summary of a millennium became increasingly simple and decreasingly credible as he aimed (successfully) for a steadily broader readership after concluding most academic research in the 1980s, but it is crucial to note that he derived his ideas from an ample body of colleagues' writings on the Crusades and early modernity.[4]

Among the numerous problems in this decades-long scholarly trend is that it interprets geopolitical power as primarily a function of knowledge, rather than acknowledging that the reverse is often the case. The idea that well-funded and prestigious academic institutions, especially those that foster study of human subjects, lead to a superior and more globally powerful culture would seem to ignore the early modern history of Western universities: during and immediately after the Renaissance, sciences and what came to be called humanities were in many cases fostered for the explicit service of imperial power. Orientalists have furthermore used an accepted definition of the Renaissance (translation, cosmopolitanism, the founding of universities, and the use of historical artefacts to improve one's own culture) as a model by which to understand medieval cultural developments. The Crusades, then, emerge as a kind of anti-Renaissance, in which Christendom and the main Islamic empire failed to understand one another. Because neither group of people was culturally outward-facing nor properly disposed to study the past as a repository of information about the future, neither contributed much useful knowledge to the world between the ʿAbbāsid 'Golden Age' and the European embrace of modernity.[5]

What philologists and historians have labelled an insular textual culture was in fact an active, dynamic producer of ideology. Rather than championing the age of Saladin as demonstrably more cosmopolitan or Western-oriented than has previously been thought – we have noted the works of literary history emerging to make that case – this chapter insists that the lament at lacking ethnography draws attention away from the key function of Crusades-era *adab*. The Ayyūbids were knowledgeable about the early ᶜAbbāsid academic programme, in which a foreign (Greek) corpus was translated for its utility, and they were at the same time keen to undertake another project because, in their eyes, the geopolitical moment required it. Their goal was to create a figure of Saladin as the dominating martial interlocutor with the *ifranj*, which would tie their sultan to the Islamic imperial past and serve as a lasting paradigm of legitimacy for his successors. The discourse of *adab*, especially poetry, centred on the idea of a competition between two bodies of belief: polytheism (*shirk*) and monotheism. This familiar opposition, laid down in the Qur'an and plumbed by Classical poetry for centuries thereafter, took on new political meaning as writers used it to distinguish Saladin from his recent predecessors. The battles being fought in the immediate present – the military struggle with a Western enemy – took shape and became intelligible in the historical competition wrought by Ayyūbid authors.

Motifs of Execution

Literary scholarship of the past three decades leaves little doubt that Arabic praise poetry is inextricably linked to political power. That premise can be extended to say that praise achieves form, in many cases, through legitimated kinds of political violence. As with the provincialism, decadence, and binary models all reviewed in the introduction and previous chapter, the topics of violence and Crusade invite facile, unproductive clichés.[6] In its starkest form, such thought explicitly attempts to link Islamic history with ceaseless warfare, and Arabic speech with armed attack and a vague eschatology of martyrdom. While such interpretations issue more from news media and the popular press than from academe, they have a disturbing currency even among some scholars. In Islamic and Middle Eastern Studies, as well as in Medieval Studies addressing the Crusades, we confront these strikingly durable clichés from both the popular media and our own academic corpus. Fortunately, theoretically minded studies of the past decade have taken on much of the critical work of revision, from which contemporary research on Islam and the Middle East is a prime beneficiary.[7] The most crucial task remaining for Classical Arabic criticism and especially for Crusades scholarship is to situate, with precision and judiciousness, the fraught ideas of political violence and propaganda in the literary tradition. Two trends stand to be reversed: (1) the dehistoricising of Classical literature itself, as was the tendency among Orientalists, and (2) the grafting of poetry and didactic *adab* on to a monolithic narrative of war.

As with many Islamic leaders, praise poetry was both Saladin's instrument and a force that instrumentalised him. To appreciate the many functions of praise (*madḥ*), and indeed its central position in imperial culture, it is necessary to explore certain military and judiciary events of political life such as those that occurred during his rise and eventual rule. The court seized upon particular executions of notables to mark his power in literature. Because those acts recalled previous major events in Islamic history, chroniclers and poets used them as performances, integrating him into a larger field of geopolitics and idealised Muslim leadership.

The poetics of Saladin's internal disputes were at first only tangentially related to the Crusades, although that would change as his power grew. The authors who affiliated with him set paradigms early in his rule that did not emphasise his later reputation as the prime antagonist to the Franks. But that initial work compelled the Ayyūbid courts to meditate on their own language and political functions – in other words, to decide what sort of literary sovereign he should become in the course of his mounting clashes with the enemy. In modernity, Saladin is of course most readily identified with the Crusades and his intense efforts to repel them, but for much of his career the pressing political challenge he faced was from the Fatimids' legacy. Their failing caliphate allowed him and his fellow generals to take power, but it also left him with real administrative challenges to address as he became responsible for the empire. Historical records indicate that Saladin's moves into the Egyptian seat of power along with his uncle, Asad al-Dīn Shīrkūh (500–64 H, 1107–69 CE), were simultaneously decisive and prudent managing their own Sunni identities ascending in a conspicuously Shīʿī regime. At the very moments at which they took power as viziers and emirs, the two leaders were hailed in court documents invoking not just Shīʿism but its Ismaili emphasis upon the genealogical legitimacy of the seven Imams beginning with Ali.[8] Likewise, the poetry and other court literature to be analysed in this chapter consistently wend between statements of Islamic unity on the one hand, and declaration of the exclusive legitimacy of the Prophet's family line as it was maintained by Ali and Fatima's marriage on the other. Even at an ontological level but more so in the practical affairs of the court, Saladin's increasing power placed a major burden upon established poets. Many of them were well accustomed to versifying Fatimid propaganda through the lens of their and their patrons' varied positions on religious questions. When the Fatimid caliphate dissolved in 567/1171, the entire upper political, cultural class was obliged to recalibrate, 'revivification of the Sunna in order to consolidate and unify Syro-Egyptian society for the war against Frank and Ismaʿili'.[9]

Although Ḥassān ibn Numayr ʿArqala' (486–567 H, 1093–1171 CE) was neither the most famous nor ambitious poet to gain Saladin's patronage, he composed praise verse with which Ayyūbid writers and anthologists would contend for at least a generation. When Saladin was just establishing his provincial authority around Syria – that is, before his court thronged with poets praising him as vizier, emir, and sultan – he was named to the Damascus *shiḥna* (post of police chief) and ʿArqala was the poet to celebrate the event (ʿArqala al-Kalbī, *Dīwān ʿarqala* 87). Later, he substantially elaborated upon the literary relationship, combining praise and retrospective *hijāʾ* in order to celebrate Shīrkūh and Saladin in their capacity as heroes of Syria, successfully moving down to the Fatimid caliphal seat in Egypt. The event to which the poem responds is the murder of the vizier Abū Shujāʿ Shāwar (*c.*500–64 H, 1106–69 CE), a turning point in the kingdom that signalled the increasing weakness of Fatimid officials in Egypt. Shāwar had alternately allied with and conspired against Shīrkūh, with whom he had at times contended for control of major parts of Egypt and Syria. His volatile career culminated in his forging an alliance with the Crusader king Amalric of Jerusalem (1136–74 CE), meant to defeat Shīrkūh but ending in spectacular failure and earning Shāwar the reputation as traitor. Hated in Egypt and with an army inferior to Shīrkūh's force, he was killed – by Saladin's own hand, according to some chronicles (Abū Shāma 1:398–9, 436; ʿAlī ibn al-Athīr 11:430). ʿArqala's *hijāʾ* serves to situate the poem in imperial history and, in so doing, it grants his short poem anthological substance:

لقد فاز بالملك العقيم خليفةٌ له شيركوهُ العاضديُ وزيرُ
كأنَّ ابن شاذي والصلاحَ وسيفهُ عليٌّ لديه شبّرٌ وشبير
هو الأسدُ الضاري الذي جلَّ خطبهُ وشاورُ كلبٌ للرجال عقورُ
بغى وطغى حتى لقد قال قائلٌ على مثلها كان اللعينُ يدورُ
فلا رحم الرحمن تربة قبره ولا زال فيها منكر ونكيرُ

1. The Successor (Caliph al-ᶜĀḍid), who has as his vizier Shīrkūh the Strong Support (al-ᶜĀḍid), succeeds in a barren realm,
2. As if Shīrkūh ibn Shādhī, Saladin, and his sword, together, were Ali, as close as the brothers Shabbar and Shabīr.
3. Shīrkūh is 'al-Asad,' the fierce lion: his great voice majestically roars. Shāwar was a dog biting at the necks of men.
4. At his tyranny and oppression, people would cry out, 'The damned wolf is circling 'round!'
5. May Merciful God have no mercy for (Shāwar's) grave, may He send Munkar and Nakīr there for a long visit![10]
   (Abū Shāma 2:40; ᶜArqala al-Kalbī, *Dīwān ᶜarqala* 52)

Classical *madḥ* of course presupposes great hyperbole, but ᶜArqala's initial reference to *al-mulk al-ᶜaqīm* (literally, 'barren reign') makes clear how ambivalent is his position in matters of religion and politics. *Mulk ᶜaqīm*'s connotations are generally negative, most often used to describe the state of affairs in Islam after Ali's death and thus the end of 'Rightly Guided' caliphates, when the Islamic community had neither a companion of Muhammad nor a son – since he had fathered only daughters – to act as leader. This site of memory and trauma for Muslims, the origin story of a rift that would in the Umayyad period take on the terminology of Sunna/Shīᶜa, allows ᶜArqala to gesture towards Fatimid legitimacy, which is based in Ali's marriage to the Prophet's daughter Fatima. The problem is that, not only is the reference to political history an anxious one, but the entire first hemistich *la-qad fāza bi-l-mulki l-ᶜaqīmi khalīfatun* depends upon the multivalent verb-preposition phrase *fāza bi*, which reads either as 'to arise victoriously in' or 'to bring about', that is, the alternate translation would be 'the *khalīfa* (Caliph) brought about a barren reign'. Therefore, when line 2 invokes Ali himself, positioning him next to two famously Sunni officials likened to the Prophet's two most illustrious grandsons including martyred Ḥusayn, the ostensible praise for the young and ineffectual Fatimid caliph al-ᶜĀḍid li-Dīn Allāh (*c.*546–67 H, *c.*1151–71 CE) becomes open to question, straddling the distinct poetic dogmas associated with Sunni and Shīᶜī regimes.[11]

It must be borne in mind that Shīrkūh and Saladin's Kurdish family was known as staunchly Sunni. As Saladin took greater control of the empire, he instituted policies in Egypt's mosques to promote Sunni dogma – although it appears he did so prudently and with a pragmatic interest in the best possible relations with the Sunni ᶜAbbāsid caliphate – reflected in much prose and poetry likening him to the Rightly Guided foursome (Ibn al-Athīr, *al-Kāmil* 11:369; Hirschler, *Medieval Arabic Historiography* 78–9). The poem stands in for many kinds of change in political history, long- and short-term: as one of the earliest examples of Saladin's praise oeuvre and a precursor to fast-approaching Ayyūbid era, it introduced a host of anxieties into the poetic court.

The true object of praise is of course Shīrkūh, overshadowing al-ᶜĀḍid in this composition and drawing attention to the event of Shāwar's murder. (The plot had been largely orchestrated by his fellow administrators even though Shīrkūh was the immediate beneficiary, entering Egypt with Saladin and assuming the vizierate with his antagonist now eliminated.) Line 3's 'al-Asad' ('the Lion') refers to Shīrkūh's Arabic honorific Asad al-Dīn, all of which alludes also to the name Shīrkūh itself: 'the Lion of the Mountains' in Kurdish. That the poem gives a sense of one vizier attacking another – a lion dispatching a craven, snapping cur – shows the poem's exertions to individualise a murder plot that was very much a group effort (Abū Shāma 2:40). The historical record suggests that Shāwar, late in his career, was more a hapless representative of the Fatimids than a bona fide tyrant, unpopular among Egyptians and increasingly at pains to triangulate between his regime and Crusader forces. His most infamous act against the kingdom's citizens, the burning of Cairo's neighbouring city Fustat, seems to have been an act of desperation when his pact with Crusaders had soured. It is quite logical that the townspeople expelled from Fustat who watched their homes destroyed on their own vizier's orders would have seen mostly treachery and cowardice in the move, therefore providing the poet with the propagandist opportunity to write *hijā'*, whose resonance would be felt well beyond the confines of high courts. We must give credit to ᶜArqala for initiating the durable poetic account of the vizier's end moves, echoed not only in subsequent poems on the topic but also in prose histories (Lev, *Saladin in Egypt* 63). Then ᶜImād al-Dīn al-Iṣfahānī (519–97 H, 1125–1201 CE), expert in both poetry and prose, delivered his panegyric of unknown date but clearly after Shīrkūh's death in 564/1169, a few months after Shāwar had been eliminated. The Shāwar incident remains fixed in the courtly imagination, for the obvious reason of its historical significance but also because of the poetic ritual continually celebrating it:

هزمتم جنود المشركين برعبكم فلم يلبثوا خوفا ولم يمكثوا ذعرا
وفرقتم من حول مصر جموعهم بكسر وعاد الكسر من أهلها جبرا
وأمنتم فيها الرعايا بعدلكم وأطفأتم من شر شاورها الجمرا
بسفك دم حطتم دماء كثيرة وحزتم بما أبديتم الحمد والشكرا
وما يرتوي الإسلام حتى تغادروا لكم من دماء الغادرين بها غدرا

13. You have defeated armies of pagans, instilling fear in them. It took no time at all for them to scare away, so quick to panic are they!
14. Smashing them, you've scattered their regiments from all around Egypt. Where once her people were the ones smashed, now you have set their bones.
15. With your just ways, you secure oversight and protection for Egypt, extinguishing the embers of Shāwar and all his evil.
16. As you shed (enemies') blood, truly it becomes a flowing torrent. Praise and thanks are heaped upon you for all that you have founded.
17. Islam's thirst will not be quenched until you spill the very last drop of blood, from the very last of those traitors!
(al-Iṣfahānī, *Dīwān ᶜimād al-dīn al-iṣfahānī* 160–1)

The effect of this poem is to reverse ᶜArqala's logic. Whereas the elder poet isolates the figure of Shāwar as a monolithic threat negated, ᶜImād al-Dīn makes the enemy a collective, thereby engaging the existential danger that the *ifranj* represented. ᶜImād al-Dīn, who is quoted in annals professing his admiration for the more senior ᶜArqala,[12] takes the opportunity to laud the Shāwar killing as the preface, or even explanation, for Shīrkūh and Saladin's victories against the Crusaders themselves. This poem builds on a previous panegyric that ᶜImād al-Dīn had composed for Shīrkūh before the emir's death, addressing him, 'You have saved mankind from the evil of Shāwar ..., he who enticed the *ifranj* with (the temptation of) the lands of Islam' (*Dīwān* 80–1). Now, with ᶜImād al-Dīn parlaying his successes as preeminent *kātib* in the Zangī dynasty preceding Saladin's sultanate – work that had brought him into the orbits of Shīrkūh and Saladin, who led Zangī armies – he saw how he may assemble the historical data of courtly intrigues in such a way that they would appear as the natural precursor to success against foreign powers. The poetic pathology that ᶜArqala applies to Shāwar, especially the insertion of doubt as he praised the Fatimid caliphate, allows ᶜImād al-Dīn to reify the high command as the Muslim community's evident saviour. ᶜArqala's paradigmatic and enabling idea is to ritualise the murder of Shāwar, to make it into an event closer to a sacrifice than an assassination. The political utility in that poetic formulation was so evident by the time of ᶜImād al-Dīn's composition that it presented him with the logical motif upon which to elaborate. Denying Shāwar's passage towards the Day of Judgement, ᶜArqala stations the corpse in two paradoxical positions: it dwells in desecrated earth while, in the poetic imaginary, it also lies out in view to demonstrate what befalls the traitor. The embers stamped out are an unequivocal reference to the torching of Fustat, but also perhaps to the hellfire that would await Shāwar.

ᶜImād al-Dīn preserves the sense of Shāwar as totem serving to ward off the long-term threat of the Crusaders but, because the poem engages the form and ideology of the ᶜAbbāsid *qaṣīda*, he performs far more evident political work than does ᶜArqala. The poem's length of twenty-one (extant) lines clearly qualifies it as a *qaṣīda* according to the criteria specified in major rhetoric of that era (Ibn Rashīq al-Qayrawānī, *al-ᶜUmda* 1:188), although it would not seem to aspire to the ᶜAbbāsid praise ideal of a tour de force perhaps twice that length. As discussed in the previous chapter, the valorisation of short poetry that had led up to the Būyid century allowed for a diversity of attitudes towards the *qiṭᶜa* vis-à-vis the *qaṣīda*. ᶜImād al-Dīn fell in line with that durable trend: his *dīwān* toggles between the two poetic formats, using the *qaṣīda*'s pomp to contrast with the witty economy of the *qiṭᶜa*. His move is altogether consistent with the poetic scheme constructed by ᶜArqala and indeed most major authors of the era, although in ᶜImād al-Dīn's case the bifurcation acquires rare historiographic significance because of his more famous chancery and historical prose.

To this poem, depicting Shāwar as a rogue ambassador to the Franks is more important than detailing the vizier's tyranny, a reversal of ᶜArqala's priorities. ᶜImād al-Dīn reflects upon the historical moment even as he seeks to take advantage of it. He supplants the previous poetic account of the decisive move that brought the Ayyūbids to power. Now, Saladin replaces the late Shīrkūh as the most powerful Fatimid emir-vizier, and the poem's panegyric content need not be diluted with caliphal niceties. The disgraced, defeated Shāwar remains so useful as a *mahjuww* (a target of *hijā'*) because the poetic text can identify him with all things local, Arab, and Muslim,[13] and therefore tap a wide set of anxieties about the loss of Arab Muslims' political control of the eastern Mediterranean. It must be borne in mind that Shāwar's appeal to the enemy was an attempt to connect two courtly, military systems: he undertook the intellectual effort of apprehending a foreign entity and cooperating with it. Taken by itself, the diplomatic act between court cultures could not always be portrayed as violent or shameful: the Fatimids had conducted diplomacy with Christian European courts in Italy when it served their commercial interests, a practice that Saladin continued even in the face of military threats from the same ostensible enemy empire (Amari, *Diplomi* 243; Heyd, *Histoire* 396–7). In order to maximise its ideological impact in the poem, and therefore use it to exhort the patron, ᶜImād al-Dīn puts the anxieties of foreign outreach to work, exerting political pressure on Saladin.

The poem seeks ultimately to perform a reverent intertextual sampling of the clichés preceding it in the canon. As it arrives at the *duᶜā'* (appeal to the patron), a hallmark of the *qaṣīda* form, the supplicatory poetic voice integrates the Crusades into the history of Islamic politics and literature. Line 19 exhorts Saladin, 'Do not neglect Jerusalem … conquer it, deflower the virgin!' (*wa-lā tuhmilū l-bayta l-muqaddasa … wa-ftarīᶜū l-bakrā*), directly addressing the patron with the promise of sexual domination. While clearly adapting the sexual metaphors popular in earlier ᶜAbbāsid poetry, ᶜImād al-Dīn seeks to outstrip antecedent texts by delineating Jerusalem's special qualities in Islamic empire. The Crusaders, who rule over the feminised city and covet Egypt, display inadequate powers of control, their panic a key part of the ᶜAbbāsid poetic matrix for representing war with Christian empire.[14] Because the long-form ode requires ᶜAbbāsid components in order to represent war, it must include allusions to sexual transactions as it depicts Saladin earning glory. According to such unspoken rules, the territory in question should be feminine in the poem; the enemy should be a submissive, failed man. Shāwar therefore bridges the dominator (the Islamic military system he was supposed to uphold) with the dominated (the Christian military system whose submission precedes the annihilation guaranteed by the poem). His act of embassy is enfolded into the larger work to sexualise all things imperial. The Shāwar–Amalric interlocution is a ritual requiring the elimination of both its participants, lending urgency to the *duʿā'* calling for Jerusalem's violation. Where ʿArqala deferred Shāwar's full punishment to the indefatigable angels, ʿImād al-Dīn makes the killing simply the first step in a series of imperial actions. The first ritual, having soiled Cairo, is only cleansed by a second, licit ritual in Jerusalem.

Finally, the geographic and political telos of the city signals ʿImād al-Dīn's shifting portrayal of Saladin in Islamic history. As Jerusalem is feminised it achieves new historical valences, not anticipated by the poem's opening. Line 19's final word echoes in poetic performance, a reminder that Jerusalem as *al-bayt al-muqaddas* and the virgin as *bakr* are deeply interlinked in Islamic history. The story of *al-isrā' wa-l-miʿrāj*, Muhammad's 'Night Journey and Ascent', is mentioned in the Qur'an (17.1, 17.60), and elaborated upon in hadith and Prophetic *sīra* (biography) sources. In it, Muhammad goes from the Grand Mosque in Mecca to 'the furthest mosque', that is, al-Aqsa, and then returns. When people in Arabia call his claim a lie, Abu Bakr insists that Muhammad is unfailingly truthful and therefore the story cannot have been fabricated (hadith numbered 680 in Abū Nuʿaym al-Iṣbahānī, *Kitāb dalā'il al-nubuwwa*). Abu Bakr confirms the actuality of the Jerusalem visit, Muhammad's claim to the supernatural experiences gained there, and therefore the original encounter of Islamic political leadership with the city of the two preceding Abrahamic faiths. *Al-isrā' wa-l-miʿrāj* proves to be one of the main poetic topoi of Saladin's age (Dajani-Shakeel, '*Jihād* in Twelfth-Century Poetry' 112).

Cairo: *Adab* of the Vizierate

Two kinds of death, then, served as the critical points by which poets mapped Saladin's rise in Fatimid politics. As authors complicated and at times replaced one another's poetic accounts of historical events, they also meditated upon the motif of replacement that made the young commander a vizier and sultan. The preeminent account, however, belongs to the world of prose. Muḥyī l-Dīn 'al-Qāḍī l-Fāḍil' (529–96 H, 1135–1200 CE), ᶜImād al-Dīn's close colleague, wrote and delivered the *taqlīd* (document of investiture) upon Saladin's succession of Shīrkūh as vizier. He would have had neither the desire nor the proper platform to celebrate the assassination motif. Having served as official *kātib* to Shāwar's son, he also wrote laudatory poems for Shāwar, including endorsements of the Amalric alliance. It was therefore with a keen sense of purpose that he honed his craft under the ascendant Shīrkūh and Saladin (Lev, *Saladin in Egypt* 20–1). As had ᶜArqala before him, he negotiated between the Fatimid affiliations that had sustained him long-term and the shift of power evident in Saladin's succession of Shīrkūh. Because this was caliphal Cairo rather than ᶜArqala's Damascus, and because al-Qāḍī l-Fāḍil had already served for roughly a decade in high administration, the situation was all the more delicate. He used some of the same techniques ᶜArqala had employed – literary intimations of both Shīᶜī and Sunni legitimacy – in poetry but, more crucially, in the prose announcements of the Fatimid court.

It is nearly impossible to overstate the significance of investiture and its documentation in literary Arabic. Because the Fatimid system had essentially combined emir- and vizier status, and because the last three caliphs were children put in place by anxious imperial officials, the empire was extraordinarily vizier-dominated (Sanders, *Ritual* 4), in many respects even more than even the Būyid East had been. Furthermore, the deaths of these superior military officials was but one of several indications of how volatile a political space Egypt had become, and how essential political acumen was to sustain a career in letters. Al-Qāḍī l-Fāḍil could rely upon the caliph's good favour, earned over at least a decade of serving high administrators. To ingratiate himself to Saladin, he used that close relationship in tandem with his literary skill, which al-ᶜĀḍid conspicuously gave him the chance to showcase in the key state ritual of *taqlīd*. The document itself is not only an intricate prose composition, it is also intricately diplomatic. Its formal purposes were to confirm al-ᶜĀḍid's soundness both as inheritor and exerciser of sound judgement, announce Saladin's vizierate, outline his credentials for the post, and describe in a very general way the acts he should perform as vizier. Its ideological purposes were not dissimilar to those that we saw in Abū l-Faḍl's correspondence: seeming to exhort its audience to carry out a wish but in fact consciously demonstrating the power of the office from which it issues, and therefore not really a request but an assured statement of future deeds. Its relationship to a much broader audience is part and parcel of its language. Its use of history, too, is more complex, necessitated by the event and the institutions for which al-Qāḍī l-Fāḍil speaks.

In a long set of statements using the formula *amīr al-mu'minīn* (Commander of the Faithful) for al-ᶜĀḍid, the *taqlīd* offers an impassioned, reassuringly confident rallying cry: 'May God, in His perfection, never turn away from the Commander of the Faithful's nation … May he never forget al-Malik al-Manṣūr' (al-Qalqashandī, *Ṣubḥ* 10:93). This durable, almost generic title for caliphs becomes a refrain but here serves as a counterpoint to al-Malik al-Manṣūr, 'the King Aided in Victory', that is, Abu Bakr. The first leader to succeed the Prophet, as cited in this text, secures a transhistorical place for the current caliph at a time when it was clear how insecure his position had become as the Fatimid figurehead. To use the epithet al-Malik al-Manṣūr has the additional effect of linking Abu Bakr phonetically to Saladin, known as al-Malik al-Nāṣir, so that both of them join in a loose conceptual triangle whose third point is al-ᶜĀḍid. Abu Bakr should in theory evoke a phase of Islamic leadership before the controversies inspiring Sunna–Shiᶜa arguments, and that clearly seems to be the intent here. The irony of his mention would not escape the Shiᶜi Fatimid officials in attendance, nor indeed the predominantly Sunni populace of Egypt who would hear the declaration: selecting Abu Bakr to succeed the Prophet as leader was an act of passing over Ali. Medieval and modern Islamic historical narratives portray this decision as a critical moment of divide in the Muslim community.[15]

Any rift or complication recalled by the text would also serve as an opportunity for amelioration as the *taqlīd* details the chain of command in righteous struggle. The concept of jihad, multivalent then as now, echoes Humphreys's observation above: Saladin acquired high political position at the exact moment in which the imperial contention for the eastern Mediterranean was at a peak. Jihad was recast in order to emphasise its martial senses – historically known as the 'lesser jihad', whose 'greater' counterpart was the striving for piety in Muslim life. Among the primary goals of this intellectual effort was to rally the literary, political class around the pressing issue of the Crusades. From the fifth/twelfth century onward, writers called upon the highest institutions (the caliphate and sultanate) and upon their own scholarly community to put the greater jihad to service to organise, promote, and take active military part in the lesser jihad. This ethical move was imagined as a means to form a class of able scholar-warriors, who would not only fight but also engage the high leaders in the kinds of challenging dialectical exchange that shaped pious policy, especially in critical moments of war against foreign invaders. While an intellectual fighting class performed work to connect the ruler with the legendary righteousness of the Prophet and early caliphs, just as important, his perennial efforts to repulse the enemy would connect his actions to his pious words.[16] Engaging the historical subtext of jihad, al-Qāḍī l-Fāḍil hails the auspicious position of the vizier-sultan for his ability to continually restore the pious community and its military body. 'It is fitting that you be the one whose face God illuminates: you among all those whom He has created in His own image, all those stationed at the sites of jihad, (you to be) the one who fulfills the sworn duties of the Commander of the Faithful' (93). In order to highlight its own function and the basic political apparatus for which it speaks, the document then addresses Saladin in the second person:

> وخرج أمره إليك بأن يوعز إلى ديوان الإنشاء بكتب هذا السجل لك بتقليد وزارته [...] فتقلد وزارة أمير المؤمنين من رتبتها التي تناهت في الإبانة إلى أن لا رتبة فوقها إلا ما جعله الله تعالى للخلافة
>
> (The Commander of the Faithful) hereby issues the order that the royal chancery record you as the head of his vizierate … Accept the investiture of the vizierate of the Commander of the Faithful, the lofty position, leading at the highest levels, the topmost, nothing outshining it except that (authority) which God reserves for the Caliph! (al-Qalqashandī, *Ṣubḥ* 10:95)

Despite his exclusively modern objects of study, Pierre Bourdieu gestures towards the transhistorical with 'the guarantee of delegation' that he insists animates language: 'The power of words is nothing other than the *delegated power* of the spokesperson' (*Language and Symbolic Power* 107, emphasis original). Because the language of this *taqlīd* is not just courtly Classical

Arabic but that of a specific court function, it draws attention to itself and the binding authority of its words. When, in the above quotation, it indicates the very institution of the chancery that publishes and archives it, the document refers to its own delegation and the power, unattainable by other kids of literature, that it wields. We have seen how praise poems, as the products of a professional class of authors earning their living from the art, contain supplications as a part of their form. The *taqlīd* is licensed – and is itself a licence – to give orders. The imperative verbs in and after the above passage (for example, *taqallad*, 'accept the investiture'; *tabawwa' minhā*, 'take your place'; *iᶜtaqil*, 'seize') issue from a voice of command distinct from ᶜImād al-Dīn's poetic order to 'deflower the virgin!' Arabic poetry's archetypal ritual privileges the individual, even as it articulates communal and institutional positions; the *taqlīd* necessarily speaks for the caliph, the chancery, and the government as an institution. Al-Qāḍī l-Fāḍil offered to the court his poetry and *kitāba* from the intimate to formal, official registers: more than different ways of composing, these works were different ways of performing delegation.

Mosul: Aspiration and Discretion at Court

Not coincidentally, Saladin's contemporaries in the literary field gravitated to him for the same reasons that subsequent historians highlighted his career. Following his dominion over Egyptian politics in 567/1171, he spent more than a decade allying with the ᶜAbbāsids to the east and organised a robust campaign against Crusader strongholds near the Mediterranean coast. With al-ᶜĀḍid dead in the same year as the *taqlīd*, Saladin as sultan now authorised to install an ᶜAbbāsid (Sunni) caliph, the task at hand was to ensure Islamic rule in contested regions of the Levant. ᶜImād al-Dīn's ideological call to take Jerusalem would echo in the prolific corpus of martial poetry addressed towards Saladin. Despite that clear sense we have of the era's literary trends, there is little detailed information on Saladin's tastes, and even less on the specific poetic interactions that occurred as authors vied for his good favour. In addition to his reputation, cited above, for having memorised poems from *al-Ḥamāsa*, he was said to enjoy the compositions of the Syrian polymath Usāma ibn Munqidh (488–584 H, 1095–1188 CE), already an elder statesman by the time of Ayyūbid ascendancy.[17] For Saladin, these compendia made up his literary formation: their function was probably in large part curricular, exercising canonical power as aspiring poets entered the court system. There are two known instances, ʿImād al-Dīn chronicling both, in which Saladin and his inner circle held competitive events for poets and prose authors. They give us a unique perspective on how the sultanate shaped and actively wielded taste as a governing tool.

In a little-studied episode from Saladin's campaign in northern Mesopotamia, he and ʿImād al-Dīn surveyed poets from the region of Mosul sometime in the years 578–81 H, 1182–5 CE.[18] ʿImād al-Dīn reports that a group of poets from the area, 'the urban and Bedouin type' alike, had gathered to welcome the sultan and his entourage with poems that they had written and collected as manuscripts (al-Iṣfahānī, *Sanā l-barq al-shāmī* 270). The Kurdish *faqīh*, or religious scholar, Ḍiyā' al-Dīn ʿĪsā al-Hakkārī (*c.*520–85 H, 1126–89 CE), an instrumental part of royal court, was delegated to collect and read the poems: ʿImād al-Dīn credits his fellow courtier with literary discernment and a magnanimous nature, thus the assignment. Saladin, upon receiving the manuscripts from Ḍiyā' al-Dīn, orders them delivered to ʿImād al-Dīn to check their quality and authenticity as compositions, who then tells his reader,

> فما استملحت أكثر ما استلمحت وفيها منتحل ومنتحل ومقول ومنقول وصحيح وسقيم ... فلو حملنا أمرهم على مقتضى الأمر لقل من استقل بالنفع وباء الباقون بالضر فضممت نشرها وطويت خبرها وسترت عيوبها ... وجئت إلى السلطان ... وقلت ما هذا أوان الانتقاء والانتقاد وتعرض الرجاء فيك للكساد وما من هؤلاء إلا من استفرغ وسعه ... وهم وفدتك وقد هدتهم نارك وحدتهم أخبارك فجد لهم على أقدارهم ولاتشعرهم بشعار أشعارهم فقال: نعم ما به أشرت ولنشره بعرفنا عرفت ونشرت ثم أحضر الأكياس وأجرى في تفريق جمعها القياس وأوجد الرجداء وأعدم اليأس وأغنى الوفد وذخر الحمد
>
> (270)

> Most of what I looked at I did not adore. There was original work and plagiarism, there was true composition and mere imported material, both robust and weak content … Had we dealt with their situation even-handedly, only a few would have merited a reward and the rest would have returned home crestfallen. So I held off publicizing the poems, folded away their contents, covered up their faults … and approached the sultan …, saying, 'This isn't the time to be picky and critical, turning to sorrow all the hope placed in you. Every one of these men gave it his utmost … They've

> come to you because your light has led them, your exploits have inspired them. So give them the impression that their quality is good. Don't let on to them about the true stature of their poems.' He replied, 'It's true, what you've pointed out. Let's make an announcement that shows our kind nature.' I acknowledged (the order) and made an announcement. Then I brought money bags and proceeded to dispense them equally, thus confirming hopes and preventing despair, enriching the entire delegation, and winning their appreciation.

As occurs in a healthy proportion of ᶜImād al-Dīn and al-Qāḍī l-Fāḍil's prose pieces, the anecdote serves its author's reputation more than that of its purported subject. Whereas al-Qāḍī l-Fāḍil implicitly attributes power and excellence to himself in the *taqlīd,* here it comes out openly. The passage is titled 'One Type of Sultan-Style Generosity', but ᶜImād al-Dīn credits himself, not Saladin, for the Solomonic approach to aspiring poets. He also shrewdly implies that he oversaw and meted out valuable material prizes, even though Ayyūbid history tells us that Saladin's monetary policy was one of the least popular aspects of his rule. He degraded the dinar currency in an attempt to retain gold for his ambitious military programme (Baadj, *Saladin, the Almohads and the Banū Ghāniya* 108–10). Because the anecdote takes place at precisely the time at which the Ayyūbids were preparing their Syrian and Palestinian campaigns, we have ample reason to doubt the heft and weight of money sacks that ᶜImād al-Dīn mentions.

A story that begins by describing a competition among poets becomes a different account of competitive challenge among peers – subtle tension develops between Ḍiyā' al-Dīn and ᶜImād al-Dīn. Of the two officials, ᶜImād al-Dīn is the one whom Saladin seems to credit with a more powerful mind for detecting plagiarism,[19] that is, ᶜImād al-Dīn is the better-read courtier, or he has the best memory for poetry, or both. Much as praise poetry would like to produce an accord between the poem's expressions of the patron's generosity and the eventual reward that the poet hopes to receive, the historical anecdote wants to show the agreement of king and *kātib.* Saladin chooses ᶜImād al-Dīn for the task of exercising literary taste, and the sultan also assents to the secretary's political calculation of how to please unfamiliar new poets in the region where the Ayyūbids were not universally welcomed.

All of that cachet symbolically feeds into the concluding scene of financial transaction. Saladin's generosity, through one last act of delegation, belongs also to ᶜImād al-Dīn.

This underscores a secondary effect of writing war and diplomacy, namely the ameliorative function that *adab* can have in a frustrated court. The sense of triumph that comes from narrating literary erudition, successful consultation, magnanimity, and the adoration of a region's poets stands in sharp contrast to Saladin's overall experience of invading Mosul. In the course of two expeditions, each involving months of encampment outside the city walls, he was unable to subdue Mosul militarily. His negotiations with its rulers were protracted and for years unproductive, until he was able to acquire much of the region through diplomacy in 581/1186. Where the Saljūq administrative heads proved recalcitrant, ᶜImād al-Dīn insists that the region's poets wished most fervently for the Ayyūbid sultan's approbation. We have seen how the poetics of conquest use the Islamic imperial past in order to invite the patron-leader to acquire glory and impose a legitimate order upon a contested city. Such a dynamic is also at work outside the frame of poetry, administrative prose, and didactic belles-lettres.

ᶜImād al-Dīn's depiction of open competition and equity above all shrewdly elides the traditional processes by which poets accessed and gained advantage with patrons. His self-quotation, 'This isn't the time to be picky and critical' (*mā hādhā awānu l-intiqā'i wa-l-intiqādi*) would seem to him magnanimous but belies the fact that one of the court's most crucial functions was precisely to select (*intiqā'*) and to criticise (*intiqād*) poetic works.[20] His chronicle was primarily written for Syrian and Egyptian audiences, so it is imaginable that he would construe Mosuli poets as inferior. More importantly, his account has it that Saladin himself never read or listened to the poems themselves. The ethos of *intiqā'/intiqād*, placed on hold in order to placate the regional community, also allows the sultan's courtiers to conduct the most important affairs in sorting and evaluating art. Because of our dependence upon second-in-command writers such as ᶜImād al-Dīn for primary source material, and because they all would logically have their own agendas as they often figure in their recorded anecdotes, it becomes clear that Saladin is less of an agent in these narratives than his political status would suggest. Nowhere is this more the case than in instances of *adab*'s negotiation, description, political marshalling, and aesthetic appraisal.

Jerusalem: Conquest, Homiletics and Poetics

The other motif of open competition explored in historical texts is the choice of imam and sermon (*khuṭba*) for the first Friday in al-Aqsa mosque, that is, subsequent to the Battle of Hattin, Saladin's foremost military accomplishment. The culmination of a string of victories, this battle in the Golan region dealt a crushing blow to the Crusader enterprise known as Kingdom of Jerusalem. The towns that their armies held to the west and south of Hattin fell in short order, and Saladin took Jerusalem itself in autumn 583/1187. It is clear that the Ayyūbid political elites saw the need to affirm the symbolism of the conquest when Saladin and his armies entered the city gates. Whether that effort manifested itself in an actual open competition among Levantine clerics, or merely in historians' retelling of the sermon story, cannot be established. In either case, the ideology of Saladin's intellectual regime emerges in sharp relief. As with the Mosul anecdote, ᶜImād al-Dīn goes to great lengths to depict an exceptional talent distinguishing himself from a wide and enthusiastic field, fellow competitors whose identities and prose submissions are not preserved in the account itself. Thanks however to his and a handful of other chroniclers' efforts, we have the sermon's text, by the Damascene legal scholar Abū l-Maᶜālī Muḥyī l-Dīn ibn Yaḥyā ibn al-Zakī (550–98 H, 1155–1202 CE).[21]

As if the sermon would need a prefatory work in order to raise Muḥyī l-Dīn's profile in Syria and guide him to Jerusalem, his selection to lead prayer was anticipated by his success as a praise poet for Saladin. In 579/1183, amidst the Mosul campaigns, the Ayyūbids secured the surrender of sultan Nūr al-Dīn's (511–69 H, 1118–74 CE) Zangī successors in northern Syria – a certain Muḥyī l-Dīn is recorded as having become chief judge of Aleppo that same year, although some historians believe that to have been a different member of the extended Ibn al-Zakī family (Eddé, *Saladin* 581n27; Margoliouth, 'Legend' 540). Our Muḥyī l-Dīn is said to have celebrated the event with a poem calling Aleppo by one of its epithets, *al-qalᶜa al-shahbā'* (the Grey Castle). Its only surviving line reads, 'Your conquest of al-Shahbā' Castle in Ṣafar brought the good tidings of conquering Jerusalem in Rajab'

(Ibn Ṭūlūn, *Quḍāt dimashq* 54)! The fact that Saladin did indeed conquer Jerusalem in the month of Rajab is extraordinarily convenient, for reasons of military and literary history. It promotes Muḥyī l-Dīn's reputation in posterity, and becomes a crucial foreshadowing note to the sermon as medieval accounts tell of it. Classical Arabic homiletics make frequent use of augural signs, much as the *taqlīd* format does: both prose forms comment upon the past when they seek to authorise a ruler, a prophet, or a cleric; they then use that affirmative view of history in order to predict or request future actions. Further, it is almost certainly a reference to Abū Tammām's indispensable Amorium *qaṣīda*, which tells of soothsayers predicting wonders to occur '*fī ṣafari l-aṣfāri aw rajabī*,' in Ṣafar or Rajab (Stetkevych, *Poetics of Islamic Legitimacy* 305). Abū Tammām had opened his poem with a near-mockery of those who could not have foreseen Amorium's fall to Islamic power in the month of Ramadan – Muḥyī l-Dīn endeavours to show how the empire has synchronised events so as to conform to licit, Islamic divination and to poetry itself.

By the time of the Jerusalem campaign ᶜAbbāsid *khuṭbas* had been delivered in mosques throughout the Ayyūbid empire for more than fifteen years, granting Muḥyī l-Dīn a rhetorical task politically more clear-cut than al-Qāḍī l-Fāḍil's had been when the vizierate passed hands in Cairo. In the sermon at al-Aqsa, the text dutifully invokes the Baghdad caliph al-Nāṣir li-Dīn Allāh (553–622 H, 1158–1225 CE) after 'the prescribed form of the Sunni bidding-prayer' (Ehrenkreutz, *Saladin* 205). It exhorts God to aid and protect the caliph along with Saladin himself. Al-Nāṣir of course lent legitimacy and symbolic privilege to the sultan but they were conjoined by official mutual understanding rather than a ceremony of selection: the Fatimid caliph had already performed that ritual just before his regime dissolved. Because of that complicated administrative history, Muḥyī l-Dīn accentuates Saladin's rise and selection as the work primarily of God. His sermon declares, addressing the leader, 'Had you not been the one whom God chose from among His servants, and the one whom he selected from the inhabitants of His lands, He would not have distinguished you with such excellence, in which no one can compete with you. May God fulfill you with ultimate reward for fulfilling (the mission of) His Prophet Muhammad' (Abū Shāma 3:250)! The selection of an imam for the occasion benefits from the frame that the imam places around that process. Saladin was selected cosmically by God, and therefore chosen to choose Muḥyī l-Dīn. The sermon calls for the mission to be advanced, Muhammad's original voyage to Jerusalem given its permanent physical tribute in situ. What must also continue, the sermon insists, is the cleansing of Islamic lands of their Frankish presence (which, of course, persisted then and long after the reestablishment of Islamic institutions in Jerusalem), the political call that would need to resonate most immediately among the congregated soldiers, officials, and war-weary townspeople.

There is nothing coincidental about the sermon's fixation upon sustained progress, for the document and its performance represented a crucial moment in Muḥyī l-Dīn's career as *khaṭīb* (orator). Marvelling at the eloquence that had reverberated through al-Aqsa, ʿImād al-Dīn remarks that the Friday address and prayer session made Muḥyī l-Dīn a fixture in Jerusalem: 'The sermon brought brilliant beams of light to the darkness of wartime, when the perils were enormous, the dangers of the abyss itself. Then the sultan placed him at the rank of *khaṭīb* to establish him there (in Jerusalem), attracting congregations for Friday prayers' (*Sanā l-barq al-shāmī* 314). With all of his success in Jerusalem, Muḥyī l-Dīn eventually returned to Syria. He became chief judge of Damascus in 587/1192 or shortly thereafter. In this post, he followed his father: because of the prominence of the Ibn al-Zakī line of judges, his appointment would have been all but assured, even had he not transcended the regional fame of his family and in such spectacular fashion.[22]

Unremarked upon in period accounts is that the Jerusalem chapter in his career stood to benefit not just Muḥyī l-Dīn but also Saladin in the long term, as the lauded *khaṭīb* resettled in his home country. Damascus was home to both of them: although the sultan resided there only sporadically after his Egyptian campaigns with Shīrkūh, he considered it his ideal seat of power, except that Cairo and Baghdad were caliphal seats and maintained larger economies. Saladin had guaranteed Muḥyī l-Dīn's fame as the sermon disseminated throughout Islamic societies, and in so doing he had guaranteed for himself a loyal *qāḍī* in the centre of Syria. Members of the Ibn al-Zakī family practised Shāfiʿī jurisprudence, Saladin's own legal school that he had funded and promoted since he took power in Egypt, and that he was keen to see as part of official doctrine throughout the kingdom (Lyons and Jackson, *Saladin: The Politics of the Holy War* 41). Muḥyī l-Dīn's series of judicial appointments in Aleppo, Jerusalem, and then Damascus, were of course attributable to the combination of his genealogic fame and to Saladin's orchestration of a maximally successful and acclaimed career.

As emphatic as ᶜImād al-Dīn is on Muḥyī l-Dīn's role in Jerusalem after the *khuṭba*, the return to Damascus was only logical, because Jerusalem's import at that time was more symbolic than administrative. When Muḥyī l-Dīn made his journey back northward, it was chiefly with symbolic capital accrued, simultaneously difficult to measure and immeasurable. In fact, each discrete characteristic of his achievement amounted to an investment in the Ibn al-Zakī familial name: the uniquely high calibre of the competition he had won, the narrative of Saladin judging entries, the city's holiness in Islamic history, and Muḥyī l-Dīn's placing a sermonic seal on to the conquest. Late in life, he affirmed his status as a conduit linking Damascus with Jerusalem and, it would follow, the material and political to the symbolic. He was buried adjacent to his home at the foot of Mount Qassioun on the edge of Damascus, a property where many generations of Ibn Zakī lived before and after Muḥyī l-Dīn. By his request, his epitaph proclaims his Jerusalem accomplishment, a recognition of where he acquired his greatest fame and his plural loyalty to those two great capitals of Islamic life (Talmon-Heller, *Islamic Piety* 166). What he deemed suitable for posterity was his success as a young man, his earning of a victory in the court of the victorious sultan.

Crusade and Counter-Crusade: Knightly Confrontations in *Adab*

Poets constantly invoked the *ifranj* in the process of fashioning Saladin as a political, cultural symbol for Muslims. As we have seen, extant medieval Arabic texts only rarely suggest an interest in engaging Western Europeans as a cultural entity, and researchers have drawn far-reaching historical conclusions from that evidence.[23] What is overlooked in such studies is the essential role that the *ifranj* played in Ayyūbid literature as it shifted Muslim imperial identity. It is true that the image of the Frankish enemy was sparsely depicted in most writings on the topic. That fact, however, makes it all the more salutary to consider how fraught a religious and political debate he entered, and what additional complications he introduced to it. In looking for premodern elements of what we now think of as anthropology, scholars have not recognised the *ifranj*'s reason for literary existence.

So far as Muslim members of court society were concerned, Crusader identity was more an expression of Middle Eastern history than of Western European culture. Because the *ifranj* fit so seamlessly into existing discourse on the Byzantines, Ayyūbid authors were able to swiftly and surely depart from the stubborn intra-Islamic problems of regime and sect into the more fecund ideological territory of inter-religious polemic. Saladin and his administrators were intensely concerned with the legacy of the Fatimids and the Zangī regime. Both of those rival factions had at various times enabled Saladin's rise to power but also had committed key political mistakes vis-à-vis Muslim groups under their rule with whom they differed on matters of religious dogma.[24] The Fatimids had been disgraced by their caliphal impotence and Shāwar's virtual takeover of Egypt as their rule dissolved. Still, vestiges of Fatimid identity persisted in Egypt for generations following the dissolution of the caliphate, an important political consideration for Saladin, even as he enjoyed more legitimacy among Egyptians than his immediate predecessors had. The Zangīs gained a reputation as enemies to Shiᶜi Muslims, not only for their military rivalry with the Fatimids but also for their antagonism of Shiᶜi subjects in Syria (EI2, 'Nūr al-Dīn Maḥmūd b. Zankī' para. 11; Möhring, *Saladin: The Sultan and His Times, 1138–1193* 97). If Saladin's regime was to acquire and maintain ᶜAbbāsid legitimacy, it would be necessary to implement ᶜAbbāsid formulas of rule in court policy and literature. The sultan led a community of great religious and ethnic diversity, much as his forebears in Iraq had done. It could not have been lost on him and his courtiers that ᶜAbbāsid rulers had strategically maintained important positions for Shiᶜi individuals and communities while promoting Sunni Islam as the official doctrine. Islamic political legitimacy in that age required a careful balance of calling for unity in literature while implementing policies geared towards the plural nature of Ayyūbid subjects. Saladin's poets carried on the tradition of praising the sultan as unifying all Islam and dominating the Crusaders – such language had been a hallmark of panegyrics for Nūr al-Dīn – but the meanings of unification and of Crusaders had changed in important ways. Through literature, the court was developing steadily more sophisticated notions of a Muslim self and a Frankish foreigner.

The parallels between the literary representation of *ifranj* and that of the *rūm* (Byzantines) are well documented. In poetry and prose, the *rūm* were the first swarm of foreign, Christian antagonists. Centuries before the ᶜAbbāsids articulated a complex discourse of ethnic identities in imperial politics, the Qur'an had told of the *rūm*'s defeat 'in the nearest land' (*fī adnā l-arḍi*) and predicted that they would return to power (30.2–3).[25] Muḥyī l-Dīn's poem on Aleppo and Jerusalem explicates the *ifranj–rūm* connection. When asked how the victory in Syria gave him a premonition of similar events to come in Palestine – and how he knew in which month Saladin would take Jerusalem – Muḥyī l-Dīn cites an exegesis of those Qur'an verses (Ibn Ṭūlūn, *Quḍāt dimashq* 54–5). He explains that it was discourse on the holy text that allowed him to understand the relationship between time's passage and the border wars, but what he does not mention is the extraordinary resonance that would be felt of the Qur'an's *adnā l-arḍi* when he celebrated the very event promised in his poem: *adnā*'s counterpart is *aqṣā* (furthest), as in al-Aqsa Mosque where he delivered his triumphalist sermon. As has been noted, the 'furthest mosque' is the distinction held by the most holy place outside of Mecca and Medina's region of Arabia, its land's remoteness marked by Muhammad's miraculous night journey. As the *rūm* had dominated Arabia, the *ifranj* violated Jerusalem.

Muḥyī l-Dīn recognised the precedent set by the Qur'an: a foreign army marked time, not ethnicity, for the Muslim Arab community. The Qur'an prescribed vigilance, with the assurance that the enemy would return; the poem reverses the geopolitical dynamic in light of Saladin's success. In a crucial respect, then, the *rūm*'s return has already occurred in Muḥyī l-Dīn's literary view, attested in the past texts informing his compositions, primarily religious prose and earlier poetry. Geopolitical events and the available metonymy between *ifranj* and *rūm* give the poet tools by which to interweave Saladin's political leadership into that of the ᶜAbbāsid caliphs and Muhammad himself. To compare the poem to *sūrat al-rūm* is to see a poem approach eschatology: the cyclical exchanges of military power described by the Qur'an take on a cosmic significance. Saladin becomes a force not just overwhelming but transcendent, reversing the cyclical course of events foretold by God and relieving the long-term anxieties of Islamic political life.

From a point early on in Saladin's career, authors cast the Crusades as a formative, even educational opportunity for him as he acquired a political identity. Al-Qāḍī l-Fāḍil's document of investiture, as it alternately lauds and instructs the new vizier, meditates upon jihad, here explicitly understood as a legal and martial organising principle of the empire. 'You nurse its milk, growing up under its protection,' the *taqlīd* declares to Saladin (al-Qalqashandī, *Ṣubḥ* 10:97), giving us a sense of the anti-Crusade's importance in administrative affairs and in the argument that Saladin was equipped to oversee them. Because waging war against the *ifranj* had initiated the ruler and would continue to legitimise his rule, the enemy played a critical role in the evolving idea of Saladin, unacknowledged in the literature itself. As al-Qāḍī l-Fāḍil marked the early stage of the process with his *taqlīd* and Muḥyī l-Dīn celebrated its peak with his sermon, Usāma ibn Munqidh articulated its maturation. Late in life, Usāma heeded the invitation to join Saladin's court in Damascus. Whether or not that move was related to the sultan's reported admiration for Usāma's poems is unknown, but extant texts indicate that the main compositions to come out of the patron–author relationship were in prose. His *Kitāb al-iʿtibār* (*The Book of Contemplation*), finished in about 579/1183, is probably the most substantive and closely observed texts on the *ifranj*. Paul Cobb notes, 'Usama's works would still be valuable and moving without accounts of the Franks, but we would have very little sense of what the crusades truly meant to medieval Muslims without them.'[26] The other singular contribution that *Kitāb al-iʿtibār* provides is an understanding of how Saladin would achieve a form of intellectual dominion over the *ifranj* via his more senior courtier.

In belletristic *sajʿ* Usāma praises his patron for having renewed the authorial licence of an old man: 'The parts of me Time had broken, he put them in splints to hold, and in his generosity he found a market for that which others had deemed unsaleable, too old' (*Book of Contemplation* 179). It seems doubtful that the writer would have lacked patronage, given his close relationship with Nūr al-Dīn before Saladin's patronage, but this note of thanks underscores how thoroughly Usāma explored the Classical theme of time's passage, especially in later works such as this when he fixates upon time's effects upon his own physical self. What is extraordinary about *Kitāb al-iʿtibār* is that it simultaneously laments that process as it afflicts the elderly Usāma and celebrates it for its tempering of *ifranj* in Islamic territory. In one anecdote, he tells of a fellow Muslim, who the text intimates was a soldier or knight serving under Usāma, invited by an official in Antioch to eat at a

Crusader's home, 'so you can observe their ways'. The Muslim assents. He reports that he and the Antiochian both visit the house.

> فأحضر مائدة حسنة وطعاما في غاية النظافة والجودة. ورآني متوقفًا عن الأكل فقال كل طيب النفس، فأنا ما آكل طعام الإفرنج، ولي طباخات مصريات ما آكل إلا من طبيخهن ولا يدخل داري لحم الخنزير، فأكلت وأنا محترز وانصرفنا فأنا بعد مجتازي في السوق وامرأة أفرنجي تعلقت بي وهي تبربر بلسانهم وما أدري ما تقول فاجتمع علي خلق من الأفرنج فايقنت بالهلاك وإذا ذلك الفارس قد أقبل فرآني فجاء فقال لتلك المرأة ما لك ولهاذا المسلم قالت هذا قتل أخي عرس وكان هذا عرس فارساً بأفامية قتله بعض جند حماة فصاح عليها وقال هذا رجل برجاسي أي تاجر لا يقاتل ولا يحضر القتال وصاح على أولئك المجتمعين فتفرقوا وأخذ بيدي ومضى فكان تأثير تلك المؤاكلة خلاصي من القتل
>
> (OIM 2:103–4)

> [The Frank] presented a very fine table, with food that was extremely clean and delicious. But seeing me holding back from eating, he said, 'Eat and be of good cheer! For I don't eat Frankish food: I have Egyptian cooking-women and never eat anything except what they cook. And pork never enters my house.' So I ate, though guardedly, and we left.
>
> After passing through the market, a Frankish woman suddenly hung on to me while babbling in their language – I didn't understand what she was saying. Then a group Franks began to gather around me and I was certain that I was going to perish. But suddenly, who should turn up but that knight, who saw me and approached. He came and said to that woman, 'What's the matter with you and this Muslim?'
>
> 'This man killed my brother ᶜUrs.' This ᶜUrs was a knight in Apamea whom someone from the army of Hama had killed.
>
> The knight shouted at her and said, 'This man is a *bourgeois* (that is, a merchant), who neither fights nor attends battle.' And he yelled at the assembled crowd and they dispersed. He then took me by the hand and went away. Thus, the effect of that meal was my deliverance from death. (*Book of Contemplation* 153–4, emphasis original, parentheses added)

It is worth asking why Usāma would include this anecdote in a book that follows the age's literary convention of wishing death upon the *ifranj*. He may have invented it. In the first place, it is a story of technical failure: the anthropological call for the Muslim to 'observe their ways' (*tarā ziyyahum*,

OIM 2:103) instead offers him a view of some of his own ways, loosely understood. Second, the European knight's period of cultural education and (partial) assimilation allows him not only to speak Arabic and appreciate the superiority of halal Egyptian food, but also to negotiate diverse forms of conflict. His intervention in the marketplace testifies to his prescience of the dangers faced by Muslims in the European quarter. To the angry Frankish woman, he portrays the Muslim fighter as a civilian,[27] which is to say that he recognises the political imperative to lie in order to fulfil his responsibilities as host. Usāma never explains precisely why Muslim cultural norms are desirable to some *ifranj*: the advantages of 'extremely clean' food seem self-evident. But, of course, the real benefit is enjoyed by the Muslim guest, whose life is saved by the foreign knight's interest in local mores. His understanding of the household and food has become an object (of study), a fixed idea of Muslims' culture and behaviour that the ecumenical Frank wishes to know and adopt, at least in part. In a span of what are probably years, not months, after submitting to the foreign systems of Arabic language and halal food, he emerges with a form of power wielded not even by the people whom he has emulated. Despite all of Usāma's requisite statements of the inherent superiority of Islamic society, there is a unique merit in acquiring culture, quite outstripping the 'observation of ways' to which he and his fellow Muslims are limited.

The book's title, *al-Iʿtibār,* means 'contemplation' but its more basic definition is 'learning by example'. How, then, do its examples function, and how do lessons accrue from one anecdote to another? We do not know whether it was originally conceived of as a presentation for Saladin but that is probable, given the dates at which the sultan patronised Usāma and the manner in which the text reflects upon past military service in order to educate contemporary military leaders. *Al-Iʿtibār* stemmed from a long tradition of instructional prose works, of which Usāma authored many. What distinguishes this book in his extant corpus and in the larger field of Classical Arabic didactic literature is its studious cultural observation of the *ifranj* and its framing conceit of Saladin's patronage. To the sultan, *al-Iʿtibār* insists that he, as the representative of Islamic empire, must control time in order to establish geographic, military advantage over the *ifranj*. The prose takes part in the poetic practice of repeatedly calling for the *ifranj*'s obliteration, a plea to God to act in the absolute, infinite realm. At the same time, individual humans such as Saladin, the hospitable Crusader, and Muslim subjects including Usāma himself all exercise discrete forms of temporal authority. They learn and acquire culture so long as they use, in a courtly way, language and their physical senses. Eating under the auspices of the knights' invitation, speaking to one another, and of course reading *adab* such as *al-Iʿtibār* are means of using time in order to learn and demonstrate knowledge. The unfolding of *al-Iʿtibār* is an opportunity for Saladin and his court to see culture acquired, even by the enemy, all of which they in turn acquire themselves. As Saladin passes from vizier 'nursing the milk' of jihad to the adult orchestrator of struggle, Usāma allows him to toggle between war-time and peace-time with the master instrument of *adab*.

Emerging from the Counter-Crusade

To investigate Saladin, and ask why he has compelled our attention for centuries, we must situate him in the conceptual relationship between courtliness and violence. For modern readers with access to the prolific literature on the sultan in European languages – the main medium of fanciful Saladinic imagery from Early Modernity to the present – he stands out for his near-constant chivalry and the ferocity with which he attacks cities like Hattin and unchivalrous foes like Reynald of Châtillon.[28] In Classical Arabic literature, too, his persona is caught between two seemingly opposed forces. The Fatimid collapse of course represented Saladin's key chance to attain the vizierate. On the other hand, that same moment of opportunity had also made Egypt as vulnerable as it ever had been to Crusader intervention, because the caliphate was so weak. We sense a hardly passed wave of worry when ʿArqala decries Shāwar as a traitor and 'a dog biting at the necks of men' in this chapter's first poetic analysis. Saladin's kingdom revelled in his growing strength, particularly during the Syrian campaigns that led to Hattin, and at the same time, the intellectuals around him anxiously pondered the news of Mediterranean fleets and Christian reinforcements preparing to depart England and continental Europe. By the time English and French monarchies had collected the dramatic-sounding 'Saladin tithe' and marshalled forces that historians would later label the Third Crusade, literature in the Islamic courts had announced the Ayyūbids as a dynasty fated to last. Arab intellectuals' efforts to create poetic, panegyric concordance – to make Saladin fit their aspirational model of a great Sunni monarch – portrayed him as the master of courtly contention and larger-scale struggles with the Franks. That is to say, panegyric concordance meant to efface the boundary between Saladin's ethical posture at court and his strategic use of violence on the battlefield.

It is in prose, most of all, that the importance of Ayyūbid poets' sustained work becomes evident. ᶜImād al-Dīn attributes to his king a past (the Mosuli poets 'have come to you because . . . your exploits have inspired them,' he tells Saladin above), supplanting Fatimid memory and clearing the way for a meaningful reign. We know from Saladin's policies that he needed to proclaim his status as an ᶜAbbāsid agent but, in the long memory that *adab* maintains, he is perhaps even better connected to the early Islamic caliphate, the key referent of al-Qāḍī l-Fāḍil in his *taqlīd*. Prose discourse, which had for centuries spoken of barbaric threats to Muslim communities, could now flesh out that threat as Usāma did and, most importantly, begin to imagine a lasting Islamic victory at the hands of the new dynasty. At the cathartic endpoint of their narratives, they placed Saladin and, more subtly, themselves as the chroniclers of the Sunna's restoration in the Levant.

Notes

1. As with many terms denoting ethnic and religious groups, *ifranj* (also *ifranja*) was liberally applied to people who did not identity as Frankish. Crusaders and their sponsors in Europe of course came from diverse parts of the continent. When reference is made to *ifranj* in this study, it is to the idea – inchoate and very much evolving during Saladin's lifetime – of a European Christian force with unclear ambitions for its Middle East occupation.
2. Saladin is quoted reciting poetry from Abū Tammām's *al-Ḥamāsa* in *Sanā l-barq al-shāmī* 147. Knowledge of *al-Ḥamāsa* was common in boys' Arabic education during Saladin's time. For the secretarial class, including Saladin's own scribes and close confidants, it was widely considered an essential source of eloquence (Sallām, *Al-Adab fī l-ᶜaṣr al-ayyūbī* 211).
3. The best-known scholars to forward such arguments are Badawi (*Modern Arabic Literature* 23); Cahen (EI2, 'Crusades'); Cardini (*Europe and Islam* 13); Gabrieli (*Arab Historians*); Irwin, who goes so far as to complain of what he considers Ayyūbid parochialism ('Image' 226); Lewis (*Muslim Discovery*); Morgan ('Persian' 210); Möhring (*Saladin* 101–2); Riley-Smith ('Islam and the Crusades

in History and Imagination' 161); and Saunders (*History*). Fortunately, critiques of this received-wisdom trend are to be found in both historical and literary studies (Dajani-Shakeel and Messier eds 41–2).

4. For Lewis's attempt to extend his view of medieval Muslims' attitudes to twentieth-century contexts, see *Crisis of Islam* 48–52. All of this may have been limited to an academic trend had Lewis not been so successful in appealing to a broad audience in the popular media and in particular the administrations of several United States presidents, including that of George W. Bush as he ordered the American invasions of Afghanistan and Iraq (Waldman, 'Historian's Take'). A decay theory that begins with the Crusades ends in wars of occupation. As Lewis portrays history, the period of Europeans' invasion of the eastern Mediterranean throws into stark relief Middle Easterners' profound, ultimately crippling, lack of receptivity to the foreign people's communal life, cultural practices, and technologies. It is furthermore compelling to consider how entrenched that general notion was among the Western academics whom Lewis, to judge from the references in his many books, was reading (Dajani-Shakeel and Messier eds 41).
5. For documentation and discussion of the Western university's ties to empire, see Cormack, *Charting* 3–5, 17–19, 223–30, and Mignolo, 'Globalization' 99. With regard to ᶜAbbāsid historiography and epistemology, the most accurate and effective rebuttal of scholars' anachronistic criteria is articulated by Samer Ali: 'As we can see from the placement of history within *adab*, the key problem modern scholars have faced in the study of historical narrative remains the difficulty of appreciating the literary performative atmosphere in which narratives are deployed, recited, and transmitted to future generations ... Abbasid historians – with rare exceptions – did not *discover* what happened in the past' (*Arabic Literary Salons* 36, emphasis original).
6. Even the most discerning of historians sometimes adopt the language of large-scale war prediction. Martin Jay, whose writing on European thought is a much-needed intellectual opposite to the simplification strategy of the Clash of Civilizations school, opines in response to the 2014 *Charlie Hebdo* cartoons and subsequent murders, 'I'm glad to see that strong protests are finally being made by the latter against the hijacking of Islam by the fanatics, for we are dangerously close to a situation, especially in Europe, in which some sort of prolonged civilizational war might break out' (Yaren, 'Interview' 140).
7. For critique of Islam–violence–eschatology linkages, see Asad, *On Suicide Bombing* and Hirschkind, 'Cultures of Death'. Bonner provides a useful review of sources that subscribe to the essentialist link in *Jihad in Islamic History* 1, 11.

8. Despite the obvious temptation to associate his vizierate and its associated literature with the ᶜAbbāsid material analysed in the previous chapter, the Fatimids understood the vizier title differently from other Islamic regimes (al-Bāshā, *Al-Alqāb* 525; Sanders, *Ritual* 95–6). There seems to be very little distinction drawn in Fatimid-era texts between vizier (*wazīr*) and emir (*amīr*), both denoting a form of authority exercised by administrators who often commanded armies. Further complicating matters of nomenclature is that Saladin was called Sultan from the time he became a Fatimid vizier, because in his case *sulṭān* denoted the authority (*sulṭa*) invested in him (Gibb, 'Achievement of Saladin' in *Studies on the Civilization* 100). As we have seen, in the Būyid age of ᶜAbbāsid empire, the emir was roughly akin to a prince and officially served by the vizier, so officials understood that one person would not hold both titles simultaneously. Saladin had sought the ᶜAbbāsid title of Sultan but was never granted it by the caliph in Baghdad (Eddé, *Saladin* 155).
9. Humphreys, *From Saladin* 6. The Ismaili enemy to whom Humphreys refers is the Assassins of Syria, not the Fatimids.
10. In Islamic tradition Munkar and Nakīr interrogate the recently deceased in order to determine whether the soul may be left in peace until the Day of Judgement. If they find the person to be a denier of God and Muhammad's messenger status, or even insufficiently a believer, they exact harsh punishment, including beating. All of this transpires at the grave site itself. They leave only when faith is satisfactorily proven, thus ᶜArqala's formulation of time – Munkar and Nakīr's remaining at Shāwar's grave means indefinite punishment, even before the presumed hellfire after Judgement.
11. Shabbar and Shabīr are names by which the Prophet is said to have referred to Fatima and Ali's sons al-Ḥasan and al-Ḥusayn, respectively (Dūlābī, *Al-Dhurriyya al-ṭāhira* 97). The latter of the two sons is the central, venerated martyr in Shiᶜi traditions. Muhammad was honouring the biblical prophet Aaron, two of whose sons are called Shabbar and Shabīr in Arabic Islamic sources. *Mulk ᶜaqīm*: in politics contemporary to ᶜArqala's era, *mulk ᶜaqīm* could mean a sultanate or emirate with no hereditary successor or, more idiomatically, something close to a lame-duck regime. In the Mamluk period that was to follow, it took on more positive associations, its logic working in some ways to the Mamluks' favour by suggesting a lack of genealogically determined nepotism around the throne (Philipp and Haarmann eds 59).
12. Aḥmad al-Jundī interprets ᶜImād al-Dīn's reminiscence of meeting ᶜArqala as

not just a sign of respect but also the memorable character of ᶜArqala's authorial persona (*Dīwān ᶜarqala*, introductory p. lettered *jīm*).

13. Shāwar was of the influential Banū Saᶜd tribe, his branch based in southern Palestine and northern Arabia.
14. By making Jerusalem a sexual metaphor, ᶜImād al-Dīn builds his poem on the complex edifice of preexisting Classical Arabic war/sex violation tropes. The ᶜAbbāsids set the main precedent. The most prominent work to merge city siege with sexual violation is Abū Tammām's Amorium poem 'Al-Sayfu aṣdaqu …' ('The Sword is More Veracious …') on which see Ḍayf, *Al-Fann wa-madhāhibuhu* 256–62 and Stetkevych, *Poetics of Islamic Legitimacy* 152–79.
15. Abu Bakr proves to be a complex historical identity. He has been consistently revered by Muslims but he was also the key part of one of the earliest major political controversies in Islam, and therefore available to narratives of a Sunna/Shiᶜa split. He was selected over the much younger Ali (as well as other Companions) for the first caliphate, although accounts vary widely about how much the deliberation focused on those two in particular. Even the level of desire that either had had for the rulership is subject to question. His story continues to fascinate, with pundits in mass media citing his ascent as evidence for a nagging, painful Sunna/Shiᶜa binary in Islamic geopolitics.
16. See especially ᶜAlī ibn Ṭāhir al-Sulamī's landmark Classical work *Kitāb al-jihād* (The Book of Jihad) in Zakkār ed., *Arbaᶜat kutub fī l-jihād*. Al-Sulamī's interest in convening scholar-warriors is discussed in Bonner, *Jihad in Islamic History* 139–40.
17. Saladin's preference for Usāma's *dīwān* is attested in al-Iṣfahānī's *Sanā l-barq al-shāmī* 111. For a useful summary of Saladin's literary preferences and how they compare to Usāma's, see Riley-Smith ed., *Oxford History of the Crusades* 232–3. He and his close associate al-Qāḍī l-Fāḍil are both said to have enjoyed the oft-dismissed shadow play (al-Ḥamawī, *Thamarāt* 47; Jacob, *Geschichte des Schattentheaters* 53).
18. On the variety of dates on which Saladin is recorded as mounting military campaigns to take Mosul, see Durand-Guédy, 'Diplomatic Practice in Salǧūq Iran' 274–5.
19. In Classical Arabic, plagiarism could be considered a fault but it was by no means a grave offence. This rhetorical theme is treated at length in Kilito, *Author* 18–28.
20. *Intiqād* (and its synonym, *naqd*, from the same root) should not be understood

as criticism in its modern sense. The meaning of the term fluctuated in the Middle Ages, generally having to do with judging authenticity, origin, and, by extension, quality (Ouyang, *Literary Criticism* 91–4).

21. The family known by the name Ibn al-Zakī was venerable in Islamic law. Especially because Aleppo figures in the literature of interest here, it should be noted that there appears to be another *qāḍī* by the same name of Muḥyī l-Dīn ibn al-Zakī, of Aleppo (Margoliouth, 'Legend' 540).
22. For the timeframe of Muḥyī l-Dīn's top-level appointment in Damascus, see Ibn Ṭūlūn 52 and Margoliouth, 'Legend' 540. The ideological power of the Ibn al-Zakī family is described and contextualised in Chamberlain, *Knowledge* 63.
23. Even if we limit our scope to preserved texts, the record from the early modern period is very different from that of the Middle Ages. The abundance of early modern geographic works in Arabic includes a great deal of writing on ethnographic topics (Matar ed., *In the Lands* xxxviii).
24. This is the general consensus of historians in the past several decades, although Ehrenkreutz is a prominent dissenter, arguing that Nūr al-Dīn had achieved greater military and administrative victories than did Saladin (*Saladin* 236).
25. Like *ifranj*, *rūm* is a blanket term. It could mean Romans (thus its etymology) or Greeks, but its most common signification is Byzantines. In all cases it connotes Christians from countries around the northeast Mediterranean. For a discussion of Sura 30 ('Al-Rūm'), including a review of disagreement among some Islamic scholars as to whether the Byzantines had been victorious or defeated in the Qur'anic telling, see El Cheikh, 'Sūrat al-Rūm'. Finally, it should be noted that Saladin conducted extended diplomatic communication with Byzantium and in fact allied with that kingdom when he felt compelled to do so by Crusader threats (Ehrenkreutz, *Saladin* 211–12).
26. *Book of Contemplation* xxiv. This and all quotations of the book in English translation are Cobb's (his treatment of Usāma titled *The Book of Contemplation*), who distinguishes his treatment of Usāma from other translations with his sensitivity to Usāma's literary style.
27. Derenbourg reads the loan word as *burjāsī* (OIM 104n1): a phonetic adaptation of 'burgess,' a non-noble head of a town's merchants. He and Cobb translate it as 'bourgeois'.
28. European writers contemporary with the Crusades tend to accuse Reynald of looting Muslims' ships and caravans. Modern artistic treatments build upon Arab chroniclers' suggestion that he had captured (and even killed) Saladin's

sister. Whether by piracy, kidnapping, or murder, Reynald violated a critical truce with the Ayyūbids, and of course numerous European ethical rules for knights. The bloodiest and most spectacular depiction of Saladin avenging himself and his family on Reynald is in Ridley Scott's film *Kingdom of Heaven* (2005).

3

Alfonso X: Poetry of Miracles and Domination

Alfonso X of Castile and León composed extraordinary contentious poetics. He also forcefully complicates the metacritical problem investigated in the previous chapter. Whereas Saladin's regime, as well as its immediate predecessors and successors, has been portrayed by modern scholars as insufficiently cosmopolitan in worldview, Alfonso is held up as the paragon of early multiculturalism. Some scholars go so far as to call him a medieval pioneer of Renaissance learning. His traditional sobriquet, dating back to the Middle Ages, is 'el Sabio' (the Learned); in the twentieth century, he has gained many new honorifics. Because of his expansive projects in manuscript culture – in addition to poetry, his court's translations of Middle Eastern science and imaginative literature – historians have dubbed him '*Stupor mundi*' and the 'Emperor of Culture'.[1] Attributing to Alfonso hints of Renaissance learning, these scholars echo precisely the Orientalist treatments of Islamic intellectual history. Orientalists valorised cultural transfer (translation especially), and viewed the activities of the Italian Renaissance as a historical necessity for ascendant political regimes. In order to more precisely appraise medieval art and thought, we must revise the academic narratives that maintain, even if inadvertently, the Middle Ages 'as a field of undifferentiated otherness against which modernity … emerged' (Cohen, *Postcolonial Middle Ages* 4). Poets at the king's court made use of his cosmopolitan self-portrayal in order to promote him but, in most of the literature attributed to Alfonso, his most pressing interest is in demarcating and enforcing rules of difference.

Prologue, Will and Testament

It could be said that Alfonso composed his last will and testament three times over: twice in prose, once in poetry. Affairs in his kingdom had grown rancorous, most pointedly on questions of royal succession, as he aged and suffered intense illnesses that may have affected his mental powers. After dictating the will in the autumn of 1283, he revised some of its stipulations, and added many personal instructions in a second and final version, delivered in early 1284. Despite the attention to detail that this revision would suggest, some of Alfonso's more symbolically potent orders went unfulfilled after his death. If indeed he was lucid at the time of the document's composition, he was surely aware of the symbolism in his order to bury his heart in Jerusalem, adding, 'only when God grants that the land be won and (my heart) might be safely delivered' (Alfonso X, *Antología* 235). Against the backdrop of Jerusalem's undeniable and long-lasting political status as an Islamic city since Saladin's victory a century before, the will's authoritative prose acknowledges the limits of its own prolepsis. Its focal point, however, was Seville, the king's adopted city and the growing capital since its capture from Muslim empire decades before his coronation. In the cathedral, a converted mosque in the tradition of Castilian conquest, Alfonso called for 'all the codices of songs praising Saint Mary to be stored in the Cathedral and that they be sung at the festivals of Saint Mary' (236).[2]

In Seville and throughout Alfonso's domain, the recitation of the songs themselves was another public expression of the king's will and testament. In his lyric poetry he couched some of his more extravagant political wishes, so that his authoritative voice would run through the ritual of venerating Mary. His *Cantigas de Santa Maria* (CSM), a collection of more than 400 sacred lyric works in a poetic language that had been exclusively profane before Alfonso's time, give sense to his imperial ambitions, figured in the overarching themes of chaste love, marriage, and death. In her capacity as deliverer, Mary saves Christians and the occasional heretic. Most importantly, however, she ensures the king's passage from life to afterlife. The CSM place Alfonso in the middle of a far-reaching imperial history and geography. Although Hispanists have made much of the songbook's depiction, through words and illuminations, of normative medieval people's habits, more striking vis-à-vis the default profane tradition is the CSM's comprehensive ideological view of empire. The *Cantigas d'escarnho e de mal dizer* ('Songs of scorn and slander') (hereafter CEM) as well as Iberian lyric of profane love and friendship all skew towards topical, conversational poetics. Alfonso, credited with authoring several dozen such works, understood how stark a counterpoint he provided to the existing Galician-Portuguese tradition by composing sacred verse on such themes as Crusade, geopolitics, theology, divine intervention, and pious governance.[3]

Alfonso's sacred verse provides a frame for his courtly enterprise. It allows him to assert ownership of a Christian empire beyond Iberia. It also makes great use of historical referents, from which the king drew authority – and in his poetry the king becomes powerfully bellicose, ruminating upon his indeterminate war against Muslims. Most importantly, his lyric persona seeks the favour of saints and of God. Although the CSM feature distinct moments of immediate material concerns, their main function to the student of Alfonsine culture is to provide a sense of his historiography and understanding of life and afterlife. This gives us a critical lens with which to inspect both his sacred and profane lyric because, in addition to his work to convert hagiography into politics, he also used mundane, quotidian methods for pursuing his political goals in literature. He made use of the CEM in order to identify literary adversaries from within his court and, by engaging them, he recast his imperial projects as lewd, lighthearted exchanges of insults. The conspicuous differences in intellectual and theological horizons mapped out between these two bodies of poetry have led critics to address CSM and CEM as largely unrelated phenomena. Alfonso's politics argue against such an approach. This chapter examines the cooperative, cumulative effect of sacred and profane in Alfonso's work to promote himself inside and outside the court.

As a songbook, the CSM begin and end with supplicating political speech, whose purpose is to imagine a future in which Alfonso gains privileges over other royal estates. More subtly, his lyrics also portray him dominating the field of poetry. The two-song *Prologo* (Prologue) legitimates its description of him as 'King of the Romans' by crediting him with winning key Iberian kingdoms from 'the Moors' (CSM A). It elides between two royal projects that, as we will see, pulled Alfonso in opposite directions during his reign. The second section of prologue, CSM B, is composed as the king's own lyric voice, a mode sustained through the hundreds of *cantigas* making up the collection. 'I pray she will approve of me as her/Troubadour' (*rogo-lle que me queira por seu/Trobador*), he declares as the prologue comes to a close,[4] plotting out his royal request that drives both CSM and CEM. Many songs later, the work introduced as the *Petiçon* (Petition: CSM 401) seeks to make the book cohere. The *Petiçon* enumerates the duties that Alfonso may fulfil before his death, the piety that legitimises his royal acts, and the state in which he should leave the kingdom. His troubadour persona exhorts Mary to advocate to God on his behalf:

queira que os encréus
mouros destrüír póssa que son dos Filistéus
com' a séus ẽemigos destrüiu Macabéus
Judas que foi gran tempo cabdélo dos judéus
... os mouros que térra d'Ultramar
tẽen e en Espanna gran part' a méu pesar
me dé poder e força pera os ên deitar
... e que el me defenda de fals' e traedor
e outrossí me guarde de mal consellador
e d'óme que mal sérve e é mui pedidor

that He might grant me the power
to destroy the disbelieving Moors – Philistines they are! –
much as Judas Maccabeus, leader of the Jews long ago,
destroyed his own enemies.
... the Moors – who hold the Holy Land
and large parts of Spain, to my regret –
may He grant me strength to expel them!
... May he protect me from the liar, the traitor,
from the bad advisor,
and from him who serves poorly but makes constant requests.
... May I see you for eternity in Paradise.

Desire, supplication, biblical and medieval warfare, and constant tensions with nobles at court – all serve to model Alfonso's lyric idea of his own rule. CSM 401's aspirational reference to Judas Maccabeus taps the power of diplomacy, not just his famous military might. The Bible relates that Judas valiantly led Israel's armies, and that he also signed what came to be known as the first Roman–Jewish Treaty, enlisting the help of the ascendant Roman Republic against Greco-Syrian forces. Perhaps the most ambitious of Alfonso's political goals, never fully realised despite his diplomacy, was to be named Holy Roman Emperor by papal authority and a plurality of fellow kings officially tied to the Vatican. The move would have simultaneously affiliated Alfonso's regime with ancient empires and a specifically medieval political ideal of Christendom conquering its supposed enemies. Alfonsine literature rested upon certain diplomatic criteria and a notion of Ancient Rome that developed in the Middle Ages, a historical imaginary closely linked to the German royalty from which he was descended on his mother's side. He adapted that story to mark both the success and frustrations of Iberian Christendom.[5] The song's litany of 'Moors' along with the Christian 'liar', 'traitor', and 'bad advisor' ('*fals*', '*traedor*', and '*mal consellador*') stakes out a field of general ideas, providing a frame for more specific antipathies and contests addressed in his other *cantigas*, both of the profane and sacred varieties. We gain a sense here of the extraordinarily personal sense of a court. The voice of a king announces his own vulnerability to malevolent courtiers, an admission rarely given in royal literature.

Alfonso's legislative works privilege poetry. Tellingly, however, they do not point out the known fact that the king himself was the most important poet in the sovereign territory to which his writs pertained. His legal magnum opus *Las siete partidas* places veracity and eloquence of speech at the centre of (1) royal conduct, (2) jesting contests of speech, and (3) the ethical life of the court. The court is defined as the space that isolates and punishes 'the slander, the trickery, and the arrogant and hollow words that degrade men' (*los escarnios et los engaños, et las palabras soberbias et natias que facen á los homes envilescer*) (2.9.27). As the treatise continues mapping the realms of acceptable and unacceptable courtly conduct, it refers to the phenomenon of Romance-language wordplay (*jugar/juego de palabras*) (2.9.29–30), which it deems acceptable for certain courtly occasions. The important stipulation that this *partida* makes is that the game be closely regulated for content. All this of course imagines the king more as the receiver of discourse than its author. Other laws in the *Partidas* describe proper education and eloquence for royals, but at the moment in which Alfonso defines the court, his priority is to instruct those to whom he grants access as knights. To *Partida* 2.9.27, his primarily responsibility is to wield 'the sword of justice' (*la espada de la justicia*), the legal and hermeneutical tool that the court is designed to house.

With the sword and his own knowledge, the ideal king is understood to be a critical listener first, only secondarily a composer. The legal treatise was intended to be revelatory, the first comprehensive set of laws written in the language that Castilians spoke rather than in the customary Latin. But it was not designed to explain the particularities of Alfonso's reign and his work with language. Nowhere does it address the question of a king's compositions, how their language was to be judged if the poet himself should be the sole bearer of *la espada*, and how poets and performers may engage the king when he participated in poetic exchanges with them.

The aim of this chapter is to address the gap left by Alfonsine prose, the lack of context that his contemporaries have left in extant works. In this way, we begin to understand his motives and techniques for writing a poetics of combat. I will argue that Alfonso preoccupied himself with two wars, one in the service of the other. As Castilian king and pretender to the throne of the Holy Roman Empire, he portrayed himself as waging a long-term campaign to lead and expand Christendom. This meant fighting Muslim armies, and struggling with fellow Christian monarchs of Western Europe, as well as with the pope. All of Alfonso's powerful interlocutors, it seems, complicated his attempt to take the title of Emperor. Perennially frustrated in this large-scale campaign for land and power, he issued a long series of triumphalist and antagonistic poetry. In the literary field where Alfonso intervened, inevitably, a central issue was his own historical, political role in the world. This chapter will analyse Alfonso's attempts to distinguish his antagonists, his poetic techniques for publicly naming them and testing them in verse. We will also see those poetic interlocutors' own means of engaging him – by name, epithet, and allusion – as they both initiated and responded to the poetic challenges he offered them. The most evident struggle between king and subject was over a limited, seemingly insignificant form of political mastery: one speaker's wit and lyric mastery over another's. Because of the imposing historical frames holding each poem together, however, they contended over issues much broader than language. Their works pressed outward, into material political matters, especially diplomacy and war. Galician-Portuguese, the predominant poetic language among the upper classes, was a uniquely Iberian currency, but when performed at court it spoke to a wide range of European political concerns. Alfonso and his interlocutors saw in the *cantiga* an opportunity to test the boundaries of domestic and foreign policy, in an idiom most often used for chaste love and provincial social matters.

Alfonso's political work with literary genre will in certain respects be familiar. As Ibn ᶜAbbād had done in a very different time and cultural space, Alfonso exploited the discourses of poetic praise and slander in order to promote himself as a governing figure. Like Saladin, he was the royal focal point of a court working assiduously to create an image of a foreign enemy, all the while internal fissions challenged the throne. Alfonsine literature invokes what we now think of as the Crusades, mentioning some of the particular Syrian and Palestinian sites of confrontation between Christian and Islamic imperial forces. The lyric of Iberia promoted the Gibraltar-to-Jerusalem notion of Crusades, a pan-Mediterranean set of pilgrimages and battles. This was, by and large, the trend throughout medieval European thought. By conflating the Levantine and Iberian wars, Alfonso made the *mouros* (Moors) into a useful foil. Against the backdrop of local wars in Iberia and Morocco, he portrayed himself as the ascendant king of Christendom in general.

As the language of Spanish troubadours, Galician Portuguese tapped its Provençal cousin's tradition of Crusades poetics. But its specifically Galician qualities meant that the *cantigas* constantly pointed towards Santiago de Compostela and its history as a pilgrimage destination. The CSM paid tribute to the Galician capital and the then-burgeoning traffic of Christians visiting the shrine of Saint James. 'The pilgrimage to Compostela and the enthusiasm for the Crusade to Jerusalem were the twin foci of a popular religious movement' (Watt, *Influence* 82). That popularity was also exploited by the most powerful official institutions, most notably Alfonso's court. To bridge Galicia with the contested Holy Land was to consciously recall the legend of Saint James's post-mortem voyage from Jerusalem to Santiago for burial. Alfonso, in turn, portrayed himself travelling that route in reverse. Just as the apostle was said to be interred in the West, so too would Alfonso's heart be transported to the East, in text if not in fact. Alfonso as a lyric figure exploited religious poetry's breadth of geography, a notable difference from the more state-centred profane verse.

Despite their self-conscious play with the sites of war and prayer, the CSM texts are not so universalist as to depict Alfonso combating Eastern Arabs. Such tropes could have served him politically, but the songs are consistent enough with documented history that they place Iberian Christian kings and knights in conflict with Andalusi and North African Muslims. They make up most of the martial CSM – a smaller group of works pitting Crusaders and Levantine churchmen against Tunisian, Syrian, Egyptian, and Iraqi *mouros*. The unstated argument running through the songbook is that Alfonso maintains the war front of immediate proximity and foremost interest to the Spanish court, while wars to the east provide more purposefully allegorical and historical evidence of Mary's interventions. Alfonso's CEM, never intended for the kind of sumptuous codex made for the sacred *cantigas*, are the very picture of the violent, kinetic power mastered by the king. He maintained a set of poetic tools, ranging from the broadest claims of a Christian empire to the most specific attacks on his courtiers. Furthermore, he made each tool clearly discernible according to its designation among the known *cantiga* varieties. Each presented history slightly differently, and each forwarded Alfonso's political programme in its own way. His versification was as precise as his legislation.

The previous chapter explored techniques by which Saladin's court used the martial poetic vocabulary of past centuries. The Ayyūbids drew their empire's attention to the immediate challenges presented by the Crusades, an artistic view of historiography so standard that it required no explicit acknowledgement. Alfonso and his songwriters also sifted the residues of the past. But, by necessity, they attempted to make both historical conjunctions and also geographic ones. 'The Crusades' is a neologism, not coined until the early modern period. Among its effects on modern discourse has been its eventual association with the struggle for Jerusalem, deemphasising the wars of North Africa and southwestern Europe. Medieval Christians, regardless of their varying ideological positions, generally understood campaigns against Muslim forces as part of one historical, pan-Mediterranean enterprise. Alfonso was determined to exploit that sense of generalisability as he plotted his discrete imperial moves against the Naṣrids of Granada and the Marīnids of Morocco. CSM 401 refers to the 'Holy Land': *terra d'Ultramar*, literally, 'the land at the far end of the sea'. It of course does not mention that, by the time of the song's composition and compilation (ca 1270–90, that is, the physical songbook was finished after his death), serious attempts at reconquering Jerusalem had ended. In that era, the European knights and settlers in the region enjoyed little material support from the Western seats of power. Only when the Ottomans rose as a new threat, a century later, were large-scale imperial forces reorganised for a war against Muslims.

What flourished instead was Iberian literature on the pan-Mediterranean idea of holy war, in poetry to be studied here as well as historical and heroic-themed prose written by royal scholars, probably during a few decades following Alfonso's death.[6] A Provençal poet, enjoying the hospitality that Castilian royals had extended to his ilk for a century, had lyrically exhorted Alfonso to unite European forces in a campaign for the Levant (Alamanon, *Le troubadour Bertran d'Alamanon* 54–60). Audiences all along the northwestern Mediterranean region therefore appreciated the tight affiliation between troubadour status and Crusades propaganda in the thirteenth century. The CSM's figure of Alfonso was both a pious troubadour and a would-be Crusader. Thus, the efficacy of his project depended upon the propagandist energy of his already-current profane lyric. In order to respond to the call eastward while privileging the western Mediterranean front, he made the rhetorical connection between Levantine Crusades, while keeping the audience's focus upon the immediate concerns of fighting Muslims in Iberia and the Maghreb. The wars in the Levant were a geographically remote idea. For Alfonso, they were more serviceable for establishing Iberian territorial campaigns in a narrative of Christendom's political expansion than they were for any concrete military or historical linkages he may make in text.

From Mosque to Cathedral, from Parent to Son

The lyric figure of Alfonso told imperial stories of far-off origins. Depicting himself as prosecuting an all-important war in Iberia, he suggested to his audience that his success or failure against the *mouros* would have major repercussions for Christian empire in general. The battle over the Holy Land had to be his own, and he inserted himself into that Levantine story by drawing parallels between his military campaigns and the illustrious legends of the eastern Crusades. All of this contrasts sharply with documented Castilian political history. Alfonso's predecessors had generally concluded that it was infeasible for them to make a substantive military intervention in conflicts several thousand miles eastward. The inferences and prolepsis of CSM 401 have demonstrated the songbook's hopeful attitude towards a victorious future; the explicitly formal means of narration seek to frame the past as full of victories, even in the preceding century of territorial losses and a dependence upon treaties with Muslim leaders for trade and safe passage of European settlers. The thirteenth century was hardly auspicious, so far as Holy Land propaganda was concerned. Therefore, Alfonso and his composers sifted through preexisting Marian stories and added a great many new ones to European textual culture. Their goal was to establish tension between epochs and regions, and the only fully conjunctive force at their disposal was the figure of the Virgin. Anticipating and specifying the *Petiçon* of 401, CSM 165 reports on events in the struggle for Ultramar, particularly in the port city of Tartus, Syria. The port was one of the Templar Knights' few remaining strongholds in the late part of the century.[7]

Even at their most propagandist and martial, the CSM retold complex social and political histories. The lyric figures often pause while conducting religious war, calling out to Mary or other saints in order to understand why they are fighting in the first place. Tartus is threatened by a Muslim juggernaut of a sultan, Bondoudar, who has singled out Christians from all other people as the main object of his hatred (*aos crischãos desamava mais que al*). His control of all the major cities in Syria leaves Tartus as a 'great prize' (*gran prez*). The name Bondoudar is a Latinisation of al-Bunduqdārī, Sultan Baybars I (ca 620–76 H, 1233–77 CE), whose biography comes to bear heavily on the Marian story. His name is a prescient, canny pun in the sung lyrics. In Galician-Portuguese it would have sounded like *bon dudar*: 'good doubt' or, more idiomatically, 'sound scepticism'. That is precisely what he displays, sending a group of soldiers to Tartus 'in order to know more about (the Christians)' and challenging the deputy who assures him the city is ripe for the taking.[8] The Christians of Tartus, seeing Bondoudar's army approaching, prays to Mary. The Moors' ethos of consultation will be trumped by the Crusaders' pure form of faith, unfettered by reasoning and debate. Although the Moorish scout is far from the *mal consellador* lamented in CSM 401, he seems so to his sultan, who finds Tartus guarded by scores of gleaming white knights. The *cantiga* is illuminated in one extant codex, Rico (221), showing the scout emerge from a vast Moorish army and shuttle back and forth between the royal courts with whom he consults. At once supplicative and knowing, he tilts his face towards an increasingly agitated Bondoudar and finally delivers news of the Virgin and heavenly knights' appearance at the city walls. The discourse between him and his sovereign reminds the audience that Mary intervenes with transcendent power, both worldly and divine. She brings her revelation to the enemies as well as to Tartus's pious Christian inhabitants – and, when Bondoudar witnesses her appearance, he responds not by accepting her faith but concluding that she is forcing him to change his military strategy. Bondoudar's constant exchange with his minion allows him to comprehend the miracle but not to appreciate its cosmic significance, namely that the faith of his enemy produces such wonders of protection while his does not.

When the CSM tell of events far-off or long past, the lyrics make constant reference to the stories' sources, never named but always 'found' or 'heard'. Bondoudar, too, consults source texts, exclaiming in his moment of indecision,

> Eno Alcorán achei
> que Santa María virgen foi sempr' e pois esto sei
> guérra per nulla maneira con ela non fillarei
> e daquí me tórno logo e fas tangê-lo tabal

> In the Qur'an I have found
> that Saint Mary remained forever a virgin. Now that I know this,
> there is no way I will fight a war with her.
> I shall turn around and have the marching-drum sounded!

So, while not a tale of conversion, CSM 165 narrates Bondoudar's acceptance of proof. The supporting documentation of the Qur'an, whose mentions of Mary's virginity are the only parts of the book acknowledged by the CSM,[9] contextualises the miracle of her becoming pregnant with Jesus. To Bondoudar's reasoning, if a miracle could occur in the ancient world attested by the Qur'an, another one can occur again. His contemplation of the text is superfluous from a strategic point of view: the white knights are so numerous that besieging Tartus would be a strategic disaster. The function of his Qur'an reference seems to be to demonstrate his ability to approach Christian truths via Islam. In recognition of Mary and in retreat, he makes a suitable witness to the fulfilment of a prayer that trumps his own force.

Understood as a detailed form of support for the *Petiçon*'s view on Moors ('who hold the Holy Land/and large parts of Spain, to my regret,' Alfonso declares), the most compelling aspect of this *cantiga* is its radical departure from Alfonso's own history with the Levantine front. Amy Remensnyder notes that the Tartus cathedral had been known for attracting both Christian and Muslim pilgrims, although it is not clear whether Alfonso's court was aware of such a fact. She cites CSM 165 as evidence that 'Christian authors could transform even apparently innocuous stories about sharing Mary into brazen narratives of Christianity victorious' (Remensnyder, *La Conquistadora* 161). Beyond Tartus's ecclesiastical history, there was ample information about Baybars circulating in Alfonsine Iberia. This problematises the *cantiga* at a deep political level. Baybars unsuccessfully attacked Tartus twice, both times in the three years before the initiation of the CSM project, but the courtly audience would have been aware that the two kings had conducted substantive diplomatic business with each other. Alfonso made it his practice to send gifts and correspondence to rulers in Egypt and the Holy Land, so that he may ingratiate himself to them.[10] He and Baybars each sent emissaries to the other and reportedly gave warm welcomes to their official guests. Although this suits historians' 'Emperor of Culture' representation of Alfonso, it was probably more a function of royal pragmatism. Egypt's control of ports and the land between the Mediterranean and Red Sea granted it major geopolitical power, even without Tartus under its reign. Alfonso's campaigns to eliminate Islamic political power from southern Iberia were difficult in their own right, as will be discussed in detail subsequently. Also, the Levantine Crusades were in shambles, as members of Castilian courts would have long known. In many respects the CSM seem an attempt to counterbalance the sense of resignation that prevailed in the Castilian government and in the networks of knights throughout the peninsula. Few of Alfonso's noblemen would have been eager to venture so far eastward when Andalusis and North Africans threatened to regain lost territory.

In the CSM's calculus of power in the East, Christian victory depends upon more than prayer and Mary's redemptive answer. It also requires that she be to the dominating Muslim, who in turn must possess the reasoning power and literacy necessary to appreciate the intervention of a higher power. It is precisely the senses of loss and vulnerability that allow for CSM 165 to ultimately celebrate a Christian *esprit de corps*. When Alfonso's sacred imperial poetry dwells upon Spain, it is in an attempt to suppress such concerns. The empire's subjects must coalesce around the king as an intermediary between population and saint. Alfonso's father Fernando III (1199–1252, r. 1217–52) loomed large as a historical figure and bequeathed tremendous legitimacy to his son. He was best known for his exceptional piety and his conqueror persona. For Alfonso, however, the memory of his paternity was also a nagging reminder of his family's imperial projects not yet realised or thwarted entirely. His texts rarely miss an opportunity to cite Fernando, and that tendency is especially significant in the CSM.

Fernando was a patron of the *cantiga* and enjoyed tremendous successes in his wars against Muslims. They came at a cost, however, namely his intense taxation of landowners (Mansilla, *Iglesia castellano-leonesa* 50–9). In contrast, Alfonso could boast chiefly of literary achievements but few material successes in the kingdom. To make matters worse for his popularity, he kept the large and onerous system of tax revenue basically unchanged from his father's era. He made a poor warrior-king, although the CSM would like to suggest otherwise. His lack of imperial acquisitions of land meant that his relatively lavish spending on academies and European diplomacy strained his treasury. Castile was beset by insurrection from important noble families, upon whom Alfonso relied for protecting and expanding the borders of his realm. Perhaps for reason of his many false starts as military commander, the king relied upon the narrative of his father's royal, martial preeminence. Alfonso seems to have built upon a major work of profane Galician-Portuguese praise lyric from his father's tenure, a composition celebrating Fernando's conquest of Seville (Iglesia, *El idioma* 2:223–4). Under both kings, Seville began to compete with Toledo as a royal seat, presaging its eventual status as the premier city of Golden Age Spain. As Alfonso stationed more and more of his imperial project in that city, he sought to sanctify Fernando's military triumph there. By extension, he celebrated the city itself.

Unable to gather resources and unite the necessary personnel to defeat the Granadan and Moroccan forces, Alfonso sought refuge in his father's narrative of conquest. In CSM 292, Fernando earns Mary's favour because of having paid her such careful tribute: accumulating successes of spiritual, political, and material nature. He reserves an expanded Christian empire for his fortunate son. Like his son after him, Fernando plays the part of Mary's chaste lover, offering her devotion and the wealth he gains in his expeditions. This is echoed in the CSM's Prologue *cantiga*, which directly addresses Mary. Alfonso asks to be made 'your troubadour', tapping the Provençal lyrical tradition, of which Alfonso (like his father had been) was a major patron. As a suitor to the Virgin, Alfonso seeks legitimacy through the stories of Fernando. Alfonso's chaste courtship becomes a sort of multi-generational saga of patronage and versification. The pious father figure 'always served her (Mary) and delivered praise to her,/and when he won any city from the Moors,/he placed her effigy in the mosque's entryway', according to the *cantiga*. That historically accurate claim conjoins Fernando and Mary beyond the chaste world of poetic courtship. The king and his saint collaborate in an act of dominance, wresting space from the Moors and marking their space with a near-sexual ritual. In order to initiate the mosque's new existence as church, Fernando leaves Iberian Christendom's enduring mark on the entryway (*pōya eno portal*). The Virgin is repurposed as phallic signifier. Likewise, Alfonso as son of course embodies the generative capacities of Fernando's sex. Having a mortal mother, he is the symbolic half-kin to the Mary effigy in the mosque's entrance. He becomes by extension the new masculine overlord of the conquered city. Fernando wrested a great many territories from the Almohad enemy but, as we have noted, Seville was the jewel. Alfonso's final order, that the CSM be regularly performed after his death, meant to ensure that his lyric voice would fill the converted mosque, much as the statue of Mary would fill the doorway.

Profane Poetry as Political Complaint

Philologists have divided the *cantiga* into three general categories: CSM, *Cantigas d'amigo*, and *Cantigas d'escarnho e de mal dizer* ('Songs of scorn and slande') (hereafter CEM), the latter of which most starkly highlight his imperial anxieties. Of Alfonso's forty-four profane songs, most of them characterised as CEM, there are two instances in which he shares authorship. They offer us an understanding of how poets contended with another, which stylistic tools they employed, and what they sought to effect through sung dialectics.[11] The *tenso* (*tenço* or *tenção* in Iberia) proved to be one of Galician-Portuguese's most important borrowings from Provençal poetry. This lyrical form featured dialogue between two troubadours vying with each other for approbation, the attentions of the beloved, or simply for artistic primacy.

In Alfonso's CEM, the lyric speaker is beset by concerns of poetic rejoinder. The poetic discourse that he uses is contentious, irreverent, and conversational. Any ridicule or outright attack that he issues also anticipates a response from the slandered party, whether or not one comes or is recorded. 'The CEM constitute poetic utterances that are fundamentally and dialogically divided against themselves' (Liu, *Medieval Joke* 14). Alfonso's troubadour identity itself is starkly divided. Instead of the CSM's troubadour of monologue and ode, here he opens equivocal, uncomfortable conversations with his subjects standing in opposition to him. This picture is fully realised in the *tenço*, but it is implicit in all of the CEM. The voice of the perturbed, often combative royal lyricist makes a conspicuous show of his historical knowledge and his place in it, much as his sacred-verse counterpart does, but in dialogue he finds relatively little reassurance in the imperial past. CEM 305, a *tenço* attributed to the king and the Galician Pae Gómez Charinho (an admiral and accomplished poet, ca 1225–95), playfully but pointedly indicts Alfonso, whose memory of Castilian conquest vexes him more than it protects him.

Ũa pregunta vos quero fazer,
senhor, que mi devedes afazer:
por que veestes jantares comer,
que ome nunca de vosso logar
comeu? Esto que pode seer,
ca vej' ende os erdeiros queixar?

Pae Gómez, quero-vos responder,
por vos fazer a verdade saber:
ouv' aqui reis da maior poder
[en] conquerer e en terras gaanhar,
mais non quen ouvesse maior prazer
de comer, quando lhi dan bon jantar.

Pae Gómez:
A question I wish to ask you,
Sire, won't you fill me in:

Why have you been coming to dine
on meals in which no one of your stature has even once partaken?
What could it be about, all this,
that I then see your heirs complaining?
Alfonso:
Pae Gómez, I'll gladly answer
so that you might know the truth:
this land has seen kings more powerful
in conquering and winning land,
but never has anyone taken more pleasure
in eating when a good meal is laid before him!

Bereft of the CSM's reassuring rituals of sanctification, the profane Alfonso finds himself conceding Pae Gómez's unflattering point. The lyric king even elaborates upon the joke, as if endorsing it. His father's achievements, inevitably brought to mind by the reference to 'kings more powerful in conquering and winning land', do not guarantee to Alfonso any lasting, multigenerational legitimacy. In fact, they only highlight the current king's failures. By readily acknowledging his modest standing vis-à-vis previous kings, Alfonso verges on self-ridicule. This royal self-ironising stance raises the possibility that Pae Gómez may well have composed the entire song himself.

The hallmark of CEM is their ability to convert large ethical, political, and economic problems into modest worldly transactions, such as eating and barter. Their lighthearted, humourous tone has led many philologists and critics to conclude that they were limited to social gamesmanship, a diversion of elites that allowed for political jokes, but exerting no real influence on the court's decisions.[12] Such an interpretation is not plausible. When we consider the lyrical rapport between Alfonso and Pae Gómez, it is policy that forms the ground for humour, rather than joking itself providing an excuse for the poets to stumble on to political topics in some kind of free-association mode. As a historical figure, Pae Gómez could harbour no shortage of complaints. He would have been a prime target for taxation, given his status as a landholder. His high position in the navy would also have invited friction with his royal commander, who was unpopular throughout the Spanish military.

In this *cantiga*, both Pae Gómez and Alfonso make plain that the issues driving their dialogue are financial policy and governmental power. What is translated above as 'meal' is *jantar*. Its primary sense of eating a meal extends into concepts of hospitality, the social tests undergone by visitor and host to show their noble standing as they exchange pleasantries and generosities. The most pertinent element *jantar*, however, for the courtly audience, was Castilian taxation policy – Alfonso's controversial, disproportionate techniques of collecting and distributing wealth (García, et al. eds, *Documentación medieval* 79). He was known to offer financial support to his favoured officials and to prop up the near-bankrupt monarchy by increasing taxes on wide swaths of the knightly class. The *jantar* functioned at once as an enforced ritual of generosity and as an alimentive symbol of the king's right to collect. It connoted an ideology of taxation but also the widespread resentment it engendered. Gradually, resistance to Castilian fiscal policies grew, during but especially after Alfonso's reign, a part of his legacy that this *cantiga* anticipates (*Fuero de Miranda del Ebro* 49).

The precise historical developments to which Pae Gómez meant to respond are impossible to know. Their range seems wide. Pae Gómez voices communal complaints of the nobility under Alfonso, but also makes plain his individual resentment at the effects of taxation on his wealth as a landowner. Implicitly, his lyrics may even bemoan the state of the navy in which he served and the insecurity of his coastal Galician province. Nevertheless, Alfonso sees enough import in the accusation that he elaborates upon the humourous metaphor, converting that economic work of miniaturisation into a wider lens on history. In his long memory of empire, he confirms Pae Gómez's insinuation of royal greed and myopia. Most importantly in the context of the Alfonsine legacy, he subverts the political ideals of his court's prose. His laws in *Las siete partidas* self-consciously pantomime Aristotle while citing Solomon in its discourse of moderation. Alfonso's legislative voice insists that kings practise moderation in thinking and behaviour, including dietary matters (2.5.2–4). Pae Gómez's complaint is so pointed because he not only exposes Alfonso's violation of model kingship, he also historicises it in the discrete political space of Castilian sovereignty. His astonished observation that the king eats that which *ome nunca de vosso logar/comeu* ('meals in which no one of your stature has even once partaken'), could also mean 'meals in which no one in your *territory* partakes'. In his lyric portrayal of Alfonso, the king indulges himself at the expense of those around him, cheating even his heirs.

The other historical factors to which this *tenço* points are Alfonso's putative neglect of his provinces. That charge has been levelled at the king as frequently by modern historians as by the king's own nobles. One CEM aimed at Alfonso sings of *vossos meus maravedis, senhor* ('your *maravedis* coins of mine, Sire'), highlighting the ambivalent quality of wealth held by royal subjects, which was then claimed and collected by the throne.[13] That sense of royal collection and confiscation, and the resentment of the taxed subject, overlaps with the ethical questions of patronage forcefully raised by al-Tawḥīdī and Abū l-Faḍl in the first chapter. When one patron and one author negotiate their relationship through poetry, courtly postures, and material payment, they inevitably distort the ontology of such relationships. Centuries before the diffuse modern institutions of publishing houses, unions, governments, and markets all intervened in the production of art, the discrete relationships between individuals at court themselves functioned as their own abstract institutions. Pae Gómez's rapport with Alfonso signifies the general idea of two poets addressing each other, as well as the conspicuously unequal relationship between nobleman and king. The *tenço* must therefore be seen for its symbolic qualities, especially those linking it to other Alfonsine *cantigas*.

All of this is to say that, when Pae Gómez engages the practice of taxation, he shows how inherently generalisable the traditional two-party model of medieval poetry is. In its performance and the space it provides for the royal patron to respond in verse, the *tenço* actively engages both the government and the larger community of imperial subjects. Much as the CSM use the troubadour–beloved binary as a structural model for pious expression, Pae Gómez and Alfonso use the song to model the patron–poet relationship that frames courtly compositions in the aggregate. In a sense, the target of parody in CEM 305 is not the unapologetic figure of Alfonso, but rather the economic system in which poets address their patrons and one another. Pae Gómez incorporates an entire community in his lyric self. He, and the corporate body of noblemen for whom he would like to speak, makes no threat of withholding wealth from the tax collector. In the face of the political joke, Alfonso casts himself as the supplicant instead of the patron per se. This allows him to appeal to his subjects for largesse, as if Pae Gómez were now a kind of patron. Effectively, Pae Gómez has no dependable means of destabilising the king's power. Even though both lyric speakers agree that Alfonso compares unfavourably to his predecessors, they also both resign themselves to the fact that he will probably continue to rule over a resentful nobility. In his parting comment, Pae Gómez reports to Alfonso that the people 'have great fear/of opposing you on this issue'. The king closes the conversation by insisting that his knights freely give to him and, besides, his excellent taste is well known. Endorsing the ridicule levelled at him, he co-opts parody's ritual of reversal for his own interests.

Alfonso was widely accused of extravagance, even profligacy. The poetry and administrative prose of his court both make it clear that his reign was a tense one, particularly in his relations with the knighthood. He came under particular scrutiny for his expensive, and ultimately unsuccessful, campaign for Holy Roman Emperor. It proved to be a decades-long conflict with papal authority that left him frustrated and, in 1275, obliged to renounce his pretentions to the title. The title of Holy Roman Emperor was, by Alfonso's time, largely symbolic. In practical terms, the empire would have included regions of Germany and Bohemia, although there was no guarantee of subjects' fealty had Alfonso been crowned their king. Primarily it would have meant his successful alliance of fellow kings of Western Europe, and of course the historical link forged between Alfonso and 'Rome' as an imperial idea. The *Partidas* and CSM 401 demonstrate how highly he prized a Roman ideal of legitimacy. He poured resources into diplomacy with kings and pope alike, seeking their support in his campaign. By doing so, however, he alienated officers and nobles such as Pae Gómez. He also irritated clergy around the kingdom, who appealed to the Vatican to intervene at the same time that Alfonso was soliciting the pope's favour. Spanish bishops sought and received a papal declaration that Alfonso was an enemy of the church.[14]

Even though he made little attempt to refute charges of economic exploitation, Alfonso had a highly effective means of dampening its impact. He identified with the CEM's stock character, the outraged but mirthful lyric speaker. Pae Gómez provides one such example – Alfonso, too, assumed the role. The key ritual is for the aggrieved troubadour to marvel at the extent of another person's ability and willingness to wrong him, inspecting the damage done in a playfully forensic performance.[15] He asserts his own power to turn the spectacle into a poetic joke. Alfonso executes that move for its political expedience and to turn historical events, both major and minor, to his advantage. His biting wit drives CEM 33, which in many respects tells the other side of the economic-policy story surveyed and exploited by CEM 305. Alfonso's expenditures were many: the most durably famous of them are the CSM's composition and illumination, and his translation schools from which Middle Eastern texts made their famous debut in Latin Christendom. But perhaps more extravagant and certainly more onerous was his campaign for the Holy Roman Empire, requiring of him protracted exchanges with the Vatican and a series of large payments to his operatives in Germany and Italy ingratiating themselves to the other kings who would vote on the matter (Ballesteros Beretta, *Alfonso X* 175–212; O'Callaghan in Burns ed., *Worlds* 57). Although many of the historical actualities surrounding CEM 33 are unknown, the material concerns are unmistakable:

Se me graça fezesse este Papa de Roma!
Pois que el[e] os panos da mia reposte toma,
que en levass'el os cabos e dess'a mi a soma;
mais doutra guise me foi el vende-la galdrapa.
Quisera eu assi ora deste nosso Papa
que me talhasse melhor aquesta capa.
Se m'el graça fezesse con os seus cardeaes,
que lh'eu desse, que mos talhasse iguaaes;
mais vedes en que vi en el[e] maos sinaes,
queand'o que me furtou, foi cobra-lo sa capa.
Quisera eu assi ora deste nosso Papa
que me talhasse melhor aquesta capa.
Se con'os cardeaes com que faça seus conselhos
posesse que guardasse nós de maos trebelhos,
fezera gram mercêe, ca nom furtar com elhos
e [os] panos dos cristãos meter sô sa capa.
Quisera eu assi ora deste nosso Papa
que me talhasse melhor aquesta capa.

If only this Pope of Rome would do me a good turn!
As long as he's going to steal the clothes from my closet,

I wish he'd at least take the bottom-shelf ones and leave me the ones up top;
In more than one way, he's tried to sell me clothes.
 So now I have a request for our Pope:
 that he make me a better cut of the cloak!
If only he'd do me a good turn with his cardinals,
that he'd give it to them a bit, so that he might cut them up in equal share.
But no, you see all the bad signs coming from him, as my description makes clear,
when that which he's stolen went to cover his cloak.
 So now I have a request for our Pope:
 that he make me a better cut of the cloak!
If only he and those cardinals, drawing up orders,
would deign to free us from our hardship,
grant us the great favour of not scamming us
and keeping the Christians' rags underneath that cloak.
 So now I have a request for our Pope:
 that he make me a better cut of the cloak!

This work ambitiously pushes the CEM genre into the diplomatic sphere, and complicates the usual social rituals of Galician-Portuguese lyric. Profane *cantigas* are almost always about fellow Iberians, usually noblemen, clerics, or performers. The *tenço* of course accommodates two voices within the text proper, but most compositions are limited to one lyric speaker and a chorus. Parties slandered in verse would have easy access to the text because they, as members of elite society, would understand the Galician-Portuguese lyric coin of the realm.[16] The fact that this song had little potential to reach the person about whom it spoke – who would not readily understand even were he to receive it – distinguishes it from most CEM. Alfonso mounts an instrumental, propagandist effort quite unlike his other songs. He makes a joke that relishes the social power of its own exclusivity, and the inevitable futility of its complaint. By being exclusive in the context of a long diplomatic struggle, Alfonso creates a sense of Iberian interiority – one conspicuously limited to Galicians and those people educated in peninsular poetry, who could understand the lyrics. He reminds his audience members of a solidarity they may not normally celebrate during this period of dissent in the knighthood and the church. Not only may he gain the sympathies of the Spaniards hearing it, he also takes the opportunity to enjoy with his audience the specifically Iberian character of the *cantiga*. It was an art form in which the king and the elite literate class under him took great pride, as well as being a kind of troubadour code for the peninsula.

It is not only Alfonso and his lyric speaker who play intricate linguistic games in CEM 33. While the song's language revels in its incomprehensibility – perhaps irrelevance – to the Pope himself, the reference to cardinals in the second stanza destabilises that position. The overarching goal is to provide a ludic, lyrical view of the dysfunctional political economy alienating the king from the Vatican. The Pope, 'drawing up orders' (*faça seus conselhos*) with the cardinals, oversees an activity the medieval Iberian audience would know was conducted in Latin. The private, near-conspiratorial quality of those imagined consultations provide a fitting counterweight to the private joke that is this poem. As each stanza – and even more so the chorus – fixates on the act of withholding, the idea of private speech blurs with the mercantile stinginess and privacy the Pope is said to commit. That privacy is compromised by the knowledge shared by audience members: the College of Cardinals naturally included many speakers of Iberian vernaculars, a sizeable portion of whom probably had significant exposure to Galician-Portuguese, given their social stature.

To reach the endpoint of its polemic, the *cantiga* wishes to speak for the greater public. In this way, Alfonso attempts to shed the elitism inherent to the Galician-Portuguese lyric language. We have seen how Pae Gómez, in his *tenço* with the king, employs the double entendre of *jantares*: both the sense of meals and that of tax policies engage communal activities, and his section of the *cantiga* only acquires force if it successfully speaks for classes of people compelled to give tribute to the royal estate. CEM 33 must exert even more effort. It uses social imagery towards a political end, because it would present the king essentially as a subject rather than a monarch. In that role, he has licence to invite other subjects to join him in a political complaint, despite the unpopularity of Alfonso's prolonged dealings with the Pope. The cloak (*capa*) on which the poetry has fixated is shown to cover something much humbler, a piece of cloth now portraying the king as a poor supplicant. By the last line, we sense this as the speaker makes claims for 'the Christians' in their 'rags' (*panos*), since whatever finery he may have owned he already lost to papal raiders. King and commoner are set at equal footing. Most importantly, the clothes that the cloak covers do not properly belong to the Pope. The last line insists that this poem's personal complaint is generalisable, that it speaks for the interests of the variegated Christian nation. The cloak, by virtue of the fine material from which it is wrought, serves as a unit of exchange only between Pope and King. Alfonso uses the sense of audience privilege (the insiders-only quality of the joke) to imagine popular opinion as his own will. When he converts his contentious relationship with the Pope into song and his subjects into lyric subjects, he effectively conscripts his people into a battle abroad.

Wars, Moors and Africa: Bodies on the Imperial Boundary

All of the *cantigas* examined thus far shed light on Alfonso's nagging problems in military and financial matters. As his armies fared poorly against Moroccan and Andalusi Muslim forces, they provided stark and painful evidence of the military consequences of his financial troubles. Following a major defeat at the hands of Arabs and Berbers northwest of Granada, the Muslim stronghold, Alfonso is said to have composed a song in disgust. His CEM 21 tells of petty-noble fighters, pallid and trembling with fear. They are routed by *genetes*: North African horsemen aiding the Granadan Andalusis' war effort. Even more astonishing to the lyric Alfonso is the sight of the mounted Christians and their *cochões* (low-class men, probably assisting the knights)

> com mui [mais] longos granhões
> que as barvas dos cabrões:
> ao som do atambor
> os deitavan dos arções
> ant' os pees de seu senhor.

> with moustaches longer
> than goats' beards,
> at the sound of the drum
> they were flung from their saddles,
> at the feet of their lord.

ᶜImād al-Dīn's poem on Shāwar and the Crusaders comes to mind, for its use of cowardice tropes and its liberal scattering of Christian bodies to mark the after-effects of treason and cowardice. CEM 21 stops short of labelling the nobles traitors, but it populates the battlefield with the same sort of pathetic warriors. They are abject victims of their own hubris, one of Alfonso's favoured poetic means of deriding his noblemen.[17] Historically, the *genete* (*jinete* in Spanish) tormented Christian Iberian armies; in lyric, he proved to be one of the most potent elements of Galician-Portuguese poetic propaganda and historiography. In both sacred and profane *cantigas*, he signifies Muslim prowess in a way that few other stock personas can. Christian knights credited the *genete* with superb horsemanship. When rendered into poetry, he uses his technical mastery to stage raids on the Spanish cavalry. Surprising his enemy, he shows the Christian forces to be disorganised – at a conceptual level he reveals the disconnect between the nobility and the royal court supposedly in commands. He also serves as a lyric reminder of the expansive nature of Alfonso's holy war. The Arab rulers of Granada could draw upon a massive force of North African allies and mercenaries. To respond, the Alfonsine *cantigas* alternately lament the kingdom's impotence (in the CEM) and invoke the divine, infinite assisting force of the Trinity (in the CSM).

CEM 21's *genete* stands out in the expansive field of Muslim enemies. He is supremely competent in war but, most significantly, he infiltrates Christendom and marks the Christian body. His exploits on horseback give him access to frontiers, which he crosses in order to engage his ignorant enemies. It is in that permeable space where Alfonso conducts his most fraught literary battle. He synthesises some of the deepest problems explored in his cantigas, namely sex, gender, ethics, holy war, and the acquisitive nature of both king and subject. Here in CEM 25, his chosen 'adversary' in the poetic field is Domingas Eanes. As a *soldadeira*, a singer and dancer at court, she mirrors her Muslim adversary in certain respects. When *cantigas* slander a *soldadeira*, they ridicule her entire professional class: singers and dancers at court, attested in court documents and rhetoric of the thirteenth century.[18] Unlike Pae Gómez, Domingas could not enjoy full courtier status, nor was she considered qualified to compose troubadour works. A non-noble, she would have been permitted entry for the purposes of entertaining the audience. *Cantigas* associate the *soldadeira* with prostitution and other illicit sexual practices. She mimics the norms of the soldier (*soldado*), the shared etymology of the two terms no coincidence since they work for *soldo*, a discrete payment. Most importantly, she crosses cultures. Her putatively loose morals grant her freedom of passage among religious groups and political factions. On campaign, she crosses the lines of battle into Arabo-Islamic society, testing (and attesting to) the skills, virility, and violence of the feared *genete*.

Domingas Eanes houve sa baralha
com um genet', e foi mal ferida;
empero foi ela i tam ardida
que houve depois a vencer, sem falha,
e, de pram, venceu bõo cavaleiro;
mais empero era-x'el tam braceiro
que houv'end'ela de ficar colpada.
O colbe [a] colheu per ũa malha
da loriga, que era desvencida;
e pesa-m'ende, porque essa ida,
de prez que houve mais, se Deus me valha,
venceu ela; mais [pel]o cavaleiro,
per sas armas e per com'er'arteiro,
já sempr'end'ela seerá sinalada.
E aquel mouro trouxe, com'arreite,
dous companhões em toda esta guerra;
e de mais há preço que nunca erra
de dar gram colpe com seu tragazeite;
e foi-a ach[a]ar com costa juso,
e deu-lhi por en tal colpe de suso
que já a chaga nunca vai cerrada.
E dizem meges que usam tal preite
que atal chaga jamais nunca cerra,
se com quanta lã há em esta terra
a escaentassem, nem cõn'o azeite;
porque a chaga nom vai contra juso,
mais vai em redor, come perafuso,
e por en muit'há que é fistolada.

Domingas Eanes had her scuffle
with a *genete*, coming out badly injured.
But she was fierce enough
to win, true enough, when all was said and done.
It's true, she beat quite a fine knight,
although he is so good with the lance
that she had to sustain some injuries.
The blow she received hit a link
in her chainmail, which was undone:
and, dear me, because at this thrust,
she was tougher – God help me! –
– she won. But then the horseman,
because of his weapons and because he was so crafty,
saw to it that she would be marked forever.
That Moor carried, along with his rod,
two 'companions' throughout this battle;
he is also known for never failing
to strike a great blow with his dart.
He went to topple her, mouth open,
and gave her such a hit from on top,
that now the wound will never be closed.
The doctors who make this their specialty say
about such a wound: 'It can never be closed
even with all the wool there is in this land,
nor with oil can it be cauterized,
because the wound doesn't go straight in –
– it goes around, like a screw,
and that's why it's been draining for so long!'[19]

The construction of feminine lyric figures is undoubtedly one of the most problematic and critically compelling features of Galician-Portuguese lyric. As a collection of songs, the CEM's use for the *soldadeira* has been aptly described as a meditation upon both the court and the intricate legal discourse of intercultural amorous coupling. The self-consciously masculine lyric voice of the Galician-Portuguese troubadour uses them to poeticise 'the consequences of female minstrelsy – the lust, the degradation, the grotesque physicality thought to be produced when a woman performs' and the ambivalence of her laughable status, since it is the court that invites her to perform (Weiss cited in Deyermond and Taylor eds, *From the* Cancioneiro da Vaticana *to the* Cancionero General 250). By ridiculing her, court attempts to relieve its own anxieties. It celebrates her as both a carnivalesque buffoon and a heroine. Those anxieties, however, are stubborn. As long as the *soldadeira* remains essential to courtly life, she animates its contentious poetry.[20]

We have seen the recruitment of the *genete* into lyric works, and how Alfonso uses this Muslim figure to portray his own knights as inadequate. With the *soldadeira,* Alfonso revisits that humourous trope, but retools it to offer a more circumspect view of his empire. His cantigas repeatedly show how deeply vexed the court is by the idea of an imperial frontier, which its forces cannot seem to master. The difference in CEM 25's mock chivalry is that the *soldadeira* achieves a kind of victory. The poem humourously tells its audience of the possibility of dominating the enemy, even though its explanation is sarcastic. The 'wound' that Domingas sustains serves as her proof of payment for the kingdom, her battle scar also the mark of an illegal sexual union.[21] She both serves the empire and tests the coherence of its laws and borders. The *genete* initiates the challenge to her, acting as a violent emissary with his weapons (they are organs: his *tragazeite,* 'small lance', as penis; his *dous companhões,* 'two companions' are his testicles). He wields them confidently, as befits his lyric reputation for military acumen. Domingas, despite her abilities, fails to maintain the integrity of her armour (clothing). She exercises only limited control over her body, lacking the chaste properties that signify the upper classes or the lyric figure of the beloved. It is only logical that Domingas should fail to protect herself, because the very strategy of protecting the body from violation is a specialty of noble women. Because of her middling position in the court economy, she is limited to performing physical labours (singing and sex) that the audience wants but cannot explicitly endorse. In the logic of the CEM, her body is prefigured as degraded but attractive. It is worthy of men's attention but ultimately expendable. It has use value, and for Domingas its defence is an end unto itself. She moves outward from the imperial centre to engage the genete but, barred from knighthood, she is not entitled to acquire any property when she emerges victorious. That is the prerogative of the *genete*, who is a perverse knight but a knight all the same. He seeks all possible loot from Christendom. His illicit sexual encounter cannot result in any legal action against him, since as a Muslim male he is not subject to the anti-miscegenation laws of Castile. What Domingas achieves is her own survival. She parries the *genete*'s blows and bests him, and the anecdote allows her to fulfil her courtly role as the provider of entertainment. In the jaundiced view that the CEM take on warfare, she occupies the dubious apex of success on the front lines.

Alfonso's choice of Domingas as his ritual adversary obscures just how dependent he is upon her as an agent of the empire. As critics have noted, the *cantiga* plays upon the Romance epic, whose archetypal hero such as the Cid gains glory for the kingdom. He employs chivalric protocol as a language through which to communicate with ally and enemy alike.[22] Even though he overpowers the Muslim armies with whom he contends for land and treasure, the only characters whom he personally targets as sworn enemies are fellow Christian noblemen who violate the rules of knighthood. In the CEM, too, chivalry is shown desecrated. Christian knights fail the tests of masculinity that give meaning to their chivalric fraternity. Pae Gómez speaks for a knightly class raided and impoverished by the king in CEM 305. Alfonso derisively laments his haughty cavalry laid low in CEM 21. In Domingas, Alfonso seizes the opportunity to repair a damaged chivalry, even if his means for doing so are the equivocal and ironic gestures of misogynist satire. Caught constantly between strength and weakness, autonomy and violation, Domingas bears the multiple identities of the tested empire itself. Alfonso's attempt to augment the tradition of *soldadeira* jokes leaves the court inspecting his own political wounds as a king.

In her violated state, the *soldadeira* nonetheless delivers sovereignty to Castile. The only other persona in Alfonso's poetry – and perhaps in the entire *cantiga* canon – capable of such an act is Mary herself. Since Ramón Menéndez Pidal's seminal study on medieval performance, literary historians and critics have suggested subtle links between sex workers and the Virgin.[23] But those connections are more forceful drivers of literature, performance, and cultural consciousness than that research has acknowledged. Because the *soldadeira* was associated with the sex trade, she also retained the unspoken political cachet of a prostitute. In medieval Spain, to deal in sex-for-payment made one 'a marker of difference, as well as an active agent in its surveillance' (Nirenberg, *Communities* 148). She communicated linguistically, artistically, and sexually with disparate groups of Iberian people, including the enemy. Even while the court condemned prostitution in its laws, it recognised this transgressive ability as a form of power. The *soldadeira*'s unique cross-border exploits serve not only as the conceit of the lyric joke, they also assure the elite masculine space of the court that the imperial borders can be crossed. By extension, a *cantiga* such as CEM 25 challenges Alfonso's knights to retrieve their lost potency. Throughout the Alfonsine lyric corpus, Christendom achieves victory only when it creates a figure of the feminine and enlists her in the fight. That is made obvious in the CSM; in martially themed CEM, it is more deeply coded, but it nonetheless gives the songs ideological weight. CEM 21's long-moustached Christian horsemen lie prostrate before exultant *genetes*. God and king witness their knights' emasculation. In CEM 25, Domingas emerges triumphant despite the ridicule aimed at her. The *genete*'s attack leaves her infected and perhaps untreatable, but she delivers a much-coveted net gain to her kingdom.

Lyric and Legal Claims of Empire

Returning to the doctrine of *Las siete partidas*, we find a telltale connection between the military iconography of the monarch and the *cantigas*' ritual function. They come together in the courtly space, where they achieve meaning. *Corte* is so named 'because there the sword of justice is kept, which is used to *cortar* (cut off) all bad deeds, material and verbal; ... as well as words of slander' (2.9.27). The term that is translated as 'words of slander' is '*escarnios*': the Spanish cognate of CEM's *cantigas d'escarnho e mal dizer*.[24] The shared etymology of *corte*/*cortar* is linguistically bogus, but it provides insight into Alfonso's legislative goals. The *Partidas* wish to conjoin eloquence and the violent work of the sword. What the laws do not mention is the potential for the words themselves to mimic weapons. Alfonso recognised the martial and hermeneutical uses of language, as his lyric compositions make particularly clear.

By adopting a troubadour persona, Alfonso reframed events and political relationships in his kingdom. Composing lyric also allowed him to actively take part in a sphere in which he had the perennial upper hand. He held informal contests with nobles, and the results almost inevitably would confirm his power at court. In this way, he could claim victory during a time in which he rarely won in war and diplomacy. By most measures, he was more successful as a combative poet than as the symbolic leader of an army in actual combat. We have scrutinised the signs of deep anxiety running through his sacred and profane lyric. Even in the triumphalist imperial hagiography of the CSM, he is at pains to recast his own projects as meeting with Mary's approval. It is as if he sought to overcome the sense of self-doubt and imperial weakness that he also writes into the sacred songbook. CSM 401's political complaint about courtiers' poor service to the throne is a cliché, but it takes on cosmic and historical significance when Alfonso articulates it in a lyric plea to the Virgin. He fears that his court cannot be relied upon to reject, on its own power, the 'liar', 'traitor', and 'bad advisor'. In other words, he doubts whether the institution will carry out the precise functions that his *Partidas* say are the most basic reason for a court to exist.

Long before Alfonso's time, the CEM had been a means of licitly bringing *escarnios* into court. His innovation with the slanderous genre was to use it as a method of *cortar*. The *Partidas* do not suggest that speech may simultaneously play both roles, that is, serving as licentious wordplay and royal enforcement of language norms. The poetic texts themselves, however, demonstrate their multiplicity when issued from the throne. When Alfonso found himself lacking – in many cases, failing to adequately prepare – the political tools necessary to achieve his imperial ambitions, he fashioned himself into a confrontational, irreverent poet. Understanding this is essential for resituating the CEM in the history of Iberia. It also sheds light on the relationship between sacred and profane literary genres. The CSM are generally thought of as his lyric of empire, but the CEM analysed here compel us to rethink that assumption. Benjamin Liu astutely takes several major twentieth-century studies to task for having adopted too simple an interpretive approach to the CEM. He argues that Hispanists tend to look for basic segments of society that the *cantigas* supposedly lampoon, when the more substantive project would be to explore the social, religious, and linguistic systems that the CEM call into question (Liu, *Medieval Joke* 113–14). Building upon Liu's critique, we see how Alfonso's CEM engage the troubled royal system. They respond to the *Partidas*' dictum that the ideal king should evaluate his courtiers' speech, and mete out rewards and legal punishments when the court organises contests. As dialogic works, these songs call out to, and answer, one another. When Alfonso entered the lyric field of play, he began to label the inherent metapoetics of CEM. He showed them to be not just poetry but also a semi-official form of royal rhetoric.

The other crucial function of the *cantigas* in the court was to exclude certain groups and individuals based on their identity rather than their speech. This is where the idea of the Moor is so crucial. Although it is documented that Muslims had access to official gatherings with Alfonso's high administration, the *cantigas* imagine a world of clear prohibitions separating religious groups. Crossings-over inevitably produce violence, as in Domingas Eanes's battle. What makes the *mouros* such a driving force in these songs is precisely their status outside of court and culture. The figure of the Muslim served to expose the court's vulnerabilities. The Spanish epic tradition had its *moro latinado* (Spanish-speaking Moor) but, in the Galician-Portuguese lyric text, Muslims were exclusively the inhabitants of the militarised frontier. They did not enter the rarefied inner sanctum of the court.[25] Muslims, as poetic personas and distant spectres, confirmed the righteousness of Christianity even as they exposed the dysfunctional relationship between Christian court and battlefield. Despite their heathen status, their commitments to fighting wars and their primitive nature make them dangerous. They make up a cohesive warrior class for their empire – the very element that Alfonso's *cantigas* complain that Spain lacks. According to the CEM, *genetes* highlight the poor ethics of Spanish knights, who fail to adhere to chivalric norms of bravery. The administrative, military conduit between court and province is frayed. Muslim fighters – and, less directly, *soldadeiras* – expose the key political breakdown in the empire. The privileged lyric language, which celebrates its own exclusivity, invents an outsider whose exclusion ironically grants him power.

Alfonso's profane *cantigas* have received a small fraction of the critical attention paid to the CSM, not only because they are fewer in number but because they do not effect the sort of formal innovation that the CSM represent in the Galician-Portuguese tradition as the king had received it. It is true that the CEM were a source of entertainment that do not offer the grand generic and ideological synthesis of the CSM, which merged existing Marian anecdotes with the Iberian troubadour language. Nevertheless, the

CEM are highly synthetic: by inviting discourse between king and courtier, and providing a lighthearted register for serious political complaints, they sharpened the artistic instrument of the court itself. Alfonso's pious but sometimes aggressive troubadour persona allowed him to rework the imperial narrative as he struggled in the quotidian matters of administration. To explain his own lacklustre record in battles against Arab armies, he turned from the grand language of holy war to mundane local matters such as unpaid taxes and Christian–Muslim sexual improprieties. In the tension between the ridiculed Spanish subject and the fiendish, captivating Muslim, the king produced a lyrical fiction of himself. His image as Iberia's benevolent, intellectual, combative, and even slanderous leader expanded the definition of court and king. It was only in the centuries to follow, when Spain turned its imperial gaze away from Gibraltar and towards the New World, that Alfonso became an international courtly ideal.

Notes

1. For these modern epithets applied to Alfonso and the pre-Renaissance theory, see Burns ed., *Emperor of Culture* 1–13 and Carrión Gutiérrez, *Conociendo a Alfonso X El Sabio* 139. *Stupor mundi* is the historical honorific for Alfonso's cousin, Frederick II of Hohenstaufen (1194–1250); Burns's attribution to Alfonso is apparently inspired by the two kings' shared genes in addition to their reputation for cosmopolitan academic projects. An important (albeit conjectural and tongue-in-cheek) alternate view of Alfonso's cultural identity is to be found in Fierro, 'Alfonso X "The Wise": The Last Almohad Caliph?' 175.
2. There are several sources of Marian praise from which Spanish performers could draw in heeding Alfonso's instructions. Many of the texts are in Latin, but the king's own songbook is clearly foremost in the context of his royal writ.
3. Alfonso is the only person, royal or otherwise, known to have composed sacred verse in Galician-Portuguese, whereas many poets' profane works (CEM, *cantigas d'amigo*, and *cantigas d'amor*) are extant.
4. The sacred-troubadour persona is shown fully formed in CSM 279: the chorus pleads with Mary to save 'your troubadour' (*vosso trobador*), indicating a generalised form of consent that Alfonso's wish has been granted.
5. See especially Alfonso's law books *Espéculo* and *Las siete partidas*, given a modern critical overview by Bernal in Martínez and Rodríguez eds, *El Scriptorium alfonsí* 17–81.

6. The main Old Spanish prose text concerning the Crusades is *La gran conquista de Ultramar*, long attributed to Alfonso's own court but now widely considered subsequent to his reign (González, *La tercera* 14).
7. In Galician-Portuguese as well as Old Spanish, Tartus is spelled Tortosa, although the two cities' names seem to have different derivations: Tartus from the Phoenician Antarados, Tortosa from the Latin Dertōsa.
8. This scouting mission brings to mind the anthropology of Usāma ibn Munqidh's testimony on the intercultural dinner at Antioch in the last chapter, although the Arab knight described by Usāma's story is not necessarily interested in learning Frankish ways for the sake of military advantage. The CSM claim, as do the stories of *Kitāb al-iʿtibār*, to be true. In contrast to Usāma's story – and, more importantly, to Alfonsine prose – the CSM emphasise unidirectional cultural encounters: in the relatively few cantigas featuring conversion and/or cross-cultural edification, Muslims learn from Christians, not vice versa. Albert Bagby has aptly observed this fact, although he misunderstands CSM 165 to take place in Tortosa, Catalonia, rather than in Tartus ('Moslem' 177, 179).
9. CSM 329 is the only other composition to mention the Qur'an. It repeats the reference to Mary's virginity.
10. For medieval Arabic documents noting Alfonso's missives to rulers in Yemen and Egypt see Ibn al-Furāt 1:106–7, 1:167, 2:83. For a detailed modern account of Alfonso's diplomacy with Mamluks see Martínez Montávez, 'Relaciones'.
11. Several major scholars have proposed that we subdivide the CEM (recounted in Nodar Manso, *Teatro menor* 12–14). On the question of authorship: as with most premodern works of literature, *cantiga* composition is very much a collaborative practice, all the more so in the case of a literary monarch as prolific as Alfonso. Although we know that Alfonso was knowledgeable about the Galician-Portuguese language, it is altogether possible that he personally composed few or none of the *cantigas*. The same could be speculated about the lengthy volumes of Latin and Old Spanish attributed to him. Ultimately it is the attribution, and the politics thereof, that are more directly a concern to Medieval Studies.
12. González Jiménez, 'Alfonso X, poeta profano' 108–9. Paredes provides a history of the 'light entertainment' reading of CEM – which he notes originally stemmed from the *cantigas*' reference to their own jocular language – in Alfonso X, *El Cancionero profano* 99–100. Helder Mecedo seeks to apologise for them as basically unpoetic songs that only barely merit serious analysis (Deyermond ed., *One Man's Canon* 69). See also Moure's insightful but apolitical reading in Smith ed., *Time in Time*, 102–8. Fortunately, such suppositions about the

anodyne nature of humourous poetry in medieval Spain have not escaped some rigorous scrutiny over the past century. See especially Buceta's studies in the early twentieth century, demonstrating the technique of folding political poemic inside jocular language among the generations of troubadours following the heyday of Galician Portuguese poetry: 'Fecha probable' 51–8.

13. For examples of historians criticising Alfonso for his provincial policies, see Burns ed., *Worlds*; Luis Martín in Mondéjar and Montoya [Martínez] eds, *Estudios alfonsíes*; and Socarrás, *Study*. The *maravedí* was, until very late in Alfonso's life, a non-circulating copper coin, generally used for accounting (Kulp-Hill in Alfonso X ('el Sabio'), *Songs* 81n5).
14. Detailed accounts of Alfonso's expensive projects are provided by Ballesteros Beretta, *Alfonso X* 175–212; and O'Callaghan in Burns ed., *Worlds* 57. Fernández-Ordóñez examines Alfonso's conflicts with Spanish clerics in Martin ed., *La historia alfonsí* 55–70.
15. The singing auteur was almost always figured as masculine, especially when identifying a troubadour (*trovador* in Iberia), as Alfonso did. Feminised voices are discernible in the larger apparatus of Galician-Portuguese tradition, however, on which see Filios, *Performing* 33–46.
16. A strong case has been made that people slandered in CEM, beyond merely comprehending the poetry invoking them, could respond to the charges and jokes made in the compositions. Building on the competitive wordplay (*jugar* or *juego de palabras*) mentioned in *Partida* 2.9.30, Montoya Martínez explores the potential overlap between that legal concern and the performance embodied in 'El carácter lúdico' (441–2). Filios inspects *juego* and poetic tradition more directly in *Performing* 41–6.
17. Typically, an Alfonsine *cantiga* imputing the nobles will accuse them of cowardice, unjustified arrogance, or both. For a broad overview of his composition on such themes, see O'Callaghan, *Alfonso X and the* Cantigas de Santa Maria 107–9.
18. For a definition of the *soldadeira* and her role in both society and poetry, see Menéndez Pidal, *Poesía juglaresca* 31–3. *Soldadeiras* are named in poems, sometimes appearing in more than one composition, although Domingas Eanes is not to be found in other extant CEM. There is archival evidence of a widow named Domingas Eanes in northwest Iberia (Boullón Agrelo, et al. eds, *As tebras* 135) but the records' dates place her almost a century after Alfonso, so if he was indeed the *cantiga*'s author, it must be about a Domingas Eanes undocumented in other known sources.

19. In the case of this song, I have used Manuel Ferreiro's edition of the manuscripts, in Arbor Aldea and Fernández Guiadanes eds, *Estudos* 246–58. Ferreiro's edition is a revision of both Lapa's CEM and subsequent treatments of the composition. It deserves to be considered the foremost edition.
20. On female identification in the CEM, see Filios, 'Jokes' and *Performing* 3–5 and 21–22; and Weiss in Deyermond and Taylor eds, *From the* Cancioneiro da Vaticana *to the* Cancionero General 245–57. On the imperial military themes worked by *soldadeira* personas in poetry, see Filios, *Performing* 55–62; Liu in Blackmore and Hutcheson eds, *Queer Iberia* 57–64; Nirenberg, 'Conversion' 1,074–5; and Villares, 'Castillos' 15–18, the latter of which explores the enduring legacy of *soldadeira* exploits in national literature.
21. Alfonso's own legal code greatly elaborated upon (and in some cases, moderated) existing laws against sex between Christians, Muslims, and Jews. See his *Partidas* 7.24.9 and 7.25.10, redacting previous local laws in Spanish kingdoms, most famously *El Fuero de Teruel* (386, 533). Whereas prior codes had called for execution of both parties when Christian women were found to have lain with Muslim, the *Partidas* stipulate that the offending woman is to be placed in the power of her (Christian, since religious intermarriage is of course forbidden) husband, who may choose to let her live or have her burned to her death.
22. See Nodar Manso, 'La parodia' 160–1, whose formal observations lay the groundwork for Liu in Blackmore and Hutcheson eds, *Queer Iberia* 57; and Rosenstein, 'Voiced' 69.
23. See Menéndez Pidal, *Poesía juglaresca* 31; and Fontes, 'Celestina' and 'On Alfonso's "Interrupted" Encounter' 97. Filios (*Performing* 72) and Liu (*Medieval Joke* 80) make similar but distinct points, likening the *soldadeira* to aspects of Christ's body.
24. The cited *partida* 2.9.27 section reads, 'Otrosi es dicho corte segunt lenguage de España, porque alli es la espada de la justicia con que se han de cortar todos los males tambien de fecho como de dicho, asi los tuertos como las fuerzas et las soberbias que facen los homes et dicen, porque se muestran por atrevidos et denodados, et otrosi los escarnios et los engaños, et las palabras soberbias et natias que facen á los homes envilescer et seer rafeces.'
25. For legal protections of Muslim visitors to the court, see *Partida* 7.25.9. In addition to the CSM illuminations, manuscripts of Alfonso's *Libros del ajedrez, dados y tablas* contain many depictions of multiconfessionalism at court, including that of the king consulting with Muslim savants on the playing of chess. As

for the *moro latinado*, his most famous (and perhaps his first) appearance is in the form of Abengalbón in *Cantar de Mío Cid*, then becoming a key part of late medieval Spanish literature.

4

Saladino Rinato: Spanish and Italian Courtly Fictions of Crusade

Court writers of the late-medieval Mediterranean received a textual version of Saladin largely divorced from the record of Crusades military operations and, in turn, integrated him into an abstract notion of the court. Thanks to French and Provençal literature, he had become a chivalric universal. He was able to converse in European languages, exchange compliments and gifts with his European knightly counterparts, engage in chaste love with Christian beloveds, and even broach the subject of conversion with relatively little sense of scandal.[1] It was not until the thirteenth century, however, that he graduated to a literary personality who compelled the Europeans around him to consider how the court should function. His prior fictional, historiographic career of battling Christians, and his subsequent entrance into the fictional version of the court, allowed him to re-engage European intellectuals in a crucial literary move beyond the traditional borders of kingly legends and knightly romances. Already courtly, he became meta-courtly.

Saladin's adaptation at the hands of Iberian and Italian authors thrust him from the role of espousing comprehensive chivalric tenets to a markedly more dialectical position, engaging fellow courtly figures in tests of wits and wisdom. One of the sultan's customary roles in European literature and admiring semi-historical texts had been to demonstrate the sociopolitical ideal of generosity, with which he could issue challenges to fellow members of the fictional court. In the late Middle Ages and the approach of the Renaissance, Saladin maintained his largesse but developed new dimensions as knight and leader. The challenge he brought to the court was now both material and, importantly, insistently conceptual. The ritual of gift-giving and refined conversation allowed him to ask difficult questions of his fellow residents of the idealised fictional court. Utilising him as a liminal, border-crossing agent, late-medieval Romance texts opened a complex literary discussion on who best represented the court and whether the court would continue to sustain high culture.

Among the writers to craft new personas out of the Muslim figure of authority, Dante (1265–1321) may now enjoy the greatest fame, but his use of Saladin is not quite representative of late-medieval Christendom. His fellow Italians Giovanni Boccaccio (1313–75) and the anonymous author(s) of the *Novellino* and *L'avventuroso ciciliano* worked directly with the extant European literary Saladin, engaging the deep intertextuality that marked the sultan's chivalric persona. Using such devices as fable and narrative framing, they worked through Romance traditions in order to present the sultan in productive discourse with his Christian counterparts. In the texts to be examined in this chapter Saladin engages pan-Mediterranean courtiers in his diplomatic projects, competitive gift exchanges, ethical debates, conundrums of how best to be a knight, and explanations of history. The most culturally intricate treatment may well be that of the Castilian notable Don Juan Manuel (1282–1348), whose exposure to Arab-themed Romance sources – and, it has been argued but not proven, to Arabic sources – compelled him to allegorise the sultan several times over. To Juan Manuel, Castile's foremost nobleman (Alfonso X's nephew) who had fought in wars against Muslims in southern Iberia, Saladin represented an alternate form of Arabness to that which he and his Iberian peers addressed in literature.[2] Using similar framing techniques as those employed by Boccaccio, Juan Manuel explores a plural notion of Muslim identity, implicitly contrasting the timeless Easterner Saladin with the legendary-yet-still-historically-specific set of Andalusi officials.

Critics and historians have made much of the similarities and key differences between the plural, equivocal Saladins of Iberia and Italy, at times interpreting literary content as a statement of national culture. That methodology, which seems to be in clear need of redress, will be scrutinised in the course of the literary analysis to follow. Academic readers have responded strongly to the apparent formal similarities between Juan Manuel's *El Conde Lucanor* (hereafter *Lucanor*) and the Italian short fiction dealing with Saladin. They note the sharp contrast between that sense of peninsula-to-peninsula formal continuity on the one hand, and on the other the undeniably greater breadth of *Lucanor*'s cultural scope as it effectively creates two wholly distinct

Muslim Arab empires, one centred in the lands straddling the Straits of Gibraltar and the other in Cairo.

The eminent Spanish historian Américo Castro, keenly aware of how controversial his views of medieval Iberia were, may not have been aware of the effect he would have on the historiography and hermeneutics of Saladin. Examining discrete Crusades legends and the trajectory of Saladin in an essay that would have profound ramifications for future studies in the field, Castro attributes to the text a *morada vital*, the dwelling-place of a people's life. He justifies such an approach by insisting upon the inner coherence of each proto-national canon: Spain, Italy, and France became metonymies for the cultures producing literature in Iberia, peninsular Italy, and the fractious French-Catalan kingdoms astride the Pyrenees. Since the dissemination of that argument in the mid-twentieth century, colleagues in Romance Studies have considered Castro's forceful conjunction of text with culture. His often polemical view of Spain as a unique multicultural product of the Middle Ages has attracted equally polemical responses. Still, virtually no scholarly interlocutors have inspected the half-century-old trend to adopt (whether actively or tacitly) Castro's tendency to generalise on the topic of Saladin. Such generalities have held back our discussion of Crusades-related literature in the centuries after Eastern crusades had effectively ceased.[3] In the course of analysing Saladin as a fixture of late-medieval Romance, this chapter aims to revisit and revise the critical narrative on Peninsular cultures.

Saladin as a Defused Threat and De-Islamicised King: Castilian Translation and Historiography

The irony of fourteenth-century Castile is that, despite the extraordinary number of Saladin legends and fabulous accounts that had circulated in Europe up to that point, the kingdom's literati had their attention fixed firmly on a version that claimed historiographic status. *La gran conquista de Ultramar* (hereafter GCU) is a translation of translations, its chief source being French vernacular versions of William of Tyre's (*c.*1130–86) *Historia rerum in partibus transmarinis gestarum*. GCU, which demands far more contemporary critical attention than it has received, was in all probability an endeavour of Alfonso X but was by no means exclusive to his court (González, *La tercera* 25–37). The translators commissioned by Alfonso and his successors lacked no knowledge of Latin but the GCU makes clear that they primarily worked from the intervening and ancillary French material. For the purposes of defining the historical enterprise of battling Muslims in the Mediterranean and developing a useful central personage in their conception of political power issuing from the Levant, they delivered martial history and the heroic exploits of vernacular-legend *Salahadin* (the Old French rendering of his name) into the larger enterprise of Alfonso's massive historiography. Probably long after the king's death and thanks to the efforts of subsequent royal courts, GCU took its place in the Castilian scriptorium with such manuscripts as Alfonso's *General estoria* and *Crónica general*.

William's text, much of which was a firsthand account of the First Crusade, provided not only the basic material for vernacular history but also a lasting theory of why the Crusades had repeatedly failed. Its portrait of a dangerous, cruel, but surely competent Saladin served as a model for his growing legend prior to the writing of GCU. Just as important, GCU's reliance upon the French traditions meant incorporating the many continuations of William's text, a corpus filled with epic and legendary material. A phenomenon that we see in the centuries following the Second Crusade, critical to the composition of GCU, is the abundant telling and transcription of legends involving not just Christians and Moors but both of those martial sides *as knightly peers*, conversant in the same set of customs. William does not seem to have anticipated such a shift in the social politics of Crusades representations, especially insofar as Saladin's portrayals are concerned (Jubb, *Legend of Saladin* 24–7). As vernacular writers appended legends about the sultan as an individual – exploits that stationed him in the vague East and throughout the European Mediterranean – they folded into William's ur-narrative an entire set of chivalric abilities, allowing the sultan to traverse places and converse with diverse peoples.

When considering the role of GCU in the evolution of Crusade chronicles, it is vital to keep in mind how much elaboration had been made upon the original *Historia* by the time it became the material for Iberian intellectual labour. William, an archbishop in the Kingdom of Jerusalem during a time of confidence among the European settlers, laments what he sees as the incompetence and cowardice of commanders around the kingdom in the latter decades of the twelfth century, when there were intimations that Saladin would successfully lay siege to Levantine cities and garrisons (William of Tyre, *History of Deeds* 2:397–509). His sense of proportionality between phases of Christendom's unsound, morally questionable rule and a rising Muslim threat would prove paradigmatic in the many continuations appended to his work.[4] Lengthening the chronicle and giving it legendary dimensions, generations of storytellers and authors fully drafted the calculus that William had only sketched: in an approximate way, the enemy's success was conversely proportionate to the uprightness of Christendom's regents and field commanders. Just as importantly, interspersed with the scorn William heaped upon Saladin, he mentions the sultan's reputation for generosity. With less frequency he notes the Islamic regime's moderate treatment of prisoners after victory.

Fashionable in William's era of Crusades history-writing and in the centuries to follow, that ethical mode of portraying political systems and military fortune would be seized upon by Juan Manuel and converted into an extraordinary new rendition of the Saladin legend. French fabulists used the existing idea of ethical balance and reprise to explain the fates of kingdoms, but they also radically individualised it, aligning it with the evolving criteria for knights. William characterises the royal commanders of Crusader armies as fearing Saladin – and here again he leaves open the possibility of morally deficient men among their ranks, whose misfortune would therefore be all but assured in the tyrannical ascendancy of their foe – because the Muslim leader is ferocious and well-supplied (William cited in *Recueil des historiens des croisades* 2:1113). The French continuations of the *Historia* could point to proliferating European legends, which claimed that Saladin's background was part Christian, to help explain why he constituted a formidable knight in battle. In the French chronicles and GCU, Saladin is both a menace to Christians and an artistically compelling focus-point of narrative, even a hero in his way.[5] In the battles of the Second and Third Crusades his moral valence is largely a function of the Christian fighters' own morals; in his individual legends he lays claim to the righteousness for which any knight could and should strive.

Juan Manuel, in turn, shapes a third version of the sultan: his *Saladín* is neither cosmic punishment nor a semi-Christian model of chivalric power, but rather a lens through which his kingdom could scrutinise itself. Where the leader of Muslim armies was a threat and moral punishment, then became an ideal as an individual epic hero, he now emerges as an admirable but flawed interlocutor on politics and moral life. His Christian counterpart with whom he interacts, but even more so the Spanish authorities in the outer frame of narrative who retell and discuss his exploits, look to him for intellectual stimulation and the ethical challenges engaged by political leaders. Through an amiable but probing dialectic, Lucanor's advisor Patronio compels him to recognise the truths and obligations of their shared chivalric existence. Saladin, himself an eloquent knight, provides one of the most potent test cases for the two Spaniards' exploration of the rules that govern them. Their combined labour then accrues to the text, composed in a cultural and political context of profound questioning. Juan Manuel himself executed the official rituals of Crusade in his capacity as a knight and leader in southern Iberia (O'Callaghan, *Gibraltar Crusade* 159). His military exploits were deeply tied to the language and ideology of land acquisition for Christendom, even though – as with a great many examples of actions termed 'crusades' – his level of personal adherence to such language cannot be known. Saladin was, for him, a figure of Muslim sovereignty altogether distinct from the Andalusis and Moroccans of whom he had personal knowledge.

With *Lucanor* the Castilian courts gained a key literary tool that divided the question of crusade, indeed the question of Moorishness, so as to preserve the discourse of the Muslim antagonist but also to reap the benefits of the alternate historiography provided by Romance legend. As Castro and others have pointed out, Christian Iberians' necessarily more complex relationship to Islamic communities and political history manifests itself in medieval literature throughout the peninsula (Gerli cited in Caspi ed., *Oral Tradition and Hispanic Literature* 261). That observation, however, is a starting-point rather than end-point to any enquiry that hopes to (1) press critically upon the notion of Iberian cultural consciousness, and (2) usefully compare Spanish and Italian literary understandings of the Crusades, an effort that represents largely uncharted territory in Romance studies. Castilian knights such as Juan Manuel fought, negotiated, and occasionally formed alliances with their neighbouring '*moros*', the same term – as we saw with Alfonso X's Galician-Portuguese lyric in the previous chapter – with which they describe the enemy occupying the Holy Land. The royal counsellor Patronio, the didactic storyteller framed in the book's narrative, declares that Lucanor's reason for existing in and presiding over Iberia is to 'serve God against the Moors' (73). Significantly, *Lucanor* does not refer to Saladin as a *moro*. In fact, he scrupulously avoids naming the sultan at all when appropriating a historical account of his forces' confrontation with Richard the Lionheart.[6] Saladin is essentially freed from the historical claims of GCU: he is neither Christian nor Moor, properly. Instead he serves as a foreigner who compels Christian knights to inspect their own ethical standing in the world.

With his tightly focused depiction of Saladin in a Mediterranean of one overarching chivalric culture, Patronio demonstrates an entirely different category of knowledge than that which the counsellor brings to bear on Andalusi Arabs. There is of course ample historical, political reason for this. *Exemplos* 30 and 41 feature Arabic phrases in local spoken dialects and take place in Andalusi capitals.[7] Lucanor and indeed the book's audience are supposed to appreciate Patronio's retention and use of the enemy's language, as well as his mastery of anecdotal tradition. His narration of Saladin's adventures in *exemplos* 25 and 50 (the book's middle- and end-points) dispenses with major considerations of language difference because the sultan is part of a politically consistent world, in which the exemplary fables that Patronio offers precisely match the ethical questions that Lucanor poses. Saladin's and Lucanor's respective predicaments are structurally the same, a feature of the text that tends to universalise the sultan. Because Saladin's chivalry is taken for granted, no important distinction may arise between him and Christian individuals. Furthermore, his status as knight compels Patronio to depict this character as a different kind of Muslim than the Iberian ones populating the text of *Lucanor*.

Lucanor's Saladin operates a court stripped down to its ideal, basic structure. The ideologies and differences that dominate other Spanish stories of the Crusades, including some of the book's other *exemplos*, are suppressed when Saladin is invoked. When the book narrates stories of al-Andalus, North Africa, and Palestine, it navigates well-worn routes of Christian–Muslim struggle and conquest. Saladin in contrast sets in motion a rhetorical struggle, at once competitive and collaborative. His primary function is to consult with, or to be consulted by, peers who are simultaneously affiliated with him with strong bonds and foreign to him. With bloodline, religion, and military rank temporarily minimised as functional boundaries, the conversants map and approach chivalric perfection. The possibility that a count (Conde) may translate to the political inferior of Saladin as sultan is made irrelevant by the discourse of the knighthood, just as potential differences of culture had been eliminated long-term in European epic treatments of Saladin.

The court's perfection has led readers to the mistaken conclusion that Saladin is himself the ideal man in *Lucanor*'s construct of the world.[8] Juan Manuel stops short of providing such individual embodied ideals in the text, since perfection emerges as the dialectical product of conversation. Those characters who come closest to perfection are the counsellors, whether Patronio or those viziers and tutors who are framed in his telling of courtly stories. They do not err, but neither are they men of action, the purview of leaders whose knowledge is incomplete. Saladin occupies such pivotal positions in the series of *exemplos* precisely because he mounts the quest pursued by Lucanor himself: an aspirational ideal, its full realisation comes only as the fiftieth episode is explained and given an epilogue in the outer frame. The dualism of the sultan's predicament is that he exercises the liberties and powers unique to knights but misunderstands chivalry just enough to make himself vulnerable. So long as the sultan maintains his station in a recognisable courtly environment, he is immune from moral failure. His wide geographic freedom of movement is a knightly prerogative, posing no danger to him in and of itself. Because the courtly environment is an ethical space described as a social enclosure, a dialogue in which differing ranks are understood (the narrative functions 'in the style of a great lord speaking with his counselor'[9]), the only move that renders him weak is his temporary displacement from the court.

What motivates the sultan and virtually every valorised character in *Lucanor* is the organising principle of the pedagogical text itself, namely *vergüença*. The term denotes both a sense of shame and honour, the signifier of manhood and the knight's ethical key to the Castilian court (*Siete partidas* 2.9.27, 2.21.2, 2.21.22). As the book concludes, in *exemplo* 50, Saladin resolves to answer a question posed to him by one of his subjects: '*quál era la mejor cosa que omne podía aver en sí, et que era madre et cabeça de todas las vondades*': 'What is the greatest thing a man might possess, the foundation and peak of all virtues' (247, 249)? Ironically, the questioner is 'the wife of a knight, his vassal' (245), an updated Bathsheba to Saladin's erring David who, unlike her biblical model, challenges the king with rhetoric.[10] Her stroke of genius is to convert his decidedly unchivalrous extramarital lust into a search for the chivalric ideal. From the mission's initiation moment, to Saladin's travel in search of an answer in Italy and France, the question by design forces Christians and Eastern Muslims to consider the limits of their own ethical knowledge. His international capabilities allow him to search for an absolute value for his own benefit but also, of course, for those of his Christian interlocutors.

Travel opens up an array of tools employed by Saladin to locate *madre et cabeça de todas las vondades*, literally 'the mother and head of all virtues'. His sojourn at the papal court yielding no answer, he integrates himself with travelling entertainers and receives an audience with an elderly French nobleman and veteran of the Eastern Crusades, who recognises the disguised sultan and teaches him the preeminence of *vergüença*. With the answer he sought, Saladin returns to his kingdom to correct his infraction of chivalry. *Exemplo* 50's motif of travel in search of edification is in some sense a reversal of the other story featuring Saladin, *exemplo* 25, 'On that which happened to the Count of Provence and Saladin, Sultan of Babylon'.[11] Lucanor scrupulously avoids placing Saladin in Jerusalem, nor even does he place him in Damascus, for the precise reason that those cities were the ones that Europeans were forced to accept would house his military and administrative legacy. Instead, he sets out for his own travels and receives Christians along the peripheries of the Holy Land. A subsidiary virtue in all things chivalric is of course hospitality, which Saladin extends to the count as his captor during a crusade to Ultramar. Even the count's capture is portrayed, not as the effect of military strategy or the wiles of combat, but as God's decision to allow him to be 'tempted' (144). The trope of *temptar* amounts to a momentary weakening of the Christian's spirit and resolve, such that the sultan himself need not be shown exerting any physical or martial force.

Saladin's virtues, and interest in their discovery and cultivation, remove him from the violence inherent in his position of leadership. He first provides his prisoner with the deference and comforts befitting a high-ranking peer, and then shows his political astuteness by consulting with the count on all important matters of governance (144). The inflections of the Prophet

Joseph's story here, with the prisoner's reversal of fortune vis-à-vis the putatively Egyptian ruler, would seem insignificant were it not for the repeated biblical allegory to come in *exemplo* 50. Effectively, Saladin appoints his captive as vizier, albeit without granting him the liberties of a high-ranking subject or the right to return home. 'So well did the count advise him, so much did the sultan confide in him that, even though he was a prisoner, he maintained a high position and great power. Throughout Saladin's land, they respected him so much, *it was if he were in his own country*' (144, emphasis added).[12] By enabling the count's ascendancy, Saladin cultivates the Islamic East as a place where both officials can exercise righteous power, and the ideology that brought the count to Ultramar disappears.

In order to pose any kind of a threat to his host, even involuntarily, the count must reverse their positions in the consultative relationship. Even though he, as the recipient of and respondent to questions from the sultan, had occupied the intellectual high ground modelled by Patronio vis-à-vis Lucanor, the count sees advantage in posing a key question to Saladin. The count's daughter must be married and Saladin agrees to help select a suitor on the basis of written descriptions of each, the documents arriving presumably by courier. 'Better to value a man for his deeds than his wealth or the nobility of his lineage' (146), Saladin advises his peer in selecting a suitor. By voicing one of *Lucanor*'s commonplace sentiments, the sultan gives little clue to the young man's own journey to Ultramar, during which he contrives an elaborate ruse in order to gain advantage over the sultan. In Saladin's capacity of advisor – helping the count maintain his blood line and, we must assume, promote the creation of more crusading knights – he unknowingly sets in motion his own capture. As a result, he and the count will parallel each other, their oscillations between power and subjugation lending narrative logic to their intellectual relationship of even exchange.

When Saladin enters into conversation with a Christian knight, he necessarily mimics the structure of the mentor–pupil dialectic running through chivalric literature, recalling the formative experience of knights and chivalric kings as they are trained early in life. Jesús Rodríguez-Velasco points out that, in Spanish and in cognate form throughout European chivalric literature, the royal tutor (*ayo*) 'is a knight and forms the knight, thereby creating the illusion of a seamless union in the horizontal structure of chivalry and, through it, the simulacrum of a political and ethical continuity within the chivalric group' (*Order and Chivalry* 75).[13] Certainly the sultan and the count accomplish a similar illusion, as will occur again in *exemplo* 50 with Saladin as the traveller abroad, demonstrating that the social telos of knights' education within Christendom also has ramifications for *Lucanor*'s journey sequences of a knight in enemy territory. Whereas the biblical backdrop to the count's imprisonment, ascension, and advisory appointment is a hazy one, the key social structures of medieval chivalric stories, predictably, affect the protocols for Christian–Muslim relationships at court. Still, residues of difference appear: as the young groom arrives in Ultramar and meets its ruler, he shrewdly refrains from ritually paying homage to him, nor does he identify himself. Saladin fails to correct the infraction of normal chivalric code, which leaves him vulnerable to his own capture when the two have departed for a hunting trip, the sultan's retinue out of sight.

Corralled and loaded on to the young man's ship moored offshore, Saladin is also enlightened on the finer points of his own code. He has been beaten not by a superior force of warriors but by the young man's prescience and his ability to exploit the intricacies of their shared chivalric world. Saladin at first fails to understand how he may be captured in his own territory without treason but, it is explained to him, he never received the European visitor's pledge of fealty upon arrival. Again, he receives a Christian's counsel on chivalry and is improved for it. The groom's goals in capturing Saladin divide between the ethical and the diplomatic: he wishes to (1) reaffirm Saladin's initial judgement that he was the finest suitor and (2) gain the count's freedom. The sultan enthusiastically gives him both. The key recognition that he makes is that the violence of his arrest is licit as a chivalric move and as a diplomatic one. Chivalry, as historians and literary critics have argued, is beset by anxiety at disorderly violence. Much of the written discourse on knighthood, then, determined to impose order upon such violence, or to help shape a juridical system as it made social order.[14] Saladin's capture, specifically the learning experience that it proves to be for him, gives us a potent reminder of the distinct forms of violence perceived by knights and the sociopolitical anxieties informing their discernment. Knights as intellectual conversants may face off as they educated one another, a multiplicity of ritual seized upon by Juan Manuel. *Lucanor* complicates the Gibraltar-to-Ultramar Crusades and, at the same time, contains Islamic power within the hermetic walls of chivalry.

It is fitting that the *Lucanor* court should distil Patronio's diverse cosmopolitan knowledge so that it fits the agenda of Castilian state legitimacy. As knight and author Juan Manuel was himself dedicated to that operation. Well after Alfonso's death, while prosecuting wars against the Muslims of al-Andalus, Castilian courts continued to fulfil the king's instructions to supervise the translation and recopying of Arabic source texts by Iberian monks and philologists. Throughout the centuries of intermittent fighting between its people and Christian forces of Spain, al-Andalus served as a rich source of knowledge for Spanish scholars. Detailing a process that he calls 'Colonizing the Frametale', David Wacks argues, 'Just as the Christian *repobladores* ('settlers') took possession of Andalusī homes and fields, Juan Manuel appropriated the frametale genre from Andalusī literary practice' (*Framing Iberia* 131). His is not only the first known appropriation of Eastern frame traditions in Europe; it is also the one whose political motivations are clearest.

Juan Manuel was vexed by his own concept of Muslims. Recalling the North African *genete* light cavalry in the previous chapter, we see Alfonso's fixation upon an enemy who shared some aspects of knights in battle but who neither had nor wanted any place in the chivalric order.[15] In Romance poetry the *genete* dominated Christian knights, infantry, and songstresses, his military skills sexualised as the text forced key imperial subjects to inspect their failures. Juan Manuel, leader of conquest missions, was not immune from such sentiments, but he found his own strategies for making them literary. His presentations of Andalusi figures, via Patronio, places the Muslim potentate in failed love schemes. Without touching upon the Saladin *exemplos*, Wacks notes an episode narrating Muslims more proximate:

> The setting in Andalusī Cordova, together with Abenabet's exaggerated extravagance in fulfilling Ramayquía's wishes, communicates the implied message that even the most powerful Muslim kings are weak-willed when it comes to pleasing their wives, and generally preoccupied with sensual matters. Underlying this criticism of Andalusī mores, however, is a begrudging and unvoiced admiration for, and perhaps jealousy of, the superior material culture of al-Andalus. (*Framing Iberia* 153)

Sensual matters are Saladin's undoing, too, as we have noted, additionally damning for his attempted intervention in his loyal vassal's marriage. But because Juan Manuel's text grants the sultan no material culture discernible from that of a Christian ruler, there is no potential for a Castilian knight to regard him with jealousy. *Lucanor* devises an elegant and ideologically useful set of dualisms with which it produces peoples, polities, communities, and of course knights along with the code that gives them a sense of self. These personas are all conspicuously partial, Juan Manuel separating them just enough from the existing legends and chronicles about them so as to figure them as incomplete, and for that reason unthreatening to the idea of Christian Castile.

At this crucial moment in the development of Spanish literature, a noble such as Juan Manuel decided that he had an obligation to depict Muslims using the strategic, selective poetics of contention. They constitute the immediate and remembered threat of al-Andalus, as Wacks notes, and the only partially remembered past frustrations of Ultramar. *Lucanor*'s Muslims point towards a trend in Iberian Romance literary history, exposing the connections between only tangentially related motifs and personas we have seen in other texts. Alfonso's lyric *genete* resembles a knight in warfare, his masculine power laying low Christian nobles. But he has no acknowledged history, nor culture. *Lucanor*'s Andalusi man of frametales and legends indeed has history and culture, but his masculine attributes are insufficient. Finally, Saladin is characterised as partial, narratively incomplete, in several key respects. His history is interrupted, redacted, and subject to excision, making him a vague hero of legends: for him to occupy historical station he would need to figure in the telling of Crusades chronicle, such as *Lucanor*'s third *exemplo*, on Richard's Jaffa assault. Effectively, then, his only culture is the aspirational calling of his manhood, that is, chivalry. At that, too, he realises only partial success. His generosity as ruler and his power over his imprisoned adversaries provide him chivalric bona fides but his sexual self-regulation fails, and he allows the flattery of gifts to make him a captive when he is accustomed to being the captor.

Such false starts and equivocal moments of the chivalric mission, along with Wacks's revelatory work on *Lucanor*'s Arab anxieties, have led to a revision of Saladin, dubbing him a figure of incompetence. His prominent placement in the middle and end *exemplos* would therefore constitute a playful picture of ridicule made of the sultan (Ana Adams, 'Ser es fazer' 150–64). That is not entirely accurate. Saladin must be trained by his moments of discourse in order to mould his masculinity, chivalry, and political legitimacy. The telos of that educational experience is his final grasping of *vergüença*, which exposes his past shortcomings but his realisation is also Lucanor's. From that moment, he has benefited in his new knowledge just as his Castilian counterpart does in the outer frame narrative. The figures with whom he is compared in the book are not Lucanor nor Patronio, nor Juan Manuel himself, but only those of his fellow inhabitants in the *exemplos*, and from that he emerges corrected and redeemed. He is the user and beneficiary of righteous prescriptive language. There is no little irony in the fact that the same language is the means by which he is contracted into serving Castile. He retains all the trappings of his dehistoricised kingdom while his virtue and authority are limited by the politics of *Lucanor*'s text.

Soldano, Papa, Torello: Engaging and Isolating Saladin

In one of the most haunting stanzas of the *Inferno*, the lyric speaker recounts his visit to Limbo, where Saladin is stationed at a distance from his neighbours and from the very tradition of representing the sultan in literature. Dante's lyric persona testifies, 'solo in parte vidi 'l Saladino': 'I saw Saladin by himself, separate' from Limbo's population of Ancient Greeks, Trojans, Romans, and even fellow Muslims Averroes and Avicenna.[16] *La Commedia*'s famous use of alliteration takes a compound form here, internal to lexical units: the first two syllables of Saladin's name are now tied to the metaphysical state connoted by *solo* (4.129). That conceptual link distinguishes the sultan but, more importantly, it marks a radical departure from Saladinic literature in Europe. Dante preserves Saladin's ontological status as knight but destabilises the consensus of extant literature. As we have seen in *Lucanor*, late-medieval exempla narratives were able to make Saladin work for the moral and intellectual good of Christian empires only because prior legends had assiduously deemphasised, corroded, and supplanted his identity as first-hand histories had previously crafted it. As the Crusader-historians' dynamic, at times fearsome central agent of Islamic empire became an epic adventurer model for knighthood, he acquired the trait of conversational prowess, which would have as much formal impact on his identity as his chivalry would have on his moral standing in the European Christian imaginary. His power was the consummate prerogative of a knight, the ability to arrive at truths by discoursing with other nobles. After history and legend shaped his persona, the *Inferno* would historicise him one more time before modernity. Here, in perhaps the first literary instance of Saladin's portrayal in the afterlife – for him an eternal silence – the discomfort is palpable.

Dante places extraordinary emphasis upon the rigours of solitude for several reasons. As a reader, he drew from a corpus of Latin and vernacular literature consistently portraying Saladin as a conversant with Christian peers. Furthermore, Dante's Limbo itself is an intensely social space. The *Inferno*'s Dante persona, with Virgil his guide, describes *un nobile castello* ('a noble castle', 4.106) inhabited predominantly by people of Antiquity. Greek and Roman poets consort with one another and greet their colleague Virgil with the familiarity of fellow residents of Limbo – and, as Boccaccio notes in his commentary upon the work, fellow poets in the tranquil first circle of Hell (*Comento* 1:334). Likewise, political figureheads of the Hellenic world speak among themselves – as well as scientists and philosophers, the Ancients and medieval mutually intelligible. Avicenna (Ibn Sīnā) and Averroes (Ibn Rushd) seem to share a language with Aristotle, to whom the text refers not by name but as the *maestro*, both master and teacher. In turn, these scholars' Greek master text serves as their shared language, the academic mother tongue made into the spoken parole even as Dante was well aware of Avicenna and Averroes's Arabophone background.[17] This adds a note of irony to Saladin's physical and social state as a dweller in Limbo, occupying a space by himself with seemingly no conversant. Why should he be both special and isolated in the netherworld? If Romance instantiations of Saladin have provided glimpses into the historical anxieties and rifts of the courts and kingdoms in which his identity was produced, what is the precise utility of this lone, unspeaking Muslim politician in Dante's political world?

The *Inferno* deprives Saladin of the court's chief product and most powerful tool: language. It also suspends his ability to implement the chivalric virtue for which he was best known in European poetics: his magnanimity. Without opportunities for elocution nor the ritual bestowal of honour upon courtly persons, he departs from his customary treatment in Romance literature. Dante's historiography therefore loses stability: when the lyric speaker ruminated upon Saladin in the *Convivio*, he exclaims that the sultan stays in Christendom's memory for the gifts he presented.[18] Saladin's physical separation and aural silence are yet more striking, spoken language of course being the very instrument that grants him his powers in Spanish texts and the other Italian works to be analysed here. The illustrious-but-unsaved fellow citizens of Dante's Limbo speak privately of their disciplines, their method of communing itself speaking of discretion and even exclusion: *parlavan rado con voci soavi*, 'they spoke sparingly, with soft voices' (1.4.114). *Lucanor*'s Saladin, stripped of almost all of his historical military qualities, had only language to grant him the key prerogatives of knight and diplomat, especially travel, the building of friendships, and courtly reasoning. For Dante, Saladin has no discipline to articulate and refine in Limbo, not because the poetic text would deprive him of knowledge but because his actual discipline would be as military strategist, raising the troublesome issue of his position as military antagonist to Christendom. Furthermore, Saladin's language poses a problem for the atmospherics of Limbo. Dante declines to attribute a Romance language to Saladin, nor a fellow Arabic speaker to accompany the sultan. Avicenna and Averroes, we must assume, communicate with their fellow scientists in the Greek of their curricular texts. Where Juan Manuel chose to elide historical data with Saladin's moral dialogue, Dante accomplishes the same elision by setting the sultan aside from speech altogether.

Saladin and the peculiar nature of his role in Dante's work shed light upon Italian debates over culture and crusade, but also help us to understand where the author himself wished to intervene in late-medieval politics. Commentators, from Dante's own contemporaries to modern critics, have wrestled with the hermeneutics of Saladin's solitude in the poem. Suzanne Conklin Akbari notes the doubled sense of separation: Limbo is itself between Hell 'proper' and the forest in which Dante's own lyric persona begins his poem before Virgil leads him through the afterlife.[19] Saladin lacks the instrument by which one may commune and be fully courtly, but it is precisely because of his long-hailed courtliness that the *Inferno* deems him a virtuous pagan. He straddles sociability and silence, much as Dante's writing depended upon both sociability and exile.

Despite the fact that Saladin shares Limbo with at least a few other medieval historical figures, he is the only person there whose merit and demerit both are tied exclusively to medieval life. His chivalric nature, which qualifies him for Limbo rather than the Inferno's wretched inner eight circles, could not be articulated in anything but a medieval idiom. At the same time, it is precisely because of his failure to embrace Christianity that he is sent to Hell's periphery; only he and other medieval personas would have had any choice in the matter, since the ancient Greeks and Romans predate Christ. Saladin can be said to have a hand in his own failure to be fully virtuous, while his ancient peers cannot not. It is as if Dante wished to remove the sultan from the discourse of Greek and Roman figures – and even from the medieval Muslims Avicenna and Averroes as potential interlocutors – so as to note that it was chivalry that had prevented Saladin from entering the inner circles of the Inferno. Certain medieval writers insisted upon the ancient roots of chivalry, looking particularly to Alexander as a model; but unlike knowledge, art, and honour (*scïenzïa*, *arte*, *onranza*, 4.73–4), it only emerged as its own political and social concept in Romance texts of the eleventh century. At least so far as legendary literature was concerned, Dante showed himself to be an avid student and intertextual author.[20] One of the trends in literary history of which he inevitably reminds us is that previous European authors had consistently moved the figure of Saladin into a written discourse of knights, in order to counterbalance and eventually erase the military threat that he had represented in recorded Crusades histories. In effect, Dante maps that work of moral recompense and salvation – even if partial, Saladin being unfit for Paradise.

The trope of the sultan's isolation gives a sense of allegorical logic to a key movement in fourteenth-century Romance Saladinic literature, treating chivalry and the anguished history of the Crusades. This Saladin presents the unsettling possibility of another language, unspoken, its distance from 'Latin' marking the far end of human existence.[21] Were he to speak he would call into the question the cohesive groupings that Dante constructs in Limbo itself and the ethics of speech in the *Inferno* as the paradigm-setting first part of *La Commedia*'s trilogy: 'the failure of language as a mode of communication in Hell, the unification of language in Purgatory, and the creation of language in Paradise' (Ferrante, 'Relation of Speech' 34). All of this, however, has a preface, a small cul-de-sac in which one persona can claim simultaneously the merits of chivalry and the exile from language. The knightly class of

Crusaders, in which Dante proudly claimed his links of ancestry, is revealed to have little in the way of a legitimate military enterprise: the pope and high courtiers have turned away from the call of Eastern crusade in favour of fomenting disastrous local wars.[22] Saladin's silence presages the testimony of Italian Christian wrongdoers, his silence and liminal status presaging the absolute quality of their punishment in the eighth circle.

Dante's use of Saladin compels the audience to consider whether Saladin may ever have been in position to convert to Christianity. That question vexes all late-medieval Italian narratives in which the sultan plays a role but the *Commedia* explores it more anxiously and probingly. As Dante's lyric valorises Saladin as a knight and alludes to his Muslim identity, could the *Commedia* imagine a world in which he fully employed his chivalrous wisdom and embraced Christian belief? From the thirteenth to the fourteenth century, translated works of Crusader history featuring Saladin were integrated into the literature of Italy. This cosmopolitan narrative linked the two peninsular traditions, Spanish and Italian; as Juan Manuel had explored the relationship between chivalric legend and Christian–Muslim encounter so did his contemporaries to the east, as well as the generations following. The differences between Castilian and Italian adaptations, though, emerge just as clearly as the general literary commonalities. By placing Saladin in his peculiar position in Limbo and calling attention to his familiar noble qualities, Dante gives notice that the sultan's religion will now become an explicit topic of contention in Italian literature.

Forza da alcuna ragion colourata: The Wiles of a Narrated Sultan

Where previous traditions of legend had tended to ignore or suppress the issue of Saladin's religious identity, or explain it away by making Saladin's genealogy part Christian, Italian authors saw the utility in placing his faith at the centre of the narrative. Some of this is attributable to the main historical source in Italy, *Conti di antichi cavalieri*, like GCU a translation but in this case from French sources. The book not only takes a keen interest in conversion, it names Saladin as the would-be convert, whereas previous French texts had posed the sultan's successors as faced with the question of choosing among religions.[23] Here, Saladin is approached by monks to convert, but the only question that comes out of the episode is whether his law requires him to kill the interlopers – an option that he, ecumenical and of course generous, declines. Declaring his fealty to an abstract law seemingly transcendent of individual Abrahamic faiths, he rejects his Islamic scholars' calls to punish the missionaries (*Conti* 9–10).

The episode, and its passage from French to Italian with the identity changes of the sultan in that process, has been characterised as a moment of self-reflection in Christian European literature, a faint but nonetheless paradigmatic statement of multiconfessional acceptance. As early as Boccaccio's commentary on the *Inferno*, Saladin receives praise (albeit backhanded) for having been undogmatic in his Muslim identification and resistant to political pressure from mosque officials. Extending that characterisation, modern scholarship would like to read the episode as Italian narrative speculation upon Christendom's own political history: 'If only the crusaders had reacted like their adversary, the sultan, if only they had given full power to the king and not to the clerics, things would perhaps have turned out quite differently.'[24] Such a didactic role of the story is indeed tempting in our modern retrospect, and the sense of political complaint is of a piece with the *Inferno*'s criticism of clerics and commanders failing to convincingly prosecute the Crusades. But Saladin's role in Italian narrative is multiple and, as a result, so are the historical allegories to which he gives voice. At this late-medieval moment, Saladin having evolved for more than 150 years in European literary culture, these Tuscan authors figure him as a capacious persona. All of the ethical work performed by chivalric moral tales had sought to minimise the historical trauma related to him, but the process was not total, nor did anyone seem to wish to assuage it altogether. The call to crusade, so deeply tied to pilgrimage, lost much of its ideological force if it was not ritually alluded to and therefore renewed.

The most popular and useful stock legend with which these writers articulated Saladin was that of 'The Three Rings', the earliest extant versions of which date from the mid-thirteenth century. In its typical telling, a father considers which of his three children – allegories for Judaism, Christianity, and Islam – should inherit his most valuable ring. Whether or not he arrives at an answer to the question varies among texts;[25] those that portray him willing the ring to one heir are of course uncomplicated valorisations of Christianity, but the Three Rings lends itself to ideology, even in its versions that refrain from the endorsement of one heir/religion. As far as the extant textual record tells us, Italian writers were the first to situate the sultan in the story – more accurately, in the frametale in which the story is delivered. As was Count Lucanor, an inquisitive Saladin arrives unsuspecting at a fable that edifies him. And, like *Lucanor*'s Saladin, this ruler is capable of base motives: he displays weakness in the face of his desires. Much as he was in *exemplo* 50, Saladin finds a vulnerable subject in the sociopolitical order upon whom to impose his will, only to find himself compelled to reevaluate his approach because of his interlocutor's savvy response.[26] His astute interlocutor challenges him in such a way that he arrives at the moral truth that is contained in the frametale's didactic value. As the Jewish subject gently confronts his king with allegory, the story's initial comment upon Crusades history – that Saladin fought at times from a position of acute weakness, despite the famous humiliations he caused Christendom in war – combines with the open-ended religious message. The motif of agenda-driven dialogue, in which each speaker hopes to get the better of his conversant, aims to problematise simpler extant narratives of military campaign and pilgrimage, and the pious and dogmatic bases upon which they were pursued in previous centuries.

There are two known versions of the Three Rings written in the century before Boccaccio composed the *Decameron*, both of which anticipate discrete parts of his dynamic intervention while giving very little clue of the sorts of claims his text would make. One of these antecedent works (the anonymously authored *Novellino*) speaks merely of a *soldano*, the other (*L'avventuroso ciciliano*, attributed to Busone da Gubbio) names Saladin and makes direct reference to his efforts at anti-Crusade. The sultan in *L'avventuroso ciciliano* is only barely chivalrous, more self-interested and militarily compromised than heroic. Lucanor, for all its equivocations in portraying Saladin – his heroism and heurism, his promiscuity and confusion – scrupulously avoids implicating him in any battles against Christendom, only a brief mention of the Provençal count's capture in unclear circumstances. *L'avventuroso ciciliano* presents the king in desperate straits:

> Saladino venne bisognio di moneta per cagione d'una Guerra che egli co' Cristiani facieva. Di che fu consigliato che prendesse la moneta da Ansalon Giudeo. (348)

> Saladin was in need of money because of a war he was prosecuting against the Christians. He was counselled to seize money from Ansalon the Jew.

European authors and relaters of legends had long implied that the sultan's storied generosity had proven a strategic liability to himself and his kingdom, but this particular telling of Saladin serves to implicate the knight in trickery and injustice. (The *Novellino*, praising Saladin, imputes only a nameless 'soldano' as carrying out the plan to fool his wealthy Jewish subject, and does not detail what had depleted the royal treasury.) He engages his subject at court:

> 'Ansalon la cagione perch'io ho per te mandato si è migliore, tra la tua, o la mia, o la Cristiana'.' Nell'animo del Saladino era, che se egli avesse la sua lodata, sì l'avrebbe poste per traditore di sua legge, e così in ogni risposta pensato avea di torgli la sua moneta. (348)

> 'Ansalon, I've summoned you for you to tell me which (religious) creed is the best: yours, mine, or that of the Christians?' Saladin's scheme was that if the Jew lauded his own faith, then Saladin could say that Ansalon had slandered him, and likewise if Ansalon lauded Christianity. If he cast any aspersions on his own faith (of Judaism), Saladin could declare him a traitor. Therefore, in any event Saladin was bound to confiscate his money.

The sense of mental challenge is of course familiar from *Lucanor*, as is the violation of chivalric ideals. But, while the former is brought to resolution, the latter problem remains to haunt the text and the Italian frametale generally. When Ansalon delivers his shrewd answer, the inheritance parable at the heart of the Three Rings, he assures the sultan that one religion is indeed the best, a crucial move not always made in tellings of that allegory.

> 'Quale sia quella, non sò. Ma ciascheduno di quelli di questa legge, si crede avere la diritta, al modo di quelli tre figliuoli.' (348–9)

> 'Which it is, I don't know, but each believer of the three faiths thinks his to be the real one, much as the three sons has thought.'

Saladin is left to ponder which it may be, a courtly meditation upon truth not to be concluded, one presumes, until his death, at which point it will be revealed to him. The unique open quality of his mental quest intimates the answers that the *Inferno* sought to provide, Saladin's inevitable state of being in life and afterlife. It also underscores the key contrasts between these Italian meditations upon Saladin's life and *Lucanor*'s teleology, in which fundamental or cosmological questions of ethics motivated him both to stop (that is, to critically review his memories of encountering the young groom and the trust he had placed in his guest in *exemplo* 25, and in *exemplo* 50 to cease his advances upon his vassal's wife) and to press forward in pursuit of knowledge. The *Novellino* and *L'avventuroso ciciliano* leave him in a state of simple arrest: he resolves to correct the error of his having sought to seize the man's wealth through trickery, and there the short narrative leaves Babilonia in political equilibrium.

When Boccaccio, shortly later, takes up the Three Rings and the increasingly complex identity of Saladin, he combines the power of a new narrative frame with that of a historical phenomenon resonating with his audience. His *Decameron* forthrightly claims its own origin story:

> nel 1348, … città di Fiorenza, oltre ad ogni altra Italica bellisima, pervenne la mortifera pestilenza: la quale per operazion de'corpi superiori, o per le nostre inique opere, da giusta ira di Dio a nostra correzione mandata sopra i mortali, alquanti anni davanti nelle parti Orientali incominciata. (1:14–15).

> In 1348 Florence, the greatest city in Italy, suffered a plague of the most horrific kind which, whether it was due to the pull of celestial bodies or was God's just punishment for our sins, emerged first in the Levant.

With that the possibility of causation echoes the historical corpus reviewed at the beginning of this chapter, the narrative inspecting an Eastern scourge for signs of God's displeasure with Christians. The plague in other words merits a very similar pained exegesis as did Saladin in the literature of prior generations, and the sultan's role in the *Decameron* necessarily taps into that hermeneutical and historiographic enterprise. As a result of the epidemic, the introductory text explains, social relationships come under new scrutiny, as some citizens of Florence scrupulously avoid any interaction with their neighbours while others take the opportunity to fraternise in a carnivalesque celebration of consumption and the pleasures of the body. The outer frametale depicts both the social alienation of a plague scare and the intimate sociability of upper-class leisure. It endorses the moderation of desires while it also celebrates indulgence. Three noblemen take leave of the city with seven unmarried women of high birth, banqueting for ten days while regaling one another with entertaining stories.

Because the plague exerts power over Boccaccio's imagined Tuscans, instilling in them not only fear but also desire, the Three Rings takes on new, clear valences in this text. Its didactic content extends beyond prior Saladin narratives, in which the honourable man needed most of all to practise Juan Manuel's *vergüença* or a variation thereon in order to distinguish himself among his peers. Now the confrontations between courtly subjects, the entanglements of speech and gestures in which they find themselves, speak indirectly towards the overarching picture of divine reward and punishment, including the plague in the shared memory of Boccaccio's own writerly voice (which introduces the book, lamenting the ravaged and perished populace around him). In the *Decameron*'s version of Saladin's Egypt, the Jewish citizen of interest is Melchisedech who, the amiable frame-storyteller Filomena offers, 'was a truly clever man, well aware that Saladin sought to trap him into saying something so as to pick some kind of fight with him': *veramente era savio uomo, s'avisò troppo bene che il Saladino guardava di pigliarlo nelle parole per dovergli muovere alcuna quistione* (1.3.8). That which in the *Novellino* had been explained by the narrator ('in any event Saladin was bound to confiscate his money') is now cogitated by the perspicacious, threatened Jewish moneylender. His realisation that the sultan planned *pigliarlo nelle parole* – literally, 'to ensnare him in speech' – grants him the power of mental apprehension of Saladin's ruse, which becomes comprehension. In fact, we see throughout this fable the peculiar, undeniable form of control wielded by Melchisedech, despite the accepted fact of Saladin's own perspicacity and eloquence, qualities transferred from the existing literary record into the *Decameron*.

Melchisedech's particular gift of intellect is that he is able to please the sultan even while performing his now-familiar performance of the Jewish interlocutor, equivocating over the question of religion. Modern readings of this episode in the *Decameron* concentrate upon the shade of difference between his conclusion and that of Ansalon: Melchisedech does not imply that there is, ultimately, a better faith. The ring over which the three sons would have fought with one another to inherit is so perfectly copied by 'a true master' (*buon maestro* (1.3.14)) jeweller that neither the father, nor the sons after his death, can discern it from the two replicas made. Knowledge of the original – a savvy audience member may well equate it with the most venerable religion of Judaism – disappears into the mix of rings as soon as the jeweller has finished. When Melchisedech brings his pacifying story to a close, Saladin approaches him anew, 'deciding to openly tell him what he wanted from him, to see if he [Melchisedech] wished to give him what he needed' (*dispose d'aprirgli il suo bisogno e vedere se servire il volesse* (1.3.17)). Saladin makes two reversals: he trades his previous canny, deceitful form of speech for forthrightness, and changes his plan to impose his will upon Melchisedech's wealth such that he now grants his subject a more honourable kind of financial agency. All of this of course benefits both parties, as Melchisedech pays out the loan and Saladin in turn makes him a lasting favourite of the royal court.

The politics of friendship have played a central role throughout the Saladinic stories and lyrical accounts we have seen thus far, a product of two major, interrelated trends in medieval thought. The first of course is chivalry: its call for reciprocity of good deeds among courtly people and, by extension, its reputation for holding together the political order. The second, more commonly associated with the Renaissance than the late Middle Ages, extends its historical gaze to more ancient discourse: the affiliative relationships of friends, which for medieval Europeans was an idea on which to consult Aristotle.[27] In a move hailed by many modern critics as an ecumenical and multicultural vision, Boccaccio concludes the novella with the lasting friendship between Saladin and Melchisedech. '*Il giudeo* liberamente *d'ogni quantità che il Saladino il richiese il serví e il Saladino … donò grandissimi doni*': 'The Jew *freely* offered the entire amount Saladin had requested of him, and Saladin … gave him the most splendid gifts' (1.3.18, emphasis added). Because he understands allegory and can orally deliver it at the proper time, he gains this *liberale* quality. The concept of Melchisedech's freedom touches upon the history of texts on Jewish religion, particularly the story of the Exodus from Egypt.[28] It is also his newfound prerogative to be generous. Whereas he began the novella a miser, he is now fit to play the courtly game of loans/gifts with the guarantor of his freedom. In fact, this encapsulates thoroughly wrought literary conventions – Jew as intelligent lender, Saladin as symbol for generosity so great it proved a burden – while signalling distance from the convention of chivalry. Melchisedech of course is ineligible for knighthood, in any medieval political imaginary, by virtue of his religion. He has access to certain tools of court, especially those having to do with education and use of fine language, without entering the space traditionally set out for courtly friends. Their friendship is not the fully formed ideal version of *Lucanor*'s *ayo*-knight and king, but rather a profitable meeting of interests. The loan-gift exchange affords long-term benefits for two persons who retain qualities foreign to each other, and foreign to the Christian audience.

Boccaccio fully clarifies the categories of friendship that pertain to Saladin in the other novella involving the sultan, in which he exchanges positions with a European nobleman who evolves into an anguished Crusader. The story falls under Panfilo's narrative purview on the tenth and final day. The choice of Panfilo as that day's ritual 'king' is significant, the frame narrator-character 'loving all' (as his Greek-derived name states of him) lamenting the frayed bonds of affiliation. He invokes Filomena's previous complaint that 'so painfully little is friendship valued these days' (*l'amistà … oggi cosí poco da' mortali esser gradita*) as a means of renewing the moral sense of plague-as-punishment and then to work through the stock tale also at the heart of Juan Manuel's *exemplo* 50, the story of Saladin's travels in search of the most important human virtue. Here, though, the travel of edification is explicitly related to the Crusades, as Saladin departs Babilonia in order to spy on Frederick Barbarossa's empire as it planned its campaign for the Holy Land. Disguised as a Cypriot merchant and, it must be assumed given his ease of travel, a non-Muslim, Saladin and his small party encounter the Italian Messer Torello, who detects nobility in the strangers.[29] The novella makes much of Torello's guile and the forcefulness with which he appoints himself host to these travellers: at every point at which they ask for directions or advice, he coerces them into staying at one of his properties around Pavia, where he treats them to feasts and courtly conversation.

What Boccaccio effects, in other words, is a reversal of the ethics and material conditions informing the Saladin-Melchisedech story. Where Muslim and Jew had deceived each other so as to preserve themselves from danger (both characters had feared bankruptcy, in both cases brought about by the sultan's own immoderation), here the mutuality is gone and Torello's every act of dissemblance means to place Saladin in more luxury. He resists the language of person-to-person transaction even as his guests convey their appreciation, insisting that they are mere agents of a cosmic favour paid to him. *Signori … so io grado alla fortuna piú che a voi, la quale a ora vi colse in cammino che bisogno vi fu di venire alla mia piccola casa*: 'Sirs … I owe more to Lady Luck than to you, she overtook you along the road when you were obliged to come to my meager house' (10.9.23). As Saladin had a *bisogno* (need) of Melchisedech's wealth, Torello celebrates the sultan's lack of agency, the *bisogno* of taking refuge in a foreign place. And, whereas Saladin and Melchisedech had first found themselves in a contest of withholding and prying, then achieved the catharsis of conspicuous generosities, Torello assures the disguised sultan that the competition of gift-giving has been won by the outset. Only then does he release his dominated guests (*Il Saladino e' compagni vinti*: 'the defeated Saladin and company') and, not coincidentally, go on to plot the Crusade with King Frederick.

It is clear that the novella draws from much of the same story structure as did *Lucanor*'s *exemplo* 25, whose elements are certainly part of late-medieval Romance traditions; Boccaccio's elaboration upon the theme is to maximise Torello's control over the knightly relationship. Dispatching Saladin to travel to enemy territory (whereas *exemplo* 25's sole travellers were Provençal nobles), the *Decameron* initiates the narrative in such a way as to politically privilege the Lombard would-be crusader. His status as a model nobleman is amply discussed in modern criticism, but not so his role as an exemplary, unsuspecting agent of empire. Saladin has largely submitted to local cultural norms, having learned to communicate in Latin or colloquial Romance, at his hosts' behest donning robes worn in Lombardy, and drinking wine in a state of joyous, relaxed sociability.[30] Torello demonstrates the proper execution of noble rituals in his capacity as host, insisting that he is neither granting Saladin favors nor placing the visitors in his debt, although it becomes clear in the course of the novella that the sultan himself senses a compulsion to match his interlocutor when given the chance. In Torello's conception the opportunity to bestow gifts and hospitality upon the travellers is a pure courtly challenge. At the ontological level is it an action of military confinement. Because Torello's courtesy serves as a synecdoche for chivalric power overall, it is precisely his magnanimous treatment of Saladin that indicates to the sultan the military threat of Europe. To his party, he confides:

> se li re cristiani son cosí fatti re verso di sé chente costui è cavaliere, al soldano di Babilonia non ha luogo l'aspettarne pure un, non che tanti, per addosso andargliene, veggiam che s'apparecchiano (10.9.35)!

> If Christian kings are to kings as this man is to knights, there is no way for the Sultan of Cairo to withstand even one of them, to say nothing of the great numbers of them we've seen readying the attack on him!

Unlike Torello, Saladin is aware of the violent potential, even the possibility of martial omen, in his encounter. As their exchange of gestures and words achieves more dimensions in the course of a crusade, Torello himself will recognise the imperial content of their courtly game.

The most basic element of power sought by the sultan and the knight is the host's prerogative. For Torello, welcoming a fellow knight means conducting a set of transactions with that person, all of which eventually benefit him as the host. The rules of courtly interactions typically guarantee him those symbolic profits (Bruckner, *Narrative Invention* 118–19). When that rule is violated in a literary account, typically the language reflects social violence. In the previous chapter, lyric served to make a wide variety of complaints on that theme, Pae Gómez calling Alfonso X a rude and greedy guest, and Alfonso in turn fashioning the pope into a raider of his royal wardrobe. Their logical, ethical reference is the rule of courtly interactions – as any encounter between knight and king, or king and cleric, should be – assigning foremost controls to the host, who in turn establishes the reciprocal friendship with the guest. In this penultimate novella of the *Decameron*, host and guest are historicised in Mediterranean empire. As they exchange positions with each other, they seek to confirm the normative ethics of hospitality. The host's material largesse brings him symbolic capital, which it is the guest's responsibility to measure in words and assurances that he himself must one day reciprocate. Therefore, the social intimacy of visitation and the geopolitical concern of crusade merge in this novella. When Saladin extols Torello's generosity in direct address and then predicts a rout should his host arrive in the Holy Land with similarly upright Christians, he is essentially making the same statement twice: the chivalric display initiates a competitive game played over time. Torello's object is to demonstrate to Saladin that he is already outdone; the sultan is then forced to consider the future as a direct challenge to him and his kingdom.

Novella 10.9's narrative of disguise and spy-craft provides a hermeneutical lens into its politics, because as a story it would like to mask its own imperial content. As does *Lucanor*, the text employs a seemingly innocuous dialogue of flattery between nobles, and, even more than did Juan Manuel, Boccaccio scrupulously avoids portraying Saladin engaged in or organising combat with Christian knights. Sharon Kinoshita points out the dynamic: 'any history of military and political conflict between Christians and Muslims is displaced in favor of the heartfelt affection linking the northern Italian knight and the Sultan of Babylon' ('Noi siamo mercatanti cipriani' 45). That explicit act of displacement, however, is also an implicit means of tying the code of the individual knight to the collective geopolitical work of empire. When the setting shifts from Italy to Egypt, the game of hosting is shown to be a game of political acquisition. Because the crusading collective fails to measure up to Torello, he finds himself captured and made to serve Saladin, without either person recognising the other. The text revisits *Lucanor*'s Joseph-in-Egypt parallels seen in *exemplo* 25; in Boccaccio's version, the skilled hunter Torello serves his captors not as a prisoner-vizier but a prisoner-falconer for the crown. He tries constantly and unsuccessfully to escape in order to reunite with his wife (whom the Lombards mistakenly presume is now widowed and should therefore be ushered into remarriage). Saladin is unwittingly preventing the idealised knight from fulfilling the chivalric ideal of living in a married state with the beloved.

The violence done to chivalry is uniquely political violence, and, when Torello and Saladin recognise one another, the debt that the sultan acknowledges to his friend would be best repaid politically. Showering Torello with gifts, the sultan declares that the most cathartic end to the tortuous story would be for the two of them to govern Egypt together, resolving in Torello any conflict between imperial affiliation and shared personal loyalty forged between the two knights. Their game of courtly one-upmanship may continue but the battle over land – more a nuisance to both of them than a resonant call to arms – would become irrelevant. As a fellow knight, though,

Saladin appreciates the pressing need to restore Torello to full domesticity. The Christian is put to sleep with sorcery and laid on a sumptuous bed designed to transport him, his body draped in jewellery of exclusively royal calibre to indicate to Italy that his magical overnight journey is Saladin's work. That is how the bonds of chivalry take political shape and restore the Christian to his household, where the game had begun. Where *Lucanor*'s Saladin had enabled a marriage but had also mishandled his domestic sphere, the *Decameron* places him in the gradual process of mastering his interlocutor. His debt to Torello paid in the process of hosting and gifting, he marks the transition of their relationship on the crusader's prostrate body. The Muslim sultan restores a Christian marriage by dressing the husband as one of his own.

Making Way for Modernity

In a chapter of charged dialogue between fictional, legendary personas, it seems fitting to close by asking how, on the topic of medieval power, dialogues function between writers themselves. Since Louis Althusser began lecturing on early modern political theory in the 1960s, he developed a deep affinity for Niccolò Machiavelli (1469–1527) who, Althusser posited, embodied and indeed pioneered 'conjuncture': political thought capacious enough to incorporate a royal governor's competence and his luck, by extension 'the definite and indefinite, the necessary and the unforeseeable' (*Machiavelli and Us* 80). In the twenty-first century, Althusser's idea of Machiavelli has received a fascinating review. Building upon the conjunctive model, Peter Haidu writes of one Renaissance thinker what more and more contemporary scholars have written about the Renaissance writ large: 'It does not detract from Machiavelli's stature if, in addition to being deeply grounded in classical history … he is read as reflecting on the practices of the historical past: the medieval past' (*The Subject Medieval/Modern* 159). That past was populated by political thinkers generally unnamed in his signature work on principalities now known as *The Prince*, but Machiavelli quotes Dante outright and, in personal correspondence, identifies his Italian forebear as a favoured source (*De principatibus* 80–1).

No less compelling than Haidu's intervention – placing the Middle Ages into the conjunctive reading of a Renaissance innovation – is the set of conjunctures we find by following his call for a new retrospective reading. By quoting and paying tribute to Dante, Machiavelli acknowledges an equally pluralist reader of history. The courtly but uncomfortable space of Limbo attests to Dante's sense of scope: he recognised the moral, ethical, and theological tensions between antique glory and his contemporary Christian moment. Ambiguities of history – was it the ancients' fault that their souls could not be saved by Christ? – haunt the thoughtful residents of Limbo, even those medieval figures such as Saladin who in theory could have chosen salvation. Dante's audience is compelled to review the criteria by which previous storytellers and writers had deemed the Muslim sultan palatable for Christian Europeans, namely his legendary courtliness. That grants him a station in Limbo but, because courtly practices are social, gestural, and conversational, Saladin's conflict is magnified in the solitary unspeaking person into which Dante moulds him.

La Commedia explicates what is implicit in *Lucanor*, *Il novellino*, and *L'avventuroso ciciliano*: despite the vaguely remembered ethos of military confrontation still inhabiting the literature, primarily Saladin vies not with his Christian peers but with himself. The anxious motif of Limbo's conjuncture signifies what is divided about the world in this literary conception. That anxiety, in turn, is focused on the person of Saladin to an extent not recognised in Medieval Studies to date. In all of these literary treatments he operates as a divided, equivocal persona. In his Spanish iteration, Saladin oscillates between his customary honour and profound moral fallibility. When he grasps the authority of the *ayo*, he is safe; when he assumes the position of pupil, he is lost without the immediate edifying presence of a mentor, forced to ask himself questions that he is not qualified to answer. In the Italian tradition, virtually all of the Saladinic narrative exploits before *Decameron* 10.9 show him to be insufficiently chivalric. His magnanimity leading to foolish immoderation and then to craven practices of withholding and connivance, until Boccaccio seeks to restabilise the idea of Saladin's virtuous generosity. As Juan Manuel had given the sultan an instructor in *exemplo* 50, Boccaccio finds in Torello the chivalric doppelgänger with whom the book transports all of Saladin's contestation from the internal field of conscience to the external arena of spoken tributes and the gift economy.

Saladin's travel on that narrative arc, the moral problem he embodies, speaks to the open quality of crusade itself. By the fourteenth century, Spaniards' and Italians' long-held doubts of whether there was any hope of dominating the Levant and North Africa had found resonance in literature. The tension seems to have first manifested as complaints from the European nobles paying for Crusades, which they voiced to the royals above them. As a result, we see diplomatic tension between European kingdoms and the Vatican that had authorised long-term campaigns for the Holy Land. By the early modern period, literature shows how common it was to deride papal authority over the subject of the Crusades. Chivalric stories that had previously lent the wars their illustrious narrative qualities now spoke ironically of a knighthood failing in the East.[31] Saladin anticipates that process and affords us a glimpse of the breakdown of what had been a functional ideology. The legends, exempla, and novellas about him meant to keep him in a position of remove from the ongoing political debates on if, how, and when the campaigns for the Levant and North Africa should be prosecuted. In this vitally important respect, though, he and the narrative discourse he inhabited are consonant with the equivocal Christian rhetoric of war. Saladin is ultimately unreconciled, disjunctive, and for that reason uncomfortably close to Europe's pained self-image as it contemplated the Crusades for centuries into the modern era.

Notes

1. Saladin as a fabulous literary persona was constructed exclusively in Europe, not in the Middle East. There exists no known evidence that writers of Middle Eastern languages, including Arabic, rekindled interest in the sultan between the time of his death until the nineteenth century, when Arab nationalists saw the great utility in telling his story as an independence-struggle saga. For a discussion of conversion in Saladin-related French literature, see Gaston Paris, *La légende de Saladin* 14–16 and Burns in O'Sullivan and Shepard eds, *Shaping Courtliness in Medieval France* 251.
2. Although European contemporaries of Saladin were sufficiently well informed to know that he was not ethnically Arab but rather Kurdish, in the long aftermath of the Third Crusade, that fact was consistently elided in literature. As a result, his precise ethnicity was neither widely known nor considered relevant to authors in the era of interest here. In certain treatments, such as Boccaccio's *Decameron*, the audience would have cause to wonder whether this Saladin was

indeed a practising Muslim (10.9). The question of whether Juan Manuel knew substantial amounts of Arabic language and, if so, whether he marshalled such knowledge as a reader and author, has been debated since the early nineteenth century. The most widely read attempt to confirm such a hypothesis is probably that of Pascual de Gayangos ed., *Escritores en prosa* xx. For a summary of and response to the long history of this debate see Hitchcock, 'Don Juan Manuel's Knowledge of Arabic'.

3. Castro's study of interest here is 'Presencia del Sultán Saladino en las literaturas románicas'. For his usage of *morada vital*, a key idea in his corpus of history writing, see 19; for his statement of internal coherence to each culture he surveys in the article, see 20. He explains these concepts at greater length in *España en su historia* 109–12. A sceptical brief engagement with Castro on Saladin is to be found in Jubb, *The Legend of Saladin in Western Literature and Historiography* 159–62. For strong, often far-reaching endorsements of Castro's argument, see Ayerbe-Chaux, *El Conde Lucanor: materia tradicional y originalidad creadora* 125–7; Lynch, 'The Uses of Saladin in Medieval and Early Modern Literature'; and Ortiz de la Rosa, 'El personaje de Saladino en la literatura hispánica'. The most important exchange of polemics on Spanish history over the past century (not touching directly on Saladinic literature) is that between Castro and Claudio Sánchez-Albornoz. Castro's terminology and historical views on Spanish culture, which would eclipse those of Sánchez-Albornoz, receive a useful critical review in Soifer, 'Beyond *convivencia*'.
4. For historians from William of Tyre's era explaining Crusader wars and political shifts in moral terms, and modern comment thereon, see Tyerman, *God's War* 175, 209–10, 336–7; and Walsh and Kennedy in William of Newburgh, *History of English Affairs* 1:15. For an analysis of that historiography in GCU specifically see González, *La tercera* 80–7.
5. Reviews of the Saladin-as-part-Christian trend in medieval literature are found in Crist, *Saladin* 200–2 and Tolan, 'Mirror of Chivalry' 32–3. For the most prominent instances of praise for Saladin in the medieval French corpus, see *Chronique d'Ernoul* 228–9, 293. For an overview of that praise and the tension between it and the customary Christian chroniclers' aspersions cast upon Saladin, see Morgan, *Chronicle of Ernoul* 168.
6. See *exemplo* 3, 'Del salto que fizo el rrey Richalte de Inglaterra en la mar contra los moros': 'About the Leap that King Richard of England made into the Sea to Oppose the Moors', Juan Manuel's telling of a historical legend about Richard the Lionheart's 1192 heroics against Saladin's forces in Jaffa.

7. *Exemplo* 47, whose geographic setting is not given, also quotes *moros* and cites an Arabic phrase of unknown provenance. The trend in *Lucanor* to quote Andalusi Arabic strongly indicates that this, too, derives from local Iberian usage.
8. See Ayerbe-Chaux, *El Conde Lucanor: materia tradicional y originalidad creadora* 129–30; Castro, 'Presencia' 42; and González-Casanovas, 'Didáctica y Bildung en *El Conde Lucanor*' 81–2. Ana Adams productively critiques the modern tendency to anoint Saladin as Juan Manuel's ideal man in 'Ser es fazer: El saber y la masculinidad de Saladín en *El Conde Lucanor*'.
9. '[C]omunicaré la manera del libro, en manera de un grand señor que flablava con un su consegero' (51–2).
10. Stories of David, including that of his indiscretion with Bathsheba, proved popular and strikingly long-lived in European discourse on Saladin, dovetailing with the consultation motif so essential to *Lucanor*. Gotthold Lessing's eighteenth-century drama *Nathan der Weise* explores the allegory in remarkable fashion, revealing intertextual connections both to *Lucanor* and Boccaccio's *Decameron*. Lessing poses Saladin in dialogue with Nathan, the same prophet who admonished David for his treachery in pursuit of another man's wife. The central conceit of *Nathan der Weise* is the medieval 'Three Rings' allegory for the debate over the one true or superior Abrahamic faith. Some permutation of the story is to be found in *Lucanor* and several Italian works to be analysed in this chapter, although not all of them specify the sultan as Saladin.
11. In *Lucanor* and, as will be shown, Italian literature, Cairo is anachronistically called Babilonia, Babylon being an ancient place name in what became a suburb of Cairo during the Middle Ages. The text of *Lucanor* also implies that he reigns also over Armenia, or at least is known for hunting there (143, 147).
12. 'Et tan bien le conseiaba el conde et tanto fiava dél el soldán que, commo quier que estaba preso, que tan grand logar et tan grand poder avía, et tanto fazían por él en toda la tierra de Saladín, commo farían en la suya misma' (144).
13. Not coincidentally, Rodríguez-Velasco cites *Lucanor*, among other Iberian texts, as evidence for this claim, adding that Juan Manuel wrote 'surely considering himself to be the ideal tutor' (245n16).
14. See Cowell, *Medieval Warrior Aristocracy* 62–3; Kaeuper, *Chivalry and Violence in Medieval Europe* 22, 28–9; and Rodríguez-Velasco, *Order and Chivalry* 5–8.
15. The *genetes*, or *jinetes* in Spanish, proved so potent a force for the Andalusis in fighting Castile that their nimble riding style would be mimicked by Christian knights (Sancho de Sopranis, *Juegos de toros y cañas en Jerez de la Frontera* 3–8).

The legacy has survived in modern Spanish: *jinete* now denotes any experienced horseback rider.

16. Dante's inclusion of Saladin with laudable courtly people is echoed by his countryman Petrarch a few decades after the composition of *La Commedia.* The younger Petrarch (Petrarca, Francesco) places Saladin in his chanted litany of praise, grouping him with fellow potentates, including his putative Christian enemies (*Il Canzionere e i Trionfi* 7:149–63).
17. Avicenna must have been a Persian speaker originally, although Dante would have been unlikely to know or prioritise such a fact.
18. See 4.11. Working with the text of *Inferno*, Boccaccio elaborates upon Dante's muted presentation of Saladin, seeking to confirm the durable laudatory view of the sultan, who 'maravigliosamente amò e onorò i valenti uomini': 'greatly esteemed and honored men of valor' (*Comento* 1:368).
19. See Akbari, *Idols in the East* 267–8. Early exegesis of Dante's portrayal and placement of Saladin is to be found in Boccaccio's own writing on his immediate predecessor (*Comento* 1:368–9). Dante's own form of personal solitude – that which was imposed upon him as an exile from Florence – is of course much more exhaustively studied than his literary isolations of people. Although outside the scope of this study, a sustained analysis of his use of solitude would represent a major contribution to Dante and Romance studies.
20. For a brief historical observation on the beginnings of official chivalric discourse, see Rodríguez-Velasco, *Chivalry and Order* 7. Dante acknowledges the historical specificity of the personas whom he places in *Inferno*'s moral order, as in the mention of legendary and historical Christian knights (5.67–72, 31.16–18); but, significantly, a very literal understanding of another line from the work has him describing courtliness as a potential quality of immutable God (2.16–17).
21. 'Latin' is Dante's term for a Romance universal language of the court, both spoken and written (Vol. 3 of the *Commedia Purgatorio* 7.16–17).
22. For Dante's dialogue with his great-great-grandfather Cacciaguida, a devout Crusader whose testimony indicts Christian leadership for having failed in their long-term missions for the Holy Land and in promoting a pious society in Florence, see Vol. 4 of the *Commedia Paradiso* 15.139–48 and 16.46–154. For Dante's suggestion that the current pope, Boniface VIII, cares more for fighting fellow Christians than Saracens, see *Inferno* 27.25–99.
23. The *Conti*'s French source texts, in telling the story of a sultan approached by friars, identify the prominent Muslim as one of Saladin's sons, al-Malik al-Muʿaẓẓam Tūrān Shāh, or as his nephew al-Kāmil, in a history-cum-hagiography

of Saint Francis's dialogue with the Islamic regime in Egypt (*Chronique d'Ernoul* 431–4; Thompson, *Francis of Assisi* 232; Tolan, *Saint Francis and the Sultan* 50–3).

24. Tolan, *Saint Francis and the Sultan* 53. For interpretations of multiconfessional broad-mindedness in the story, see Stewart in Weaver ed., *The Decameron First Day in Perspective* 89–91,103–4. Boccaccio's praise for Saladin's resistance to dogma is to be found in his *Comento* 1:368.
25. In the earliest extant version, a Latin work, the father figure's legitimate and illegitimate daughters vie for the ring (Stephen of Bourbon (Stephanus de Borbone), *Anecdotes historiques, légendes et apologues* 281–2). In the French histories of the Crusades, Saladin is said to have been interested in locating the 'best' Abrahamic faith (Jubb ed., *Critical Edition of the* Estoires d'Outremer 235). For a consideration of the Three Rings' origins in literary tradition, taking into account the evidence of Semitic-language and Persian sources, see Shagrir, 'The Parable of the Three Rings'.
26. The vassal's wife whom Saladin attempts to woo calls herself a woman *de pequeña guisa* (246) 'of simple means' but also 'of little ability'.
27. For syntheses of Ancient Greek definitions of friendship with evolving medieval chivalry, see *Partidas* 4.27.1–7. Dante's understanding of courtly friendships indicates the Italian trend, leading up to and throughout the Renaissance, of muting the explicit references to knightly codes in favour of an explicit Aristotelian conversation on friendship (*Convivio* 3.3.11). For analysis of Dante and Boccaccio's work in that vein, see Masciandaro, *Stranger as Friend.*
28. In Boccaccio's age the most famous usage of the narrative of Israelites' Exodus from Egypt undoubtedly belongs to Dante. *La Commedia* makes direct and indirect reference to it throughout *Purgatorio* and slightly less in *Paradiso.* For a contextualisation of Exodus in Christian theology relevant to Dante, see Freccero, *Dante: The Poetics of Conversion* 55–68.
29. The merchant disguise is a trope of espionage in medieval European literature, on which see Kinoshita, '"Noi siamo mercatanti cipriani"' 41n2.
30. On Torello's assumption of late-medieval Italian models of chivalry, see Surdich, *La Cornice di Amore* 258–71. The question of Saladin's languages hangs upon the literary idioms of Boccaccio's era: Saladin and his companions *tutti sapevan latino* (10.9.16), which would seem to a modern eye to mean 'they all knew Latin' but would more fittingly mean 'they all knew a spoken language of Italy', given the fact that the travellers converse easily with nobles not fully members of the discursive space of the court, such as Torello's wife. As with all the texts of

Italy examined in this study, Boccaccio's was a written exploration of his spoken language: the picture of courtly encounters conducted in such a spoken register would serve his interests. The figure of the Romance-speaking (and therefore a great member of the imagined court) Muslim is a critical component of medieval Spanish literary culture, most famously in the form of Abengalbón, *el moro latinado* of the *Cid* epic.

31. For Dante's unflattering portrayals of popes and crusading kings see *Inferno* 27.79–102. The tradition of satirising chivalric, crusading romances is detailed in Kelly, *Performing Virginity* 79–81 and Cooper, *English Romance in Time* 39–40.

Conclusion: The Ministry of Culture

Power in the Poetry Festival

Researching the Middle Ages from a modern perspective compels us to closely inspect the political world in which we live. This book has noted the historicist attitudes of Orientalism, in particular the difficulty of separating them from our ongoing critical discussion of religion, Mediterranean cultural history, and especially the Crusades. Just as troublesome and thought-provoking is modern military regimes' fondness for the ancient past. It has had the potential to take on the qualities of extremism – historians and critics offer a lengthy discourse on fascist uses of Antiquity. The trend is impossible to ignore when surveying twentieth-century Europe and parts of the Middle East. Less emphasised, but crucial to dictatorships' populist efforts to consolidate power, is the official gesture towards medieval literature: linking the Cid Campeador to fascist rulers of Spain, adapting the mystery play drama of sacrifice in fascist Italy and Vichy France, the Nazi elites' Arthurian fantasy of Wewelsburg Castle, enshrining counter-Crusade in Syria and Iraq, and so on. In the Mediterranean and the Middle East, military regimes have derived political profit from fetishising the knighthood, celebrating imperial aesthetics, and reviving the art forms that had served past empires.

Few figures of political authority valued those gestures more highly than Saddam Hussein. The self-styled modern Saladin was determined to exploit the ancientness of Mesopotamia as well as the medieval identity arguments of modern Iraq.[1] There are two cultural events hosted by this talented anachronist (although far less gifted litterateur) that are particularly illuminating. One is the Babylon International Festival, chiefly a musical event. By design, it brought together the ancient and medieval so as to promote modern Iraq as an ideal of secular order. In addition to military governments' perennial favourites of orchestral music, folkloric shows, and historical reenactments with scored accompaniment, the festival featured a parallel academic seminar for its inaugural year, 1987. Spanish musicologist and medievalist Manuela Cortés García published a glowing summary report. Referring to herself in the third person, she notes that her lecture and presentation of putatively Eastern instruments depicted Alfonso X's *cantigas* manuscripts. In her view, those artefacts comprise evidence that Iraqi and Spanish cultural traditions are durably linked ('Presencia Española' 367–8, translation mine). As she praises the showcase of international music, 'along with the ancient cultures that took shape in the land of the two great rivers', the Tigris and Euphrates, she voices appreciation for the organiser, Minister of Culture and Information Laṭīf Nuṣayyif Jāsim. She reports that Jāsim has been 'honoured ... by Mister President Saddam Hussein for his constant work to foster culture in the country' (366–7). Alfonso's multiculturalism, then, redounds to these two high officials in the Baath Party, whose vision for international participation is reflected in the historical plurality of Babylon the city.

The regime's second and most extraordinary effort to align itself with the premodern was the Mirbad Poetry Festival, which Jāsim also organised. Mirbad featured two scripted moments of climax, one in which the president would enter the halls to take in performances, the other the awarding of the Saddam Hussein Prize upon a poet and several prose writers. The festival attracted its highest international participation in the late 1980s, when Iraq hosted not only poets from all over the Middle East but also a large group of Arab, European, and American scholars. I once spoke with a colleague of mine who, in 1988, was among the invitees receiving lavish hospitality from the then-wealthy government. He and I met in a cafe one evening, after he had adjourned a seminar he was teaching on Classical Arabic poetry. He told me of the uncanny experience of watching poets perform new versions of ᶜAbbāsid panegyric, the anachronism of it and the constant poetic references to Saddam Hussein as the ᶜAbbāsids' natural successor. Internationally famous and local authors alike took the stage in turns. Each one strove to outdo the other in praising the host cities of Baghdad and Basra, the ruling party, and of course the president, who ceremoniously entered the hall for short stints.

Hussein seemed to relish the lines comparing him to ʿAbbāsid caliphs, to Saladin, and to the supremely powerful poetic beloved. I asked, 'How did Hussein respond to the performance?' My colleague explained that the ruler looked not at his poets but off into the distance. It was as if it would have been unpresidential to directly acknowledge each poet eligible for the Saddam Prize.[2] After about an hour of listening at a time, Hussein would exit with his coterie of ministers and generals, leaving the audience to witness the praise spectacle that had been organised for him. He would periodically return, unannounced, and repeat the ritual.

In the years since I first learned of the Mirbad Festival, what has clung to my memory most of all in that anecdote is Hussein's askew gaze. How may we interpret his stance and the spectacle of a patron, consciously appropriating medieval cultural models? What interests of his did it serve for him to refrain from directly acknowledging the poets' competitive efforts to praise him? To read the moment for its historicity, it is impossible to avoid the Iran–Iraq War going on all around the poetic gathering in Basra. Much as the medieval literary competitions we have examined only rarely resulted in the declaration of a clear winner,[3] the war with Iran would end ambiguously so far as the two regimes were concerned. But, unlike the courtly game, the geopolitical contest promised no cathartic post-contest moment for those involved. Iraq was in the middle of a generations-long period of mourning, official and unofficial remembrances, economic crises, followed of course by the next devastation of the 1991 Gulf War. Whatever bravado Hussein may have displayed in the shrinking area of the world where he had freedom of travel, in 1987 he must have known that the war was a strategic lost cause for both Iraq and Iran. The only way one of these ravaged nations may purport itself a winner was in the pronouncements of official media, or indeed in officially sanctioned literature. Hussein's eyes are fixed on a place neither here nor there, not quite at his panegyrist nor at the audience around him. His position is more self-questioning than a dictator would wish to admit. Perhaps what he sought in the spectacle was to hear a competitor voice a perfect articulation of power, the poetic construct that would give an aura of truth to the myth of benevolence and his promise of Iraq's success.

The Mirbad Festival was designed to rally and awe its own citizens, and also to impress its guests from abroad. Text (triumphalist poetry) and subtext (the horrific war with Iran) came together, neither one fully confronted by Hussein in the performance hall but surely considered in silence by the Iraqis and visitors taking part in the congratulatory ceremony. The famous Iraqi poet and perennial Mirbad fixture ᶜAbd al-Razzāq ᶜAbd al-Wāḥid addressed both his homeland and the president in performing these lines, which officially won him the Saddam Prize:

يا سيد الارض يا ضعفي ، ويا هوسي

...

يا سيدي ، كل حرف فيك أكتبه احسه من نياط القلب يغترف

...

يا مستفزا وسيف الله في يده ونصب عينيه بيت الله والنجف

('ᶜAbd al-Razzāq ᶜAbd al-Wāḥid: shāᶜir bi-ḥajm al-qamar', par. 4)

> Master of the earth, my weakness, my obsession! …
> My master, each letter I write of you I write with feeling, pouring forth from the depths of my heart. …
> You, the one charging into battle with God's sword in hand, with eyes firmly fixed on the Kaaba and on Najaf!

Consciously conflating Hussein with Iraq, ᶜAbd al-Wāḥid figures the president as a national saviour and the protector of Islam. But even during the last moments of the war with Iran, the poet is at pains to acknowledge Mirbad as a world-wide event. Years later, he reflected upon his Saddam Prize and the poem with which he officially won it. ᶜAbd al-Wāḥid depicts himself as the festival's main event, performing for the two greats in attendance: Hussein and 'the great Orientalist, Professor Jacques Berque', who 'translated much of my poetry into French'. According to the poet, Hussein was emotionally moved by the performance, while Berque maintained his serious, scholarly respect in front of the audience. The Orientalist stood up from his seat and called out to attendees, pointing out the poem's excellent structure and rhyme ('Qaṣā'idī amām ṣaddām hiya ḥubb wa-laysat shiᶜran,' par. 3). Even in the emotive climate of recitation, ᶜAbd al-Wāḥid insists that he won the Saddam Prize with international academic support, not just with the blessing of the president he had praised.

It would be easy to dismiss Hussein's use of historical tropes, both for their superficiality and crass ambition. So much about Mirbad folds into his overdetermined self-image. Having cast himself as the inheritor of Mesopotamian glory through Babylon, he acquired more artistic credentials and the Islamic political righteousness attributed by Classical Arabic praise. But Mirbad provided the setting for a project much larger than Hussein's collection of historical icons to glorify himself. The festival aggregated and tried to unify very disparate cultural signs. Poets contended with one another to declare the Classical tradition as singular. Their task was to distil Arab identity into a unitary language of praise and, in some of their compositions, into the individual presidential patron. The audience itself, selected for its cosmopolitanism as well as its interest in Arabic literature, had been assembled to confirm this statement of cultural unity. Likewise, the scandal of an unwinnable war against a Persian-speaking enemy needed to be simplified, and portrayed as an imminent victory in Classical panegyric. At a variety of levels, the festival aimed to convert an unruly outside world into a cohesive unity. To organise poets, with their memorised and rehearsed compositions, to take turns reenacting a medieval ideal was to enforce a general form of order.[4] The Mirbad Festival went far beyond the plain ideologies of Hussein's cult of personality. It reassured the Baath Party that its violent tactics were necessary to protect a venerable, functional culture.

The Baath Party's show sharply focuses our attention upon the disciplinary politics of praise ceremony. During those peak years of the Mirbad Festival, Hussein cast himself as more than a terrifying-but-magnanimous strongman. He wanted to showcase a type of controlled violence in official culture. The appearance of a court – the formal invitations, Hussein's political coterie in the seats immediately around him, and of course the poets' hopeful extension of praise – evinced order of a kind seldom found in modern communities. Fascist movements of the last century have promoted themselves as the solution to the perceived chaos and decadence of nation-states. In turn, their nostalgia for the premodern is attributable in part to the regulatory power of courts. Fifty years before the Baathist Mirbad, Heinrich Himmler fixated on the crusading guilds of the Teutonic Knights and Arthur's Round Table. To him, these legendary brotherhoods were precedents for his community of Nazi officers. He saw in chivalry an ideological commitment to orderly warfare. Hussein, as he worked with a related but distinct premodern syllabus, noticed the ideological benefit in showcasing *qaṣīda* performances.[5] Whereas literary awards are generally given in recognition of tactile written texts, Mirbad went a step further. Hussein engaged the Classical praise economy itself. He made use of its tradition of identifying acceptable language, and he exercised the patron's unique prerogative to approve or disapprove of each performance.

In their eagerness for useful premodern narratives, fascist officials tap the regulatory discourse of the Middle Ages, which modern academic writers have been slow to acknowledge. We as a community of scholars have only begun to assertively counter the notion of the Middle Ages as a chaotic interregnum between Antiquity and the Renaissance, in spite of medieval thinkers' fixation upon the disciplining of imperial subjects. The competitive element in literary history provides ample material for the revision currently in progress. Chivalry, to cite an example at the centre of this study, takes shape as a courtly class through 'a process that transforms disorderly violence into institutionally regulated violence' (Rodríguez Velasco, *Order and Chivalry* 1). That regulating telos of the court is also at work in poetic texts. The court takes a prescriptive attitude towards literary creation, and displays that rhetorical power through the ritual of contest. The texts that successfully engaged adversaries or the motif of competition sustained their host courts by demonstrating that their empire contained its enemies, that it isolated a problem, and, oftentimes, found a violent solution. The literature prized by patrons and prominent members of the audience expressly sought out the sources of the court's social and political anxieties, absorbed them, and reformulated them as performances of skill. When the court looked outward at wars and social changes for which it was inadequately prepared, it created a sense of order by issuing literature whose telos was well-articulated. The pugilistic tradition – spectacular, aspirational, reproducible, self-stoking – was one of the most appealing and indispensable means of accomplishing that regulatory work. The more ambitiously that littérateurs sought to master one another and the genres in which they worked, the more decisively their patrons could hope to master their imperial subjects.

Even as an exclusive culture within a culture, the court wrestled with the distinct smaller groupings that comprised it. While it vigilantly enforced the barriers between its space and the society around it, courtly people recognised that they would also need to pay as much attention to its internal ritual activities, which developed into their own tributary subcultures. That is why competition proved so enduring and multifaceted. It is also why the literary language was indispensable for the articulation of larger ideas of difference in empire: religious dogmas, ethnic shifts, and social classes' divisions and resentments. Among the court's population, exceptionally discerning patrons and writers engaged the very notion of difference. Even as they naturalised their own positions of authority in the court by showing their mastery of literary registers of language, the texts that they produced explored the fissures that most vexed the court. It was no matter of mere stylistic experimentation that secretaries promoted their craft by showcasing the unequal power between addresser and addressee, viziers and kings wrested the power of ridicule and poetic aggression from its traditional masters in the poets' class, and that narrative authors pulled apart the totalising discourse of interreligious chivalry. Each of these movements in one way or another harnessed the court's empirical energies and the perennial gamesmanship of its members.

The Court in Retrospect

Charting discrete lifespans of official culture, this book would ultimately like to provide an insight into such processes going on all around us. As anachronistic as the Mirbad Festival was, at our current historical moment the very concept of the nation-state appears similarly out of time.[6] The discourse of the postnational is so common, both in academe and popular media, that it has become its own cliché, despite the very substantive questions from which it arises. It is worth asking whether state-sponsored cultural ceremonies will still matter by the end of this century. Whether because of troubled national history or because of elements of prizewinners' biographies, states have undercut the authority that they would like to grant with their awards. Günter Grass retained his Büchner Prize, the German government's highest literary award, after he very belatedly disclosed his early life history as an SS member. As his level of culpability is a subject of much debate even after his death, so is the question of his suitability as a laureate. Sonallah Ibrahim made a major display of his rejection of the Egyptian Ministry of Culture's Arabic Novel Prize, calling the government insufficiently legitimate to offer such an award; ten years later, after the democracy movements of 2011, he professed and then qualified his support for a military regime. His reasoning was that dictatorship may be necessary to wrest Egypt from Islamist politics (Ibrahim, 'Bayān'; Lindsey, 'A Voice of Dissent').

The biographies, accusations, and recriminations of literary figures do not by themselves undermine the state as an idea. They do, however, suggest that states, in the act of selecting and promoting cultural citizens, reveal their own weakness at least as much as their cohesion. Perhaps most tellingly, the Iraqi vernacular poet ᶜAbbās Jījān fell from his briefly held position as a favourite panegyrist of Hussein. He became an exiled antagonist of the regime, writing invective about the Baath Party. Finally, he reannointed himself as an elegist for the executed former president. Jījān's most recent major recitations include an appearance on the talent show *Amīr al-shuᶜarā'* (*Prince of Poets*), whose organising principle is competition among authors of all Arab nations. Gone are the sunglasses he wore when Hussein would invite him to official readings in Iraq. In the Emirati hall, his eyes flash with the drama of the moment. He shoots his arms outward towards the audience and declares himself 'son of the Euphrates … son of Baghdad'. Now, instead of appealing to a national figure or institution, the contestant must impress the pan-Arab judges and audience between commercials for laundry powder and cellular data services.

The court's history of course extends far before and after the span covered in this book, but we have seen a kind of beginning and end within the Middle Ages. For the last generations of ᶜAbbāsids as well as late-medieval Spaniards and Italians, key political organising principles of culture could no longer be taken for granted, and would in fact be replaced in early modernity. The last exportable models for Classical Arabic literature, and the techniques by which rank was acquired through it, were ᶜAbbāsid. While individual kingdoms and regions reworked the tradition in extraordinary ways throughout what has been problematically termed the Post-Classical era, their innovations never achieved the near-universal status of Iraqi imperial courts' products. As the polestar faded completely by the seventh/thirteenth century, many literary constellations continued to flourish, taking their own dynamic shapes and breaking up into new groupings.

Long after an empire had contracted, competition in literary discourse remained indispensable to the ruling classes. It averred the unity of courtly language, not just in the face of the inevitable ethnic and religious differences addressed in this study, but also amidst the imperial contractions themselves. I have argued that in Europe, during the last part of the Mediterranean Middle Ages and especially in the collapse of the Crusades, competition moved from the social spectacle of poetic exchange into narrative. Dante straddles both fields, and his perspective is telling. He articulates his general fear that the ideology of conquest is not firmly held by the popes and kings around him. Patronage is dissipating, in his view, scattered among the noble families that would come to define Renaissance culture. The material rewards offered to ambitious writers still hold substance, but Dante's nostalgic voice of poetry wonders if the great imperial proving-ground is consigned to the past. Almost plaintively, he asks,

> E cui non è ancora nel cuore Alessandro per li suoi reali benefici? Cui non è ancora lo buono re di Castella, o il Saladino? Quando de le loro messioni si fa menzione … amore hanno a la memoria di costoro. (*Convivio* 4.11)

> Who could not still have a place in his heart for Alexander, for his regal acts of generosity? Or the good king of Castile, or Saladin? When mention is made of the gifts they bestowed … people treasure these men in their memory.

Emphasising patrons' stature, Dante speaks to the power of court competition. The ritual seems to mystify even a chronicler such as him. As a cultural organising principle, competition's ostensible purpose in the Middle Ages was to perfect authors and performers. They strove towards formal ideals while seeking the approbation of the highest political authority. But we have seen imperial poetics without an emperor. Although individual courtiers conducted this work on themselves in ways that the court prescribed, the overarching goal of competition was to perfect relationships rather than individuals per se. It confirmed the protocols followed by adversaries; by addresser and addressee; patron and supplicant; monarch and administrator; and text and audience. Most importantly, competition defined the court's relationship to its empire. The disciplining ritual was effective precisely because its message to audiences was indirect. By legitimating each key component of the court, authors portrayed the whole institution as desirable. They maintained that courtly rewards were worthy of the community's attention and efforts. Properly laden with the promise of function and reward, these markers of connection appeared unbreakable. As long as they held, the empire seemed impervious to the threat posed by outside forces. The court performed and narrated circumscribed literary battles that, by their design, made sense to imperial subjects. Making critical sense of them now is to inhabit the space between the anxious, articulate members of the court.

Notes

1. Hussein identified as author of a romance novel set in medieval Iraq, *Zabība wa-l-malik*, whose heroine Zabība falls in love with a medieval royal version of Hussein. For citations and images of Hussein-as-Saladin, see Allen and Amt, eds, *The Crusades* 421. Many commentators have noted the irony of Hussein's Saladinic self-conceit: although they both claimed Tikrit as their place of birth, Hussein had little to gain from acknowledging Saladin's Kurdish ethnicity, especially given the atrocities that the Iraqi government committed against its Kurdish population in the late twentieth century.
2. We see this structure of panegyric addresser and addressee reproduced in the Syrian parliament shortly after the revolt of 2011, which unlike the Mirbad events is widely available on video recording. Bashar al-Assad addresses the assembly with the inevitable platitudes of dictators challenged by popular revolt, insisting that he must see out the will of his people, that his army will rescue true Syrians from the 'sedition' of foreign-supported conspirators. At key moments in the speech, certain members of parliament rise to issue praise- and military solidarity-building poems. Al-Assad maintains a look of pleasant surprise and appreciation during these interludes, smiling toward no one in particular, as if these moments were not clearly scripted elements of the session.
3. Precise evidence is lacking for the competitive protocols observed at various points of al-Mirbad's medieval history. The modern Mirbad Festival fostered its own routine, drawing inspiration from early Islamic iconography but structuring itself more in line with other twentieth-century secular state festivals. After more than a decade in effect, starting in 1986 the organisers awarded separate Saddam Prizes for poetry, narrative works, philology, literary analysis, etc., each winner receiving $30,000 (Bejarano Escanilla, 'Al-Mirbad' 208n4; Mason, 'Impressions' 157).
4. Herbert Mason lightly complains of the attending Iraqi citizens' diversity of ages

and social classes at one venue at the 1988 festival, calling it 'bizarre as a series of organized happenings involving extremely disciplined artists', but that discipline, he notes with approval, wins the day ('Impressions' 157).

5. Hussein's identification with chivalry extends beyond the heroism of *Zabība wa-l-malik* and his Saladinic persona in literature, murals, and sculpture. His panegyrist ᶜAbd al-Wāḥid remembers him as 'the knight whom the Arab nation had awaited' ('Al-Shāᶜir al-ᶜirāqī ᶜabd al-wāḥid' par. 3).
6. The Mirbad event continues to be held in Iraq, although its nationalist performances no longer include extended praise of individual leaders, and the Saddam Prize no longer exists.

Bibliography

Primary Texts

Abū Nuwās, Al-Ḥasan. *Der Dīwān des Abū Nuwās*. Eds Ewald Wagner and Gregor Schoeler. 7 vols. Beirut: Dār al-Nashr, 2001–6.

Abū Shāma. *Kitāb al-rawḍatayn fī akhbār al-dawlatayn*. Eds Muḥammad Aḥmad and Muḥammad Ziyāda. 3 vols. Cairo and Beirut: Lajnat al-ta'līf wa-l-tarjama wa-l-nashr, 1956–62.

——. ᶜAbd al-Raḥmān. *Kitāb al-rawḍatayn fī akhbār al-dawlatayn al-nūriyya wa-l-salāḥiyya*. Ed. Ibrāhīm Shams al-Dīn. 5 vols. Beirut: Dār al-Kutub al-ᶜIlmiyya, 2002.

Abū Tammām, Ḥabīb ibn Aws al-Ṭā'ī, and al-Khaṭīb al-Tabrīzī. *Dīwān abī tammām bi-sharḥ al-khaṭīb al-tabrīzī*. Ed. Muḥammad ᶜAzzām. 4 vols. Cairo: Dār al-Maᶜārif, 1957–65.

Āl Yāsīn, Muḥammad Ḥasan, ed. *Nafā'is al-makhṭūṭāt*. 4 vols. Baghdad: Maṭbaᶜat al-Maᶜārif (Dār al-Maᶜārif li-l-Ta'līf wa-l-Tarjama wa-l-Nashr), 1952–6.

Alamanon, Bertran d'. *Le troubadour Bertran d'Alamanon*. Ed. J. Salverda de Grave. Toulouse: Édouard Privat, 1902.

Alfonso X ('el Sabio'). *Las siete partidas del rey don Alfonso el Sabio*. 3 vols. Madrid: Real Academia de la Historia, 1807.

——. *Opúsculos legales del rey Don Alfonso el Sabio*. 2 vols. Madrid: Real Academia de la Historia, 1836.

——. *General estoria*. Ed. Antonio Solalinde, et al. 2 vols. Madrid: Centro de Estudios Históricos, 1930.

——. *Antología*. Ed. Antonio G. Solalinde. Buenos Aires: Espasa-Calpe, 1941.

——. *Setenario*. Ed. Kenneth H. Vanderford. Buenos Aires: Instituto de Filología, 1945.

——. *Primera crónica general.* Ed. Ramón Menéndez Pidal. 2 vols. Madrid: Credos, 1955.

——. *Cantigas de Santa María.* Ed. Walter Mettmann. 3 vols. Madrid: Castalia, 1986–9.

——. *Libros del ajedrez, dados y tablas.* Valencia and Madrid: Vicent García Editores and Ediciones Poniente, 1987.

——. *Espéculo.* Ed. Robert MacDonald. Madison: Hispanic Seminary of Medieval Studies, 1990.

——. *Songs of Holy Mary of Alfonso X, the Wise.* Trans. Kathleen Kulp-Hill. Tempe: Arizona Centre for Medieval and Renaissance Studies, 2000.

——. *El Cancionero profano de Alfonso X el Sabio.* Ed. Juan Paredes [Juan Paredes Nuñez]. Rome: Japadre editore – L'Aquila, 2001.

——. *Las Siete Partidas.* Ed. Robert I. Burns. Trans. Samuel Parsons Scott. 5 vols. Philadelphia: University of Pennsylvania Press, 2001.

——. *Libros del saber de astronomía del rey D. Alfonso X de Castilla.* Ed. Manuel Rico y Sinobas. Frankfurt: Institut für Geschichte der Arabisch-Islamischen Wissenschaften an der Johann Wolfgang Goethe-Universität, 2002.

Amari, Michele, ed. and trans. *I diplomi arabi del R. Archivio Fiorentino.* Florence: Le Monnier, 1863.

Arbor Aldea, Mariña, and Antonio Fernández Guiadanes: see under 'Critical and Ancillary Texts'.

^{c}Arqala al-Kalbī, Ḥassān ibn Numayr. *Dīwān ^{c}arqala al-kalbī.* Ed. Aḥmad al-Jundī. Damascus: Maṭba^{c}at Dār al-Ḥayāt, 1970.

Austin, J. L. (John Langshaw). *How to Do Things with Words.* Cambridge, MA: Harvard University Press, 1962.

^{c}Awfī, Muḥammad. *Lubāb al-albāb.* Ed. Sa^{c}īd Nafīsī. Tehran: Kitābkhānah-yi Ibn Sīnā, 1957.

al-Baghdādī, al-Khaṭīb. *Ta'rīkh Baghdād.* 14 vols. Cairo: Maktabat al-Khānjī, 1931.

Barrios García, Ángel, Alberto Martín Expósito, et al., eds. *Documentación medieval del Archivo Municipal de Alba de Tormes.* Salamanca: Ediciones Universidad de Salamanca, 1982.

Berceo, Gonzalo de. *Obras completas.* Ed. Carlos Clavería. Madrid: Fundación José Antonio de Castro, 2003.

——. *The Collected Works of Gonzalo de Berceo in English Translation.* Ed. Annette Grant Cash. Trans Jeannie K. Bartha, Annette Grant Cash, and Richard Terry Mount. Tempe: Arizona Center for Medieval and Renaissance Studies, 2008.

Bible, Hebrew: see Jewish Publication Society of America.

Boccaccio, Giovanni. *Il Comento di Giovanni Boccaccio sopra la Commedia.* 2 vols. Florence: Felice le Monnier, 1863.

——. *Decameron.* Ed. Vittore Branca. 2 vols. Turin: Einaudi, 1992.

Busone da Gubbio. *Fortunatus siculus, ossia L'avventuroso ciciliano.* Florence: Tipo. all'insegna di Dante, 1832.

Cancioneiro da Ajuda. Ed. Carolina Michäelis de Vasconcelos. 2 vols. Halle: Max Niermeyer, 1904.

[*Cancioneiro da Ajuda.* Facsimile.] *Fragmento do Nobiliario do Conde Dom Pedro. Cancioneiro da Ajuda. Edição Fac-similada do códice existente na Biblioteca da Ajuda.* Ed. Instituto Português do Patrimonio Arquitectónico e Arqueológico. Lisbon: Távola Redonda, 1994.

Cancioneiro portuguez da Vaticana. Ed. Teófilo Braga. Lisbon: Imprensa Nacional, 1878.

Cantar de Mío Cid. Eds Alberto Montaner Frutos and Francisco Rico. Barcelona: Crítica, 1993.

La Chanson de Roland. Eds Luis Cortés Vázquez and Paulette Gabaudan. Paris: Librairie Nizet, 1994.

Chronique d'Ernoul et de Bernard le Trésorier. Paris: Renouard, 1871.

Conti di antichi cavalieri. Ed. Pietro Fanfani. Florence: Baracchi, 1851.

Crist, Larry, ed. *Saladin: suite et fin du deuxième Cycle de la Croisade.* Geneva: Textes Littéraires Français, 1972.

Dūlābī, Muḥammad. *Al-Dhurriyya al-ṭāhira.* Ed. Muḥammad al-Jalālī. Beirut: Mu'assasat al-iᶜlāmī (al-aᶜlāmī), 1988.

The Epic of Gilgamesh: The Babylonian Epic Poem and Other Texts in Akkadian and Sumerian. Trans. Andrew George. London: Penguin, 2003.

Critical Edition of the Estoires d'Outremer et de la naissance Salehadin. Ed. Margaret Jubb. London: Committee for Medieval Studies, Queen Mary and Westfield College, University of London, 1990.

Dante Alighieri. *La Commedia secondo l'antica vulgata.* Ed. Giorgio Petrocchi. 4 vols. Milan: Mondadori, 1966–7.

El Fuero de Teruel. Ed. J. Castañé Llinás. Teruel: Teruel Perruca, 1991.

Fuero de Miranda del Ebro. Ed. Francisco Cantera y Burgos. Miranda de Ebro: Fundación Cultural 'Profesor Cantera Burgos', 1998.

Gayangos Pascual de, ed. *Escritores en prosa anteriores al siglo XV.* Madrid: M. Rivadeneyra, 1860.

Ghurāb, ᶜUmar, 'ᶜAbd al-Razzāq ᶜAbd al-Wāḥid: shāᶜir bi-ḥajm al-qamar'. *Al-Dīwān*

15 December 2010. <http://www.aldiwan.org/12923.html> (last accessed 31 January 2017).

al-Ḥamawī, Ibn Ḥijja. *Thamarāt al-awrāq fī l-muḥāḍarāt*. Ed. Mufīd Muḥammad Qumayḥa. Beirut: Dār al-Kutub al-ʿIlmiyya, 1983.

Hussein, Saddam (Ṣaddām Ḥusayn). *Zabība wa-l-malik*. Baghdad: n.p., *c.*2001.

Ibn ʿAbbād al-Ṭālqānī, Abū al-Qāsim Ismāʿīl ('Al-Ṣāḥib'). *Al-Kashf ʿan masāwī shiʿr al-Mutanabbī*. Ed. Muḥammad Ḥasan Āl Yāsīn. Baghdad: Maktabat al-Nahḍa, 1965.

——. *Dīwān al-Ṣāḥib ibn ʿAbbād*. Ed. Muḥammad Ḥasan Āl Yāsīn. Baghdad: Maktabat al-Nahḍa, 1965.

——. *Al-Zaydiyya*. Ed. Nājī Ḥasan. Beirut: Al-Dār al-ʿArabiyya li-l-Mawsūʿāt, 1986.

—— and Abū l-Ṭayyib al-Mutanabbī. *Al-amthāl al-sā'ira min shiʿr al-mutanabbī wa-l-rūznāmaja*. Ed. Muḥammad Ḥasan Āl Yāsīn. Baghdad: Maktabat al-Nahḍa, 1965.

Ibn ʿAbd Rabbih, Aḥmad ibn Muḥammad. *Al-ʿIqd al-farīd*. Eds Aḥmad Amīn, Aḥmad al-Zayn, and Ibrāhīm al-Ibyārī. Cairo: Lajnat al-ta'līf wa-l-tarjama wa-l-nashr, 1965.

Ibn Abī al-Damm, Ibrāhīm. *Kitāb adab al-qaḍā'*. Ed. Muḥammad Muṣṭafā al-Zuhaylī. Beirut: Dār al-Kutub al-ʿIlmiyya, 1987.

Ibn Abī Ṭāhir Ṭayfūr, Aḥmad. *Kitāb Baghdād*. Ed. Muḥammad Zāhid al-Kawtharī. Cairo: Maktabat Nashr al-Thaqāfa al-Islāmiyya, 1949.

Ibn al-Athīr, ʿAlī ʿIzz al-Dīn. *Al-Kāmil fī l-ta'rīkh*. Ed. Carolus Johannes Tornberg. 12 vols and index. Beirut: Dār Ṣādir, 1964–7.

Ibn al-Athīr, Najm al-Dīn Aḥmad. *Jawhar al-kanz*. Ed. Muḥammad Zaghlūl Sallām. Alexandria: Munsha'at al-maʿārif, 1974.

Ibn Dāniyāl, Muḥammad. *Three Shadow Plays*. Eds Paul Kahle and Derek Hopwood. Cambridge: E. J. W. Gibb Memorial Trust, 1992.

Ibn al-Furāt, Muḥammad. *Ayyubids, Mamlukes and Crusaders: Selections from the Tārīkh al-Duwal wa'l-Mulūk*. Eds and trans U. and M. C. Lyons. Cambridge: W. Heffer and Sons, 1971.

Ibn Munqidh, Usāma. *Ousâma ibn Mounḳidh, un émir syrien au premier siècle des croisades (1095–1188)*. Ed. Hartwig Derenbourg. 2 vols. Paris: Ernest Leroux, 1886.

——. *The Book of Contemplation: Islam and the Crusades*. Trans. Paul Cobb. London: Penguin Classics, 2008.

Ibn al-Nadīm, Muḥammad. *Kitāb al-fihrist*. Eds Gustav Flügel and Johannes Rödige. 2 vols. Leipzig: Vogel, 1871–2.

Ibn Qutayba, Abū Muḥammad ('Ibn Qotaïba'). *Introduction au livre de la poésie et des poètes: muqaddimatu kitābi š-šiʿri wa š-šuʿarāʾ*. Ed. Michael Johan de Goeje. Trans. Maurice Gaudefroy-Demombynes. Paris: Les Belles Lettres, 1947.

———. *Al-Shiʿr wa-l-shuʿarāʾ*. Ed. Aḥmad Muḥammad Shākir. 2 vols. Cairo: Dār al-Maʿārif, 1966–7.

Ibn Ṭūlūn, Shams al-Dīn. *Quḍāt dimashq*. Ed. Ṣalāḥ al-Dīn al-Munajjid. Damascus: al-Majmaʿ al-ʿIlmī al-ʿArabī, 1956.

Ibrahim, Sonallah (Ṣunʿ Allāh Ibrāhīm). 'Bayān min al-kātib ṣunʿ allāh ibrāhīm'. *Al-Akhbār* n.d. <http://www.al-akhbar.com/node/189692> (last accessed 31 January 2017).

al-Iṣbahānī, Abū Nuʿaym. *Kitāb dalāʾil al-nubuwwa*. Hyderabad: Majlis Dāʾirat al-Maʿārif al-ʿUthmāniyya, 1977.

al-Iṣfahānī, Abū l-Faraj. *Kitāb al-aghānī*. Ed. Muḥammad Abū l-Faḍl Ibrāhīm. 24 vols. Cairo: Dār al-Kutub al-Miṣriyya, 1927–70.

al-Iṣfahānī, ʿImād al-Dīn. *Sanā l-barq al-shāmī*. Ed. Fatḥiyya al-Nabrāwī. Cairo: Maktabat al-khānjī, 1979.

———. *Dīwān ʿimād al-dīn al-iṣfahānī*. Ed. Nāẓim Rashīd. Mosul (al-Mawṣil): Jāmiʿat al-Mawṣil, 1983.

al-Iṣfahānī, al-Rāghib. *Muḥāḍarāt al-udabāʾ*. Ed. ʿUmar al-Ṭabbāʿ. Beirut: Dār al-arqam, 1999.

al-Jāḥiẓ, Abū ʿUthmān. *Al-Bayān wa-l-tabyīn*. Ed. ʿAbd al-Salām Muḥammad Hārūn. 4 vols. Cairo: Maṭbaʿat Lajnat al-Taʾlīf wa-l-Tarjama wa-l-Nashr, 1948–50.

———. *Al-Bukhalāʾ*. Eds Abū Bakr al-Baghdādī and Abū ʿAbd Allāh Julaymī. Beirut: Muʾassasat al-Kutub al-Thaqāfiyya, 2000.

al-Jahshiyārī, Muḥammad ibn ʿAbdūs. *Kitāb al-wuzarāʾ wa-l-kuttāb*. Beirut: Dār al-Fikr al-Ḥadīth, 1988.

Jewish Publication Society of America. *The New English Translation of the Bible*. Philadelphia: Jewish Publication Society of America, 1917.

Juan Manuel. *El Conde Lucanor*. Ed. José Manuel Blecua. Madrid: Castalia, 1969.

———. *Obras completas*. Ed. José Manuel Blecua. 2 vols. Madrid: Gredos, 1982–3.

al-Jumaḥī, Ibn Sallām. *Ṭabaqāt al-shuʿarāʾ*. Leiden: Brill, 1916.

al-Jurjānī, Aḥmad ibn Muḥammad, Muḥammad Shams al-Ḥaqq Shamsī, and Abū Manṣūr ʿAbd al-Malik al-Thaʿālibī. *Al-Muntakhab min kināyāt al-udabāʾ wa-ishārāt al-bulaghāʾ*. Hyderabad: Maṭbaʿat Majlis Dāʾirat al-Maʿārif al-ʿUthmāniyya, 1983.

Keller, John, trans. *The Book of the Wiles of Women*: see *Sendebar*.

Lapa, Manuel Rodrigues, ed. *Cantigas d'escarnho e de mal dizer dos cancioneiros medievais galego-portugueses*. Lisbon: Edições J. Sá da Costa, 1995.
Libros del saber de astronomía: see Alfonso X ('el Sabio').
Machiavelli, Niccolò. *Il principe (De principatibus)*. Ed. Brian Richardson. Manchester: Manchester University Press, 1979.
al-Masʿūdī, Abū l-Ḥasan. *Murūj al-dhahab*. Ed. Charles Pellat. Beirut: al-Jāmiʿa al-lubnāniyya (Lebanese University), 1966.
Matar, Nabil, ed. *In the Lands of the Christians: Arabic Travel Writing in the Seventeenth Century*. London and New York: Routledge, 2003.
al-Māwardī, Abū l-Ḥasan. *Al-Wizāra: adab al-wazīr*. Eds Muḥammad Dāwūd and Fuʾād ʿAbd al-Munʿim. Alexandria: Dār al-jāmiʿāt al-miṣriyya, 1976.
Miskawayh, Abū ʿAlī. *The Tajârib al-Umam, or History, of Ibn Miskawayh: Reproduced in Facsimile from the Ms. at Constantinople in the Ayâ Sûfiyya Library*. Intro. Leone Caetani. Leiden: E. J. W. Gibb Memorial (Brill), 1909.
——. Abū Shujāʿ al-Rudhrāwarī, and Ibrāhīm ibn Hilāl al-Ṣābī. *Tajārub [sic] al-umam* and *Dhayl tajārib al-umam*. Ed. H. F. Amedroz. Baghdad: Al-muthannā, 1916.
——. *The Eclipse of the 'Abbasid Caliphate (Tajārib al-umam)*. Eds and trans H. F. Amedroz and D. S. Margoliouth. 6 vols. Oxford: Basil Blackwell, 1920–2.
——. *Miskawayh: The Muntakhab ṣiwān al-ḥikmah of Abū Sulaimān al-Sijistānī*. Ed. D. M. Dunlop. The Hague: Mouton, 1979.
——. *Tajārib al-umam wa-taʿāqub al-himam*. Ed. Sayyid Kasrawī Ḥasan. Beirut: Dār al-Kutub al-ʿIlmiyya, 2003.
Monroe, James, ed. and trans. *Hispano-Arabic Poetry: A Student Anthology*. Berkeley: University of California Press, 1974.
Morgan, Margaret, ed. *The Chronicle of Ernoul and the Continuations of William of Tyre*. Oxford: Oxford University Press, 1973.
——. *Dīwān al-mutanabbī*. Beirut: Dār Bayrūt li-l-Ṭibāʿa wa-l-Nashr, 1983.
Neves, Orlando, ed. *Trovas medievais obscenas: cantigas de mal dizer*. Lisbon: Matéria Escrita, 1998.
Petrarch (Petrarca, Francesco). *Il Canzionere e i Trionfi*. Ed. Andrea Moschetti. Milan: Vallardi, 1908.
al-Qalqashandī, Aḥmad. *Ṣubḥ al-aʿshā*. Ed. Muḥammad Shams al-Dīn. 15 vols. Beirut: Dār al-Kutub al-ʿIlmiyya, 1987–9.
Qurʾan (al-Qurʾān). *The Holy Qurʾan: Text, Translation and Commentary*. Ed. and trans. Yusuf Ali. Elmhurst, NY: Tahrike Tarsile Qurʾan, 2008.

Rabelais, François. *Gargantua and Pantagruel.* Trans Thomas Urquhart and Pierre Le Motteux. New York: W. W. Norton, 1990.

Rasā'il ikhwān al-ṣafā' wa-khullān al-wafā'. 4 vols. Beirut: Dār Ṣādir, 1957.

Real Academia Española. 'Breve historia'. 4 pars. <http://www.rae.es/rae/gestores/gespub000001.nsf/voTodosporId/CEDF300E8D943D3FC12571360037CC94?OpenDocument&i=0> (last accessed 17 July 2010).

al-Rūmī, Yāqūt al-Ḥamawī: see 'Yāqūt'.

al-Ṣābī, Hilāl. *Tuḥfat al-umarā' fi ta'rīkh al-wuzarā': The Historical Remains of Hilāl al-Ṣābī's 1st Part of his Kitab al-Wuzara.* Ed. H. F. Amedroz. Beirut: Catholic Press (al-Maṭba^{c}a al-kāthūlīkiyya), 1904.

Sendebar. Ed. Jesús Lacarra. Madrid: Cátedra, 1989. English translation: *The Book of the Wiles of Women*. Trans. John Keller. Chapel Hill: University of North Carolina Press, 1956.

Stephen of Bourbon (Stephanus de Borbone). *Anecdotes historiques, légendes et apologues*. Paris: Librairie Renouard, 1877.

al-Ṭabarī, Abū Ja^{c}far. *Ta'rīkh al-rusul wa-l-mulūk*. Ed. Muḥammad Abū l-Faḍl Ibrāhīm. 11 vols. Cairo: Dār al-Ma^{c}ārif, 1960–4.

——. *The History of al-Ṭabarī*. Ed. Ehsan Yarshater. Trans Clifford Edmund Bosworth, Franz Rosenthal, Everett Rowson, George Saliba, et al. 40 vols. Albany: State University of New York Press, 1996–2007.

al-Tanūkhī, al-Muḥassin. *The Table-Talk of a Mesopotamian Judge*. (Ed. and trans. of *Nishwār*.) Ed. D. S. Margoliouth. 2 vols. London: Royal Asiatic Society, 1921–2.

——. *Nishwār al-muḥādara*. Ed. ^{c}Abbūd al-Shāljī. 8 vols. Beirut: Dār Ṣādir, 1971–3.

al-Tawḥīdī, Abū Ḥayyān. *Mathālib al-wazīrayn: akhlāq al-Ṣāḥib Ibn ^{c}Abbād wa-bn al-^{c}Amīd*. Ed. Ibrāhīm al-Kaylānī. Damascus: Dār al-Fikr, 1961.

——. *Akhlāq al-wazīrayn, mathālib al-wazīrayn al-Ṣāḥib ibn ^{c}abbād wa-bn al-^{c}amīd*. Ed. Muḥammad bin Tāwīt al-Ṭanjī. Damascus: Maṭbū^{c}āt al-Majma^{c} al-^{c}Ilmī al-^{c}Arabī bi-Dimashq, 1965.

——. *Kitāb al-imtā^{c} wa-l-mu'ānasa*. Ed. Haytham Khalīfa al-Ṭa^{c}īmī. Sidon and Beirut: al-Maktaba al-^{c}Aṣriyya, 2006.

al-Tha^{c}ālibī, Abū Manṣūr ^{c}Abd al-Malik. *Yatīmat al-dahr*. Ed. ^{c}Alī Muḥammad ^{c}Abd al-Laṭīf. 2 vols. Cairo: Maṭba^{c}at al-Ṣāwī, 1934.

——. *Yatīmat al-dahr*. Ed. Muḥammad Muḥyī al-Dīn ^{c}Abd al-Ḥamīd. 2 vols. Cairo: Maṭba^{c}at al-Sa^{c}āda, 1956.

——. *Laṭā'if al-ma^{c}ārif*. Eds Ibrāhīm al-Abyārī and Ḥasan al-Ṣayrafī. Cairo: ^{c}Īsā al-Bābī al-Ḥalabī, 1960.

——. *Kitāb khāṣṣ al-khāṣṣ*. Ed. Ḥasan Amīn. Beirut: Dār Maktabat al-Ḥayā, 1966.

——. *Yatīmat al-dahr*. Ed. Mufīd Muḥammad Qumayḥa. 5 vols. Beirut: Dār al-Kutub al-ᶜIlmiyya, 1983.

William of Tyre. *Historia rerum in partibus transmarinis gestarum*: see *Recueil des historiens des croisades*.

——. *History of Deeds Done beyond the Sea*. Trans Emily Babcock and A. C. Krey. 2 vols. New York: Columbia University Press, 1943.

Wolfram von Eschenbach. *Willehalm*. Berlin: Walter de Gruyter, 2003.

Aḥmad ibn Abī Yaᶜqūb ('Yaᶜqūbī'). *Kitāb al-buldān*. Ed. T. G. J. Juynboll. Leiden: Brill, 1861.

Yāqūt al-Ḥamawī al-Rūmī ('Yāqūt'). *Muᶜjam al-buldān*. Beirut: Dār Ṣādir, 1977.

——. *Muᶜjam al-udabā': irshād al-arīb*. Ed. Iḥsān ᶜAbbās. 7 vols. Beirut: Dār al-Gharb al-Islāmī, 1993.

al-Yazdādī, ᶜAbd al-Raḥmān. *Kamāl al-balāgha*. Cairo: al-Maktaba al-Salafīya, 1922.

Zakkār, Suhayl, ed. *Arbaᶜat kutub fī l-jihād min ᶜaṣr al-ḥurūb al-ṣalībiyya*. Damascus: al-Takwīn, 2007.

Zamora, Juan Gil de. *Milagros de Santa María del «Liber Mariae»*. Trans. and ed. Francisco Rodríguez Pascual. Zamora, Spain: Semuret, 2007.

Critical and Ancillary Texts

ᶜAbd al-Wāḥid, ᶜAbd al-Razzāq. 'Al-Shāᶜir al-ᶜirāqī ᶜabd al-wāḥid: ṣaddām inḥanā amāmī'. *Al Arabiya* 11 January 2012. <http://www.alarabiya.net/articles/2012/01/11/187756.html> (last accessed 5 February 2017).

——. 'Qasā'idī amām ṣaddām hīya ḥubb wa-laysat shiᶜran'. *Al-Zamān* 2 December 2014. <http://www.azzaman.com/?p=90243> (last accessed 5 February 2017).

Ackerlind, Sheila. *King Dinis of Portugal and the Alfonsine Heritage*. New York: Peter Lang, 1989.

Adam, G. Mercer. *Spain and Portugal*. Philadelphia: J. D. Morris, 1906.

Adams, Ana. 'Ser es fazer: El saber y la masculinidad de Saladín en *El Conde Lucanor*'. *La corónica* 40.2 (2012): 145–68.

Ahsan, Muhammad Manazir. *Social Life under the Abbasids: 170–289* AH, *786–902* AD. London and New York: Longman, 1979.

Akbari, Suzanne Conklin. *Idols in the East: European Representations of Islam and the Orient, 1100–1450*. Ithaca: Cornell University Press, 2009.

—— and Karla Mallette, eds. *A Sea of Languages: Rethinking the Arabic Role in Medieval Literary History*. Toronto: University of Toronto Press, 2013.

Akehurst, F. R. P. and Judith Davis, eds. *A Handbook of the Troubadours*. Berkeley and Los Angeles: University of California Press, 1995.

Algazi, Gadi and Rina Drory. 'L'amour à la cour des Abbasides. Un code de compétence social'. *Annales: Histoire, Sciences Sociales* 6 (2000): 1,255–82.

al-ᶜAlī, Ṣāliḥ, ed. *Al-Adab al-ᶜarabī fī āthār al-dārisīn*. Beirut: Dār al-ᶜIlm li-l-Malāyīn, 1961.

Ali, Samer M. *Arabic Literary Salons in the Islamic Middle Ages: Poetry, Public Performance, and the Presentation of the Past*. Notre Dame, IN: University of Notre Dame Press, 2010.

Ali, Tariq. *The Clash of Fundamentalisms: Crusades, Jihads and Modernity*. London: Verso, 2002.

Allen, S. J. and Emilie Amt, eds. *The Crusades: A Reader*. Toronto: University of Toronto Press, 2014.

Althusser, Louis. *Lenin and Philosopy, and Other Essays*. Trans. Ben Brewster. New York: Monthly Review Press, 1971.

Althusser, Louis. *Machiavelli and Us*. Trans. Gregory Elliot. London: Verso, 1999.

Alvar, Carlos. *Traducciones y traductores*. Alcalá de Henares: Centro de Estudios Cervantinos, 2010.

Amīn, Aḥmad. *Zuᶜamā' al-iṣlāḥ fī l-ᶜaṣr al-ḥadīth*. Cairo: Maktabat al-Nahḍa al-ᶜaṣriyya, 1949.

——. *Ḍuḥā l-islam*. 3 vols. Cairo: Maktabat al-Nahḍa al-ᶜaṣriyya, 1956.

Amorós, Andrés and José María Díez Borque, eds. *Historia de los espectáculos en España*. Madrid: Castalia, 1999.

Anglés, Higinio. *La música de la Cantigas de Santa María del Rey Alfonso el Sabio*. 3 vols. Barcelona: Diputación Provincial de Barcelona, 1958.

Aniz, Iriarte C. and Martín L. V. Díaz. *Santo Domingo de Caleruega, en su contexto socio-político, 1170–1221*. Salamanca: Editorial San Esteban, 1994.

Antoon, Sinan. *The Poetics of the Obscene in Premodern Arabic Poetry*. New York: Palgrave Macmillan, 2014.

The Arabian Nights Encyclopedia. Eds Ulrich Marzolph and Richard van Leeuwen. 2 vols. Santa Barbara: ABC-CLIO, 2004.

Aragão, Ludumila. 'O tema da velha nas Cantigas d'escárnio e maldizer'. *Revista da Faculdade de Letras «Línguas e literaturas»* 20 (2003): 357–79.

Arbor Aldea, Mariña and Antonio Fernández Guiadanes, eds. *Estudos de edición crítica e lírica Galego-Portuguesa*. Santiago de Compostela: Universidade de Santiago de Compostela, 2010.

Arte de trovar do Cancioneiro da Biblioteca Nacional de Lisboa. Ed. Giuseppe Tavani. Lisbon: Colibri, 1999.

Asad, Talal. *On Suicide Bombing*. New York: Columbia University Press, 2007.

Ashtiany, Julia et al., eds. *ᶜAbbasid Belles-Lettres*. Cambridge: Cambridge University Press, 1990.

Ashurst, D. 'Masculine Postures and Poetic Gambits: The Treatment of the *Soldadeira* in the *Cantigas d'escarnho e de mal dizer*'. *Bulletin of Hispanic Studies* [Liverpool] 74 (1997): 1–6.

Al-ᶜAskarī, Abū Hilāl. *Dīwān al-maᶜānī*. 2 vols. Cairo: Qudsī, 1352 H (1933–4 CE).

Aristotle. *Poetics*. Trans Penelope Murray and T. S. Dorsch. *Classical Literary Criticism*. Ed. Penelope Murray. New York: Penguin Classics, 2001.

Auerbach, Erich. *Mimesis: The Representation of Reality in Western Literature*. Trans. Willard R. Trask. Princeton: Princeton University Press, 2003. Trans. of *Mimesis: dargestellte Wirklichkeit in der abendländischen Literatur*. Bern: A. Francke, 1946.

ᶜAwaḍ, Muḥammad. *Al-Ḥurūb al-Ṣalībiyya*. Giza: ᶜAyn li-l-Dirāsāt wa-l-Buḥūth al-Insāniyya, 1999.

Ayerbe-Chaux, Reinaldo. *El Conde Lucanor: materia tradicional y originalidad creadora*. Madrid: Ediciones José Porrúa Turanzas, 1975.

Baadj, Amar. *Saladin, the Almohads and the Banū Ghāniya*. Leiden: Brill, 2015.

Bacharach, Jere. '*Laqab* for a Future Caliph: The Case of the Abbasid al-Mahdī'. *Journal of the American Oriental Society* 113.2 (1993): 271–4.

Badawi, Muhammad Mustafa (Muṣṭafā Muḥammad Badawī). 'From Primary to Secondary Qaṣīdas: Thoughts on the Development of Classical Arabic Poetry'. *Journal of Arabic Literature* 11 (1980): 1–31.

——, ed. *Modern Arabic Literature*. Cambridge: Cambridge University Press, 1992.

Bagby, Albert. 'The Moslem in the *Cantigas* of Alfonso X, El Sabio'. *Kentucky Romance Quarterly* 20.2 (1973): 173–207.

Bakhtin, Mikhail. *The Dialogic Imagination*. Trans. Michael Holquist. Austin: Texas University Press, 1981.

——. *Rabelais and His World*. Trans. Hélène Iswolsky. Bloomington: Indiana University Press, 1984.

Balbale, Abigail Krasner. 'Cacophony'. *Journal of Medieval Iberian Studies* 5.2 (2013): 123–8.

Ballesteros Beretta, Antonio. 'Un detalle curioso de la biografía de Alfonso X'. *Boletín de la Real Academia de la Historia* 73 (1918): 408–19.

——. *Alfonso X el Sabio*. Barcelona: Salvat, 1963.

Barros, José D'Assunção. 'Poesia e poder – o trovadorismo ibérico no século XIII e a poesia satírica'. *Revista de Letras da Universidade Católica de Brasília* 3.1–2 (2010): 22–36.

al-Bāshā, Ḥasan. *Al-Alqāb al-islāmiyya fī l-tārīkh wa-l-wathā'iq wa-l-āthār*. Cairo: Maktabat al-Nahḍa al-Miṣriyya, 1957.

Bataille, Georges. *Erotism: Death and Sensuality*. Trans. Mary Dalwood. San Francisco: City Lights Books, 1986.

Baubeta, Patricia Anne Odber de. *Anticlerical Satire in Medieval Portuguese Literature*. Lewiston, NY: Edwin Mellen Press, 1992.

Baumiller, Susan Gibson. 'Satire in Tawhidi's *Akhlaq Al-wazirayn*'. Conference paper. Middle East Studies Association of North America, 1990.

Baxter, Charles. 'Dysfunctional Narratives or 'Mistakes Were Made'. *Ploughshares* 20.2/3 (autumn 1994): 67–82.

Bejarano Escanilla, Ingrid. 'Al-Mirbad: un festival de poesía en Iraq'. *Sharq Al-Andalus* 6 (1989): 207–39.

Bell, Aubrey. 'The *Cantigas de Santa Maria* of Alfonso X'. *The Modern Language Review* 10.3 (1915): 338–48.

Belting, Hans. *Florence and Baghdad: Renaissance Art and Arab Science*. Cambridge, MA: Belknap Press of Harvard University Press, 2011.

Beltran, Vincenç. 'Trovadores en la corte de Alfonso X'. *Alcanate* 5 (2006–7): 163–90.

Beltrán de Heredia, Vicente. *Bulario de la Universidad de Salamanca, 1219–1549*. 4 vols. Salamanca: Universidad de Salamanca, 2001.

Beltrán Pepió, Vicente. *Poética, poesía y sociedad en la lírica medieval*. Santiago de Compostela: Universidade de Santiago de Compostela, Servizo de Publicacions e Intercambio Científico, 2007.

Bencheikh, Jamel-Eddine. 'Les Secrétaires poètes et animateurs de cénacles aux IIe et IIIe siècles de l'Hégire'. *Journal Asiatique* 263 (1975): 265–315.

Benjamin, Walter. *The Origin of German Tragic Drama*. Trans. George Steiner. London: Blackwell Verso, 1998.

Bin Balqāsim, Nūr al-Dīn. *Aṣdā' al-mujtamaʿ wa-al-ʿaṣr fī adab Abī Ḥayyān al-Tawḥīdī*. Tripoli, Libya: al-Munsha'a al-ʿĀmma li-l-Nashr, 1984.

The Biographical Encyclopedia of Astronomers. Eds Thomas Hockey, et al. New York: Springer, 2007.

Blackmore, Josiah. 'Locating the Obscene: Approaching a Poetic Canon'. *La corónica* 26.2 (1998): 9–16.

—— and Gregory S. Hutcheson, eds. *Queer Iberia*. Durham, NC: Duke University Press, 1999.

Blevins, Jacob, ed. *Dialogism and Lyric Self-Fashioning: Bakhtin and the Voices of a Genre*. Selinsgrove, PA: Susquehanna University Press, 2002.

Bonebakker, Seeger. *Ḥātimī and his Encounter with Mutanabbī: A Biographical Sketch*. Amsterdam: North-Holland, 1984.

Bonner, Michael. *Jihad in Islamic History: Doctrines and Practice*. Princeton: Princeton University Press, 2006.

Booth, Marilyn. 'Colloquial Arabic Poetry, Politics, and the Press in Modern Egypt'. *International Journal of Middle East Studies* 24.3 (1992): 419–40.

Borovsky, Zoe. 'En hon er blandin mjök': Women and Insults in Old Norse Literature'. *Cold Counsel: Women in Old Norse Literature and Mythology*. Eds Sarah Anderson and Karen Swenson. London and New York: Routledge, 2002.

Bosworth, Clifford Edmund. 'Manuscripts of Thaʿalibi's "Yatimat Ad-Dahr" in the Suleymaniye Library, Istanbul'. *Journal of Semitic Studies* 16.1 (1971): 41–9.

——. *The Mediaeval Islamic Underworld*. 2 vols. Leiden: Brill, 1976.

Bouhdiba, Abdelwahab. *Sexuality in Islam*. Trans. Alan Sheridan. London and New York: Routledge & Kegan Paul, 1983.

Boullón Agrelo, Ana Isabel, Xosé Luís Couceiro Pérez, and Francisco Fernández Rei, eds. *As tebras alumeadas: estudos filolóxicos ofrecidos en homenaxe a Ramón Lorenzo*. Santiago de Compostela: Universidade de Santiago de Compostela, 2005.

Bourdieu, Pierre. *Outline of a Theory of Practice*. Trans. Richard Nice. Cambridge: Cambridge University Press, 1977.

——. *Distinction: A Social Critique of the Judgement of Taste*. Trans. Richard Nice. Cambridge, MA: Harvard University Press, 1984.

——. *In Other Words*. Trans. Matthew Adamson. Stanford: Stanford University Press, 1990.

——. *Language and Symbolic Power*. Ed. John B. Thompson. Trans Gino Raymond and Matthew Adamson. Cambridge, MA: Harvard University Press, 1991.

——. *The Rules of Art*. Trans. Susan Emanuel. Stanford: Stanford University Press, 1996.

——. 'The Forms of Capital'. Trans. Richard Nice. *Education: Culture, Economy, and Society*. Eds A. H. Halsey, Hugh Lauder, et al. Oxford: Oxford University Press, 1997.

Branco, António Manuel. 'O 'obsceno' em Afonso X'. *Colóquio/Letras* 115–16 (1990): 65–72. <http://coloquio.gulbenkian.pt/bib/sirius.exe/issueContentDisplay?n=115&p=65&o=r > (last accessed 5 February 2017).

Brener, Ann. *Isaac Ibn Khalfun: A Wandering Hebrew Poet of the Eleventh Century*. Leiden: Brill, 2003.

Brice, William Charles, ed. *An Historical Atlas of Islam*. Leiden: Brill, 1981.

Brittain, Frederick. *Medieval Latin and Romance Lyric*. Cambridge: Cambridge University Press, 2009.

Brookshaw, Dominic. 'Mytho-Political Remakings of Ferdowsi's Jamshid in the Lyric Poetry of Injuid and Mozaffarid Shiraz'. *Iranian Studies* 48.3 (2015): 463–87.

Browne, Edward. *A Literary History of Persia*. 2 vols. New York: Charles Scribner's Sons, 1902 and 1906.

Bruckner, Mathilde. *Narrative Invention in Twelfth-Century French Romance: The Convention of Hospitality (1160–1200)*. Lexington, KY: French Forum, 1980.

Buceta, Erasmo. 'Fecha probable de una poesía de Villasandino y de la muerte del poeta'. *Revista de Filología Española* 16 (1929): 51–8.

Bumke, Joachim. *Courtly Culture: Literature and Society in the High Middle Ages*. Trans. Thomas Dunlap. Berkeley: University of California Press, 1991.

Burns, Robert, ed. *The Worlds of Alfonso the Learned and James the Conqueror*. Princeton: Princeton University Press, 1985.

——. *Emperor of Culture: Alfonso X the Learned of Castile and his Thirteenth-Century Renaissance*. Philadelphia: University of Pennsylvania Press, 1990.

Busse, Heribert. *Chalif und Grosskönig: die Buyiden im Iraq (945–1055)*. Beirut and Wiesbaden: F. Steiner, 1969.

Cachia, Pierre. 'The Use of the Colloquial in Modern Arabic Literature'. *Journal of the American Oriental Society* 87.1 (1967): 12–22.

Callcott, Frank. *The Supernatural in Early Spain Studied in the Works of the Court of Alfonso X, El Sabio*. New York: Instituto de las Españas en los Estados Unidos, 1923.

Camille, Michael. *Image on the Edge: The Margins of Medieval Art*. Cambridge, MA: Harvard University Press, 1992.

Cardini, Franco. *Europe and Islam*. Trans. Caroline Beamish. Oxford: Blackwell, 2001.

Carmona, Fernando and Francisco J. Flores, eds. *La lengua y la literatura en tiempos de Alfonso X*. Murcia: Universidad de Murcia, 1985.

Carrión Gutiérrez, José. *Conociendo a Alfonso X El Sabio*. Murcia: Editora Regional de Murcia, 1997.

Caspi, Mishael, ed. *Oral Tradition and Hispanic Literature: Essays in Honor of Samuel G. Armistead*. New York: Garland, 1995.

Castro, Américo. *España en su historia*. Buenos Aires: Editorial Losada, 1948.
——. 'Presencia del sultán Saladino en las literaturas románicas'. *Semblanzas y estudios españoles*. Princeton: Princeton University Press, 1956.
——. *The Spaniards: An Introduction to Their History*. Trans Willard King and Selma Margaretten. Berkeley: University of California Press, 1971.
Chamberlain, Michael. *Knowledge and Social Practice in Medieval Damascus, 1190–1350*. Cambridge: Cambridge University Press, 1994.
Clarke, Dorothy. 'Alfonso X: Questions on Poetics'. *Bulletin of the Cantigueiros de Santa Maria* 1.1 (1987): 11–15.
Classen, Albrecht and Connie Scarborough, eds. *Crime and Punishment in the Middle Ages and Early Modern Age*. Berlin: Walter de Gruyter, 2012.
Clayton, Jay and Eric Rothstein. *Influence and Intertextuality in Literary History*. Madison: University of Wisconsin Press, 1991.
Cobb, Paul. *The Race for Paradise: An Islamic History of the Crusades*. Oxford: Oxford University Press, 2014.
Cohen, Jeffrey Jerome, ed. *The Postcolonial Middle Ages*. New York: Palgrave Macmillan, 2001.
Cohen, Rip. 'The Poetics of Peace: Erotic Reconciliation in the *Cantigas d'amigo*'. *La Corónica* 39.2 (2011): 95–143.
Cole, Juan. 'Review of Bernard Lewis' "What Went Wrong: Western Impact and Middle Eastern Response"'. <http://electronicintifada.net/content/review-bernard-lewis-what-went-wrong-western-impact-and-middle-eastern-response/3441> (last accessed 10 June 2014) (Original URL now inactive; see: <http://www.juancole.com/essays/revlew.htm> (last accessed 10 June 2014).
Cook, Michael. *Commanding Right and Forbidding Wrong in Islam*. Cambridge and New York: Cambridge University Press, 2000.
Cooper, Helen. *The English Romance in Time*. Oxford: Oxford University Press, 2004.
Cooperson, Michael. 'Baghdad in Rhetoric and Narrative'. *Muqarnas* 13 (1996): 99–113.
Corfis, Ivy and Ray Harris-Northall, eds. *Medieval Iberia*. Woodbridge: Tamesis, 2007.
Cormack, Lesley. *Charting an Empire: Geography at the English Universities, 1580–1620*. Chicago: University of Chicago Press, 1997.
Cortés García, Manuela. 'Presencia española en los dos primeros festivales internacionales de música de Babilonia'. *Revista de musicología* 12.1 (1989): 366–8.
Cowell, Andrew. *The Medieval Warrior Aristocracy*. Cambridge: D. S. Brewer, 2007.

Craddock, Jerry. '*El Setenario*: Ultima [*sic*] e inconclusa reundición alfonsina de la primera Partida'. *Anuario de historia del derecho español* 56 (1986): 441–66.

——. *The Legislative Works of Alfonso X, El Sabio: A Critical Bibliography*. London: Grant and Cutler, 1986.

Craig, Bruce, ed. *Ismaili and Fatimid Studies in Honor of Paul E. Walker*. Chicago: Middle East Documentation Center, 2010.

Cueto, Leopoldo Augusto de, Marqués de Valmar. *Estudio histórico, crítico y filológico sobre las Cantigas del rey Don Alfonso el Sabio*. Madrid: Real Academia Española, 1897.

Curtius, Ernst. *European Literature and the Latin Middle Ages*. Trans. Willard Trask. New York: Pantheon, 1953.

Daftari, Farhad and Josef Meri, eds. *Culture and Memory in Medieval Islam: Essays in Honour of Wilferd Madelung*. London: I. B. Tauris, 2003.

Dagenais, John. '*Cantigas d'escarnho* and *serranillas*: The Allegory of Careless Love'. *Bulletin of Hispanic Studies* [Liverpool] 68.2 (1991): 247–63.

Dajani-Shakeel, Hadia. 'Jihād in Twelfth-Century Poetry: A Moral and Religious Force to

Counter the Crusades'. *The Muslim World* 66.2 (1976): 96–113.

—— and Ronald Messier, eds. *The Jihād and Its Times*. Ann Arbor: Center for

Near Eastern and North African Studies, 1991.

Daniel, Norman. *The Arabs and Mediaeval Europe*. London: Longman, 1975.

Ḍayf, Shawqī. *Al-Fann wa-madhāhibuhu fī l-shiʿr al-ʿarabī*. Cairo: Dār al-Maʿārif, 1960.

——. *Tārīkh al-adab al-ʿarabī*. Cairo: Dār al-Maʿārif, 1980.

Deyermond, Alan. 'Baena, Santillana, Resende and the Silent Century of Portuguese Court Poetry'. *Bulletin of Hispanic Studies* [Liverpool] 59.3 (1982): 198–210.

——, ed. *One Man's Canon: Five Essays on Medieval Poetry for Stephen Reckert*. London: Department of Hispanic Studies, Queen Mary and Westfield College, 1998.

—— and Barry Taylor, eds. *From the* Cancioneiro da Vaticana *to the* Cancionero General*: Studies in Honour of Jane Whetnall*. London: Department of Hispanic Studies, Queen Mary, University of London, 2007.

Díaz-Plaja, Guillermo, ed. *Historia general de las literaturas hispánicas*. 7 vols. Barcelona: Barna, 1949.

Donohue, John. *The Buwayhid Dynasty in Iraq 334*H.*/945 to 403*H.*/1012: Shaping Institutions for the Future*. Leiden: Brill, 2002.

Donovan, Richard B. *The Liturgical Drama in Medieval Spain*. Toronto: Pontifical Institute of Mediaeval Studies, 1958.

Dunne, Bruce W. 'Homosexuality in the Middle East: An Agenda for Historical Research'. *Arab Studies Quarterly* 12.3–4 (1990): 55–82.

——. 'Power and Sexuality in the Middle East'. *MERIP* 28.206 (1998): 8–12.

Durand-Guédy, David. 'Diplomatic Practice in Salǧūq Iran'. *Oriente Moderno* 88.2 (2008): 271–96.

Al-Dūrī, ᶜAbd al-ᶜAzīz. *Tārīkh al-ᶜiraq al-iqtiṣādī fī l-qarn al-rābiᶜ al-hijrī*. Beirut: Markaz dirāsat al-waḥda al-ᶜarabiyya, 1999.

Eagleton, Terry. *Walter Benjamin: Towards a Revolutionary Criticism*. London: Verso, 1981.

Eddé, Anne-Marie. *Saladin*. Trans. Jane Marie Todd. Cambridge, MA: Harvard University Press, 2014.

Ehrenkreutz, Andrew. *Saladin*. Albany: State University of New York Press, 1972.

Eisenberg, Daniel. 'The *General Estoria*: Sources and Source Treatment'. *Zeitschrift für romanische Philologie* 89 (1973): 206–27.

El Cheikh, Nadia. '*Sūrat al-Rūm*: A Study of the Exegetical Literature'. *Journal of the American Oriental Society* 118.3 (1998): 356–64.

El-Hibri, Tayeb. *Reinterpreting Islamic Historiography: Hārūn Al-Rashīd and the Narrative of the ᶜAbbāsid Caliphate*. Cambridge: Cambridge University Press, 1999.

Encyclopedia of Arabic Literature. Eds Julie Meisami and Paul Starkey. 2 vols. London: Routledge, 1998.

Encyclopædia Iranica. Eds Ehsan Yarshater, Elton Daniel, et al. New York: Encyclopædia Iranica Foundation, 1985–2008. <http://www.iranica.com> (last accessed 5 February 2017).

Encyclopaedia of Islam, Second Edition. Eds P. J. Bearman, Th. Bianquis, C. E. Bosworth, E. van Donzel, and W. P. Heinrichs. Leiden: Brill Online, 2009. <http://www.brillonline.nl/subscriber/entry?entry=islam_title_islam> (last accessed 5 February 2017).

Entwistle, William. *The Spanish Language*. London: Faber & Faber, 1962.

Epstein, Julia and Kristina Straub, eds. *Body Guards: The Cultural Politics of Gender Ambiguity*. London and New York: Routledge, 1991.

Faci, Javier. 'Economía y sociedad en Castilla en la época de Alfonso X'. *Alfonso X: Toledo 1984*. Ed. unknown. Toledo, Spain: Ministerio de Cultura, 1984.

Fakhrī, Mājid, ed. *Al-Ḥarakāt al-fikriyya wa-ruwwāduhā al-lubnānīyūn fī ᶜaṣr al-nahḍa, 1800–1922*. Beirut: Dār al-Nahār li-l-Nashr, 1992.

Fanjul, Serafín. *Al-Andalus contra España: la forja del mito*. Madrid: Siglo XXI de España Editores, 2000.

Farrin, Raymond. *Abundance from the Desert: Classical Arabic Poetry*. Syracuse, NY: Syracuse University Press, 2011.

Farrūkh, ᶜUmar. *Tārīkh al-adab al-ᶜArabī*. Beirut: Dār al-ᶜIlm lil-Malāyīn, 1965.

Ferrante, Joan. 'The Relation of Speech to Sin in the Inferno'. *Dante Studies* 87 (1969): 33–46.

Ferreira, Ana Paula. 'A "Outra Arte" das Soldadeiras'. *Luso-Brazilian Review* 30.1 (1993): 155–66.

Ferreira, Manuel P. *O som de Martin Codax*. Lisbon: UNISYS, 1986.

Fierro, Maribel. *'Abd al-Rahman III: The First Cordoban Caliph*. Oxford: Oneworld, 2005.

——. 'Alfonso X "The Wise": The Last Almohad Caliph?' *Medieval Encounters* 15.2/4 (2009): 175–98.

Filios, Denise K. 'Women Out of Bounds: Soldadeiras, Panaderas, and Serranas in the Poetry of Medieval Spain'. Dissertation. University of California, Berkeley, 1997.

——. 'Jokes on *Soldadeiras* in the *Cantigas de escarnio e de mal dizer*'. *La corónica* 26.2 (1998): 29–39.

——. 'Female Voices in the *Cantigas de escarnio e de mal dizer*: Index and Commentary'. *Bulletin of Spanish Studies* 81.2 (2004): 135–55.

——. *Performing Women in the Middle Ages*. New York: Palgrave Macmillan, 2005.

Flory, David A. *Marian Representations in the Miracle Tales of Thirteenth-Century Spain and France*. Washington, DC: Catholic University of America Press, 2000.

Fontes, Leonardo Augusto Silva. 'A função política das *Cantigas de Santa Maria* no reino de Afonso X (Castela e Leão, 1252–1284)'. *Revista do Corpo Discente do Programa de Pós-Graduação em História da UFRGS* 2.2 (2009): 313–20.

Fontes, Manuel da Costa. 'Celestina as antithesis of the Virgin Mary'. *Journal of Hispanic Philology* 15 (1991): 7–41.

——. 'On Alfonso's "Interrupted" Encounter with a *Soldadeira*'. *Revista de Estudios Hispánicos* 31.1 (1997): 93–101.

Foster, David William, Daniel Altamiranda, and Carmen Urioste-Azcorra. *Spanish Literature. Current Debates on Hispanism*. New York: Garland Pub, 2001.

Foucault, Michel. *The Care of the Self: The History of Sexuality Volume 3*. Trans. Robert Hurley. New York: Vintage, 1986.

——. *The History of Sexuality: Volume 1: An Introduction*. Trans. Robert Hurley. New York: Vintage, 1990.

——. *The Use of Pleasure: The History of Sexuality Volume 2*. Trans. Robert Hurley. New York: Vintage, 1990.

——. *The Hermeneutics of the Subject*. Ed. Frédéric Gros. Trans. Graham Burchell. New York: Palgrave Macmillan, 2005.

——. *The Order of Things: An Archaeology of the Human Sciences*. [Trans. not noted.] London and New York: Routledge Classics, 2005.

Fraker, Charles F. *The Scope of History: Studies in the Historiography of Alfonso el Sabio*. Ann Arbor: University of Michigan Press, 1996.

Freccero, John. *Dante: The Poetics of Conversion*. Cambridge, MA: Harvard University Press, 1986.

Fuentes, Carlos. *The Buried Mirror: Reflections on Spain and the New World*. Boston: Houghton Mifflin, 1992.

Gabrieli, Francesco. *Arab Historians of the Crusades*. Trans. E. J. Costello. London and New York: Routledge, 2010.

García González, Javier. 'El contacto de dos lenguas: los arabismos en el español medieval y en la obra alfonsí'. *Cahiers de linguistique hispanique médiévale* 18–19 (1993): 335–65.

Gelder, Geert van. *Beyond the Line: Classical Arabic Literary Critics on the Coherence and Unity of the Poem*. Leiden: Brill, 1982.

——. 'Against Women and Other Pleasantries: The Last Chapter of Abū Tammām's "Ḥamāsa"'. *Journal of Arabic Literature* 16 (1985): 61–72.

——. *The Bad and the Ugly: Attitudes towards Invective Poetry (*Hijā'*) in Classical Arabic Literature*. Leiden: Brill, 1988.

——. 'Mixtures of Jest and Earnest in Classical Arabic Literature'. *Journal of Arabic Literature* 23 (1992): 83–108.

——. 'Mixtures of Jest and Earnest in Classical Arabic Literature. Part II'. *Journal of Arabic Literature* 23 (1992): 169–90.

——. 'Al-Mutanabbī's Encumbering Trifles'. *Arabic and Middle Eastern Literatures* 2.1 (1999): 5–19.

——. 'Some Brave Attempts at Generic Classification in Premodern Arabic Literature'.' *Aspects of Genre and Type in Pre-Modern Literary Cultures*. Eds Bert Roest and Herman Vanstiphout. Groningen: Styx, 1999. 15–31.

——. *Close relationships: Incest and Inbreeding in Classical Arabic Literature*. London: I. B. Tauris, 2005.

Genette, Gérard. *Narrative Discourse*. Trans. Jane Lewin. Ithaca: Cornell University Press, 1980.

——. *Palimpsests: Literature in the Second Degree*. Trans Channa Newman and Claude Doubinsky. Lincoln, NE: University of Nebraska Press, 1997.

Gibb, Hamilton (H. A. R.). *Studies on the Civilization of Islam*. Boston: Beacon, 1962.

Giffen, Lois Anita. *Theory of Profane Love among the Arabs: The Development of the Genre*. New York: New York University Press, 1971.

Glünz, M. 'The Sword, the Pen, and the Phallus: Metaphors and Metonymies of Male Power and Creativity in Medieval Persian Poetry'. *Edebiyât* 6 (1995): 223–43.

Goffman, Erving. *Stigma*. New York: Simon & Schuster, 1986.

Goitein, Shelomo. *A Mediterranean Society: The Jewish Communities of the Arab World as Portrayed in the Documents of the Cairo Geniza, 1900–1985*. 6 vols. Berkeley: University of California Press, 1967.

Goldberg, Jonathan. *Sodometries*. New York: Fordham University Press, 2010.

Goncalves, Elsa. '"*Triplici correctus amore*". A propósito de una nota de Angelo Colocci no Cancioneiro da Biblioteca Nacional de Lisboa'. *Cultura neolatina* 66.1–2 (2006): 83–104.

González, Cristina. *La tercera crónica de Alfonso X: «La gran conquista de ultramar»*. London: Tamesis, 1992.

González-Casanovas, Roberto. 'Didáctica y Bildung en *El Conde Lucanor*: Del consejo a la educación de Saladino'. *Anuario Medieval* 2 (1990): 78–90.

González Jiménez, Manuel. 'Alfonso X, poeta profano'. *Boletín de la Real academia Sevillana de Buenas Letras: Minervae Baeticae* 35 (2007): 105–26.

Goody, Jack. *The Domestication of the Savage Mind*. Cambridge: Cambridge University Press, 1977.

——. *The East in the West*. Cambridge: Cambridge University Press, 1996.

Greenia, George. 'The Politics of Piety: Manuscript Illumination and Narration in the *Cantigas de Santa Maria*'. *Hispanic Review* 61.3 (1993): 325–44.

Gregg, Joan. *Devils, Women, and Jews*. Albany: State Univerity of New York Press, 2012.

Gruendler, Beatrice. *Medieval Arabic Praise Poetry: Ibn Al-Rūmī and the Patron's Redemption*. London: RoutledgeCurzon, 2003.

Guerrero Lovillo, José. *Las Cántigas, estudio arqueológico de sus miniaturas*. Madrid: Consejo Superior de Investigaciones Científicas, 1949.

Guillory, John. *Cultural Capital: The Problem of Literary Canon Formation*. Chicago: University of Chicago Press, 1994.

Gully, Adrian. *The Culture of Letter-Writing in Pre-Modern Islamic Society*. Edinburgh: Edinburgh University Press, 2008.

Gutas, Dimitri. *Greek Thought, Arabic Culture*. London and New York: Routledge, 1998.

Hachmeier, Klaus. 'Private Letters, Official Correspondence: Buyid *Inshā'* as a Historical Source'. *Journal of Islamic Studies* 13.2 (2002): 125–54.

Haidu, Peter. *The Subject Medieval/Modern: Text and Governance in the Middle Ages*. Stanford: Stanford University Press, 2004.

Ḥajjār, Najma. *Madīḥ al-nabī fī l-shiʿr wa-l-ghinā' al-ʿarabī*. Beirut: Bīsān, 2012.

Halasā, Ghālib. *Al-ʿĀlam, mādda wa-ḥaraka*. Beirut: Dār al-Kalima li-l-Nashr, 1980.

Hallberg, Robert von, ed. *Canons*. Chicago and London: University of Chicago Press, 1984.

Hamori, Andras. *On the Art of Medieval Arabic Literature*. Princeton: Princeton University Press, 1974.

——. 'The Silken Horsecloths Shed their Tears'. *Arabic and Middle Eastern Literatures* 2.1 (1999): 43–59.

Hampton, Timothy. *Writing from History: The Rhetoric of Exemplarity in Renaissance Literature*. Ithaca: Cornell University Press, 1990.

Hanawalt, Barbara and Michal Kobialka, eds. *Medieval Practices of Space*. Minneapolis: University of Minnesota Press, 2000.

Hanne, Eric J. *Putting the Caliph in His Place: Power, Authority, and the Late Abbasid Caliphate*. Madison and Teaneck: Fairleigh Dickinson University Press, 2007.

Heemskerk, Margaretha. *Suffering in the Muʿtazilite Theology*. Leiden: Brill, 2000.

Hermes, Nizar. *The [European] Other in Medieval Arabic Literature and Culture*. New York: Palgrave Macmillan, 2012.

Heyd, Wilhelm. *Histoire du commerce du Levant*. Leipzig: Harrassowitz, 1923.

Hillenbrand, Carole. *The Crusades: Islamic Perspectives*. London and New York: Routledge, 2000.

Hirschkind, Charles. 'Cultures of Death: Media, Religion, Bioethics'. *Social Text* 26.3 (2008): 39–58.

Hirschler, Konrad. *Medieval Arabic Historiography: Authors as Actors*. London and New York: Routledge, 2006.

Hitchcock, Richard. 'Don Juan Manuel's Knowledge of Arabic'. *The Modern Language Review* 80.3 (1985): 594–603.

Hitti, Philip. *History of Syria Including Lebanon and Palestine*. Piscataway: Gorgias Press, 2002.

Hodgson, Natasha. *Women, Crusading and the Holy Land in Historical Narrative*. Suffolk: Boydell Press, 2007.

Holsinger, Bruce. *The Premodern Condition: Medievalism and the Making of Theory*. Chicago: University of Chicago Press, 2005.

Holt, P. M. et al., eds. *The Cambridge History of Islam*. 2 vols. Cambridge: Cambridge University Press, 1977.

Huart, Clément. *A History of Arabic Literature*. Trans. Edmund Gosse. New York: D. Appleton, 1903.

Humphreys, R. Stephen. *From Saladin to the Mongols: The Ayyubids of Damascus, 1193–1260*. Albany: State University of New York Press, 1977.

Ḥusayn, Ṭāhā. *Maᶜa al-Mutanabbī*. Cairo: Dār al-maᶜārif, 1962.

——. *Mustaqbal al-thaqāfa fī miṣr*. Beirut: Markaz dirāsāt al-wiḥda al-ᶜarabiyya, 1994.

Ibn Ḥazm, Abū Muḥammad. *Rasā'il*. Ed. Iḥsān ᶜAbbās. Cairo: Maktabat al-khānjī, 1954.

Ibn Jaᶜfar, Qudāma: see Qudāma.

Ibn Khallikān, Shams al-Dīn. *Kitāb wafayāt al-aᶜyān: Ibn Khallikan's Biographical Dictionary*. Trans. William MacGuckin Slane. 4 vols. Paris: Oriental Translation Fund of Great Britain and Ireland, 1842.

——. *Wafayāt al-aᶜyān wa-abnā' al-zamān*. Ed. Iḥsān ᶜAbbās. 8 vols. Beirut: Dār Ṣādir, 1968–77.

Ibn Manẓūr, Muḥammad. *Līsān al-ᶜarab*. Eds Yūsuf Khayyāṭ and Nadīm Marᶜashlī. 4 vols. Beirut: Dār Līsān al-ᶜArab, 1970.

Ibn Maᶜṣūm al-Madanī. *Anwār al-rabīᶜ fī anwā' al-badīᶜ*. Ed. Shākir Hādī Shukr. 7 vols. Najaf: Maṭbaᶜat al-Nuᶜmān, 1968–9.

Möhring, Hannes. *Saladin: The Sultan and His Times, 1138–1193*. Trans. David Bachrach. Baltimore: Johns Hopkins University Press, 2008.

Ibn al-Muᶜtazz, ᶜAbd Allāh. *Ṭabaqāt al-shuᶜarā'*. Ed. ᶜAbd al-Sattār Aḥmad Farrāj. Cairo: Dār al-Maᶜārif, 1956.

Ibn Rashīq al-Qayrawānī, Abū ᶜAlī. *Al-ᶜUmda fī maḥāsin al-shiᶜr wa-ādābihi wa-naqdihi*. Ed. Muḥammad Muḥyī al-Dīn ᶜAbd al-Ḥamīd. 2 vols. Beirut: Dār al-Jīl, 1981.

Iglesia, Antonio. *El idioma gallego: su antigüedad y vida*. 3 vols. La Coruña: La voz de Galicia, 1886.

Irwin, Robert. 'The Image of the Byzantine and the Frank in Arab Popular Literature of the Late Middle Ages'. *Mediterranean Historical Review* 4.1 (1989): 226–42.

——. 'Mamluk Literature'. *Mamlūk Studies Review* 7 (2003): 1–30.

——. 'Political Thought in *The Thousand and One Nights*'. *Marvels & Tales* 18.2 (2004): 246–57.

Izquierdo Benito, Ricardo and Ángel Sáenz-Badillos, eds. *La sociedad medieval a través de la literatura hispanojudía*. Cuenca: Universidad de Castilla-La Mancha, 1998.

al-Jābirī, Muḥammad ᶜĀbid. *al-Khitāb al-ᶜarabī al-muᶜāṣir*. Beirut: Dār al-ṭalīᶜa, 1982.

Jackson, Gabriel. *The Making of Medieval Spain*. London: Thames and Hudson, 1972.

Jacob, Georg. *Geschichte des Schattentheaters im Morgen- und Abendland*. Hannover: Orient-Buchhandlung Heinz Lafaire, 1925.

Jakobson, Roman. *Language in Literature*. Eds Krystyna Pomorska and Stephen Rudy. Cambridge, MA: Belknap Press of Harvard University Press, 1987.

—— and Jurij Tynjanov. 'Problems in the Study of Language and Literature'. Trans. Herbert Eagle. *Poetics Today* 2.1A (1980): 29–31.

Jayyusi, Salma Khadra, Renata Holod, Attilio Petruccioli, and André Raymond, eds. *The City in the Islamic World*. 2 vols. Leiden: Brill, 2008.

Jensen, Frede. *The Earliest Portuguese Lyrics*. Odense: Odense University Press, 1978.

Jensen, Kurt Villads, Kirsi Salonen, and Helle Vogt, eds. *Cultural Encounters during the Crusades*. Odense: University Press of Southern Denmark, 2013.

Jorgensen, Cory. 'Jarīr and al-Farazdaq's *Naqā'iḍ* Performance as Social Commentary'. Dissertation. University of Texas, 2012.

Jubb, Margaret. *The Legend of Saladin in Western Literature and Historiography*. Lewiston, NY: Edwin Mellen Press, 2000.

Kabir, Ananya and Deanne Williams, eds. *Postcolonial Approaches to the European Middle Ages: Translating Cultures*. Cambridge: Cambridge University Press, 2005.

Kabir, Mafizullah. 'Cultural Development under the Buwayhids of Baghdād'. *Journal of the Asiatic Society* [Pakistan] 1 (1956): 25–45.

——. *The Buwayhid Dynasty of Baghdad, 334/946–447/1055*. Calcutta: Iran Society, 1964.

Kadhim, Hussein. 'The Poetics of Postcolonialism: Two *Qaṣīdah*s by Aḥmad Shawqī'. *Journal of Arabic Literature* 28.3 (1997): 179–218.

Kaeuper Richard. *Chivalry and Violence in Medieval Europe*. Oxford: Oxford University Press, 2001.

Kafadar, Cemal. 'A Rome of One's Own: Reflections on Cultural Geography and Identity in the Lands of Rum'. *Muqarnas* 24 (2007): 7–25.

Kahl, Oliver and Zeina Matar. 'The Horoscope of aṣ-Ṣāḥib ibn ᶜAbbād'. *Zeitschrift der Deutschen Morgenländischen Gesellschaft* 140 (1990): 28–31.

Kamen, Henry. *Imagining Spain: Historical Myth and National Identity*. New Haven: Yale University Press, 2008.

Keller, John E. *Pious Brief Narrative in Medieval Castilian and Galician Verse*. Lexington: University Press of Kentucky, 1978.

Kelly, Kathleen Coyne. *Performing Virginity and Testing Chastity in the Middle Ages*. London and New York: Routledge, 2002.

Kelty, Christopher. 'Geeks, Social Imaginaries, and Recursive Publics'. *Cultural Anthropology* 20.2 (2005): 185–214.

Kennedy, Philip F. *The Wine Song in Classical Arabic Poetry: Abū Nuwās and the Literary Tradition*. Oxford: Clarendon Press, 1997.

——. *Abu Nuwas: A Genius of Poetry*. Oxford: Oneworld, 2005.

Khalidi, Tarif. *Arabic Historical Thought in the Classical Period*. Cambridge: Cambridge University Press, 1994.

Khān, M. A. Muᶜīd. 'Aṣ-Ṣāḥib ibn ᶜAbbād as a Writer and Poet'. *Islamic Culture* 17 (1943): 176–205.

Kilito, Abdelfattah (ᶜAbd al-Fattāḥ Kīlīṭū). *Al-Maqāmāt: al-sard wa-al-ansāq al-thaqāfiyya*. Trans. ᶜAbd al-Karīm Sharqāwī. Casablanca: Dār Tūbqāl li-l-Nashr, 1993.

——. *The Author and His Doubles: Essays on Classical Arabic Culture*. Trans. Michael Cooperson. Syracuse: Syracuse University Press, 2001.

Kinberg, Naphtali. *Studies in the Linguistic Structure of Classical Arabic*. Leiden: Brill, 2000.

Kingdom of Heaven. Dir. Ridley Scott. 20th Century Fox, 2005.

Kinkade, Richard P. 'Alfonso X, *Cantiga* 235, and the Events of 1269–1278'. *Speculum* 67.2 (1992): 284–323.

Kinoshita, Sharon. '"Noi siamo mercatanti cipriani": How to Do Things in the Medieval Mediterranean'. *Philippe de Mézières and his Age*. Eds Renate Blumenfeld-Kosinski and Kiril Petkov. Leiden: Brill, 2012. 41–60.

Kraemer, Joel L. *Humanism in the Renaissance of Islam: The Cultural Revival during the Buyid Age*. Leiden: Brill, 1986.

——. *Philosophy in the Renaissance of Islam: Abū Sulaymān al-Sijistānī and his Circle*. Leiden: Brill, 1986.

Kurke, Leslie. *The Traffic in Praise*. Ithaca: Cornell University Press, 1991.

Lagrange, Frédéric. 'The Obscenity of the Vizier'. *Islamicate Sexualities*. Eds Kathryn Babayan and Afsaneh Najmabadi. Cambridge, MA: Harvard University Press, 2008. 161–203.

Laiou, Angeliki and Roy Mottahedeh. *The Crusades from the Perspective of*

Byzantium and the Muslim World. Washington, DC: Dumbarton Oaks, 2001.

Landes, David. *The Wealth and Poverty of Nations.* New York: W. W. Norton, 1999.

Lane, E. W. *Arabic-English Lexicon.* Cambridge: Islamic Texts Society, 1984. First published 1863–93.

Lange, Christian and Songul Mecit, eds. *The Seljuqs: Politics, Society and Culture.* Edinburgh: Edinburgh University Press, 2011.

Lapa, Manuel Rodrigues. *Vocabulário galego-português.* Coimbra: Editorial Galaxia, 1965.

——. *Liçoes de literatura portuguesa, época medieval.* Coimbra: Coimbra editora, 1970.

Larkin, Margaret. *Al-Mutanabbi: Voice of the 'Abbasid Poetic Ideal.* Oxford: Oneworld, 2008.

Lefever, Harry. '"Playing the Dozens": A Mechanism for Social Control'. *Phylon* 42.1 (1981): 73–85.

Lefevere, André. *Translation, Rewriting, and the Manipulation of Literary Fame.* London and New York: Routledge, 1992.

Legman, G. *Rationale of the Dirty Joke: An Analysis of Sexual Humor.* New York: Simon & Schuster, 2006.

Lemaire, Jacques. *Les visions de la vie de cour dans la littérature française de la fin du Moyen Âge.* Paris: Klincksieck, 1994.

Lev, Yaacov. *Saladin in Egypt.* Leiden: Brill, 1998.

Lévi-Strauss, Claude. *The Elementary Structures of Kinship.* Ed. Rodney Needham. Trans James Bell and John von Sturmer. Boston: Beacon Press, 1969.

Levy, Reuben. *The Social Structure of Islam.* Cambridge: Cambridge University Press, 1969.

Lewis, Bernard. *The Muslim Discovery of Europe.* 2001. Reprint. New York: W. W. Norton, 1982.

——. *Islam and the West.* Oxford: Oxford University Press, 1993.

——. *What Went Wrong?* Oxford: Oxford University Press, 2002.

——. *The Crisis of Islam: Holy War and Unholy Terror.* New York: Random House, 2004.

Lindsey, Ursula. 'A Voice of Dissent Joins the Nationalist Chorus'. *Mada Masr* 6 October 2013. <http://www.madamasr.com/sections/culture/voice-dissent-joins-nationalist-chorus> (last accessed 5 February 2017).

Linehan, Peter. *The Spanish Church and the Papacy in the Thirteenth Century.* Cambridge: Cambridge University Press, 1971.

——. 'The Politics of Piety: Aspects of the Castilian Monarchy from Alfonso X to Alfonso XI'. *Revista Canadiense de Estudios Hispánicos* 9.3 (1985): 385–404.

——. *Spain, 1157–1300: A Partible Inheritance*. Oxford: Blackwell, 2008.

Lings, M. 'Unique Arabic Manuscript. (Al-Muḥīṭ fī l-Lugha of Ismāᶜīl Ibn ᶜAbbād.)'. *British Museum Quarterly* 29 (1965): 15.

Liu, Benjamin M. *Medieval Joke Poetry: The Cantigas d'escarnho e de mal dizer*. Cambridge, MA: Harvard University Press, 2004.

——. 'Joke Work and Sex Work: Courtiers and *Soldadeiras*'. *Revista Eletrônica de Estudos Literários* 1.5.5 (2009): 1–9.

Lodge, David and Nigel Wood, eds. *Modern Criticism and Theory: A Reader*. 3rd edn. Harlow, London, and New York: Pearson Longman, 2008.

Lowry, S. Todd and Barry Lewis, eds. *Ancient and Medieval Economic Ideas and Concepts of Social Justice*. Leiden: Brill, 1998.

Lucas, E. V. *A Boswell of Baghdad*. New York: George H. Doran Co., 1917.

Lynch, James. 'The Uses of Saladin in Medieval and Early Modern Literature'. Dissertation. Indiana University, 2011.

Lyons, M. C. and D. E. P. Jackson. *Saladin: The Politics of the Holy War*. Cambridge: Cambridge University Press, 1982.

McCash, June Hall. 'Negotiating the Text: Women Patrons in the Poetic Process'. *Romance Philology* 57 (2004): 27–43.

McKinney, Robert C. *The Case of Rhyme Versus Reason: Ibn al-Rūmī and his Poetics in Context*. Leiden: Brill, 2004.

Madden, Marie. *Political Theory and Law in Medieval Spain*. New York: Fordham University Press, 1930.

Madden, Thomas, James Naus, and Vincent Ryan, eds. *Crusades: Medieval Worlds in Conflict*. Surrey: Ashgate, 2010.

Madelung, Wilfred. 'The Assumption of the Title Shāhānshāh by the Būyids and "The Reign of the Daylam (*Dawlat Al-Daylam*)"'. *Journal of Near Eastern Studies* 28.2 (1969): 84–108.

——. *Religious Schools and Sects in Medieval Islam*. London: Variorum Reprints, 1985.

Maḥmūd, Ibrāhīm. *Al-Mutʿa al-maḥẓūra*. Beirut: Riyāḍ al-Rayyis li-l-Kutub wa-l-Nashr, 2000.

Makkī, al-Ṭāhir. *Dirāsa fī maṣādir al-adab*. Cairo: Dār al-fikr al-ᶜarabī, 1999.

Malik, M. Mubariz. 'Life and Works of Al-Sahib-Ibn Abbad with a Critical Edition of His Al-Muhit (First 60 Folios)'. Dissertation. University of the Punjab, 1985.

Mann, Vivian, Thomas Glick, et al., eds. *Convivencia: Jews, Muslims, and Christians in Medieval Spain*. New York: G. Braziller, 1992.

Mansilla, Demetrio. *Iglesia castellano-leonesa y curia romana en los tiempos del rey San Fernando*. Madrid: Consejo Superior de Investigaciones Científicas, 1945.

Marcenaro, Simone. 'Tipologías de la equivocatio en la lírica gallego-portuguesa'. La *corónica* 38.1 (2009): 163–89.

Mardam, Khalīl. *Al-Ṣāḥib ibn ʿAbbād*. Damascus: Maṭbaʿat al-Taraqqī, 1932.

Margoliouth, David Samuel. 'The Legend of the Apostasy of Maimonides'. *Jewish Quarterly Review* 13.3 (1901): 539–41.

——. 'Indices of the Diwan of Abu Tammam'. *Journal of the Royal Asiatic Society* 37.4 (1905): 763–82.

Márquez Villanueva, Francisco. 'Las lecturas del deán de Cádiz'. *Studies on the Cantigas de Santa Maria: Art, Music, and Poetry*. Eds Israel J. Katz and John E. Keller. Madison, WI: Hispanic Seminary of Medieval Studies, 1987. 329–54.

——. *El concepto cultural alfonsí*. Madrid: MAPFRE, 1994.

——. 'Ways and Means of Science in Medieval Spain'. *European Review* 16.2 (2008): 145–57.

—— and Carlos Alberto Vega, eds. *Alfonso X of Castile:* Cambridge, MA: Department of Romance Languages and Literatures of Harvard University, 1990.

Marsot: see Al-Sayyid-Marsot.

Martin, Georges, ed. *La historia alfonsí: el modelo y sus destinos (siglos XIII–XV)*. Madrid: Casa de Velázquez, 2000.

Martínez Montávez, Pedro. 'Relaciones de Alfonso X de Castilla con el sultán mameluco Baybars y sus sucesores'. *Al-Andalus* 27.2 (1963): 343–76.

Martínez Pereiro, Carlos Paulo. 'Del combate singular al singular combate sexual en la sátira trovadoresca medieval gallego-portuguesa'. *Floema* 5.5 (2009): 17–32.

Masciandaro, Franco. *The Stranger as Friend: The Poetics of Friendship in Homer, Dante, and Boccaccio*. Florence (Firenze): Firenze University Press, 2013.

Mason, Herbert. 'Impressions of an Arabic Poetry Festival'. *Religion & Literature* 20.1 (1988): 157–61.

Masson, Georgina. *Frederick II of Hohenstaufen: A Life*. London: Secker & Warburg, 1957.

Mazrui, Ali. 'African Islam and Competitive Religion: Between Revivalism and Expansion'. *Third World Quarterly* 10.2 (1988): 499–518.

Medieval Iberia: An Encyclopedia. Ed. E. Michael Gerli. London and New York: Routledge, 2003.

Meisami, Julie Scott. 'Dynastic History and Ideals of Kingship in Bayhaqi's *Tārīkh-i Masʿūdī*'. *Edebiyât* 3.1 (1989): 57–77.

——. 'Arabic *Mujūn* Poetry: The Literary Dimension'. *Verse and the Fair Sex*. Ed.

Frederick De Jong. Utrecht: Publications of the M. Th. Houtsma Stichting, 1993. 8–30.

——. *Structure and Meaning in Medieval Arabic and Persian Poetry: Orient Pearls.* London: RoutledgeCurzon, 2003.

Menéndez Pidal, Gonzalo. 'Cómo trabajaron las escuelas alfonsíes'. *Nueva revista de filología hispánica* 5.4 (1951): 363–80.

Menéndez Pidal, Ramón. *España, eslabón entre la cristiandad y el islam.* Madrid: Espasa-Calpe, 1956.

——. *Poesía juglaresca y juglares: aspectos de la historia literaria y cultural de España.* Madrid: Espasa-Calpe, 1962.

Menocal, Maria Rosa. *The Ornament of the World.* Boston: Little, Brown and Company, 2002.

Mez, Adam. *The Renaissance of Islam.* Trans Salahuddin Khuda Bakhsh and D. S. Margoliouth. New Delhi: Kitab Bhavan, 1995.

Michelson, Peter. *Speaking the Unspeakable: A Poetics of Obscenity.* Albany: State University of New York Press, 1993.

Mignolo, Walter. 'Globalization and the Geopolitics of Knowledge'. *Nepantla: Views from South* 4.1 (2003): 97–119.

Miles, George Carpenter. *The Numismatic History of Rayy: Numismatic Studies, no. 2.* New York: American Numismatic Society, 1938.

Möhring, Hans. *Saladin: The Sultan and his Times, 1138–1193.* Trans. David Bachrach. Baltimore: Johns Hopkins University Press, 2008.

Mondéjar, José and Jesús Montoya [Martínez], eds. *Estudios alfonsíes.* Granada: University of Granada, 1985.

Monroe, James T. *The Art of Badīʿ Az-Zamān Al-Hamadhānī As Picaresque Narrative.* Beirut: Center for Arab and Middle East Studies, American University of Beirut, 1983.

—— and Mark F. Pettigrew. 'The Decline of Courtly Patronage and the Appearance of New Genres in Arabic Literature'. *Journal of Arabic Literature* 34 (2003): 138–77.

Montgomery, James E. *The Vagaries of the Qaṣīdah.* Cambridge: E. J. W. Gibb Memorial Trust, 1997.

Montoya Martínez, Jesús. 'El milagro de Teófilo en Coinci, Berceo y Alfonso X el Sabio. Estudio comparativo'. *Berceo* 87 (1974): 151–85.

——. 'El carácter lúdico de la literatura medieval'. *Homenaje al profesor Antonio Gallego Morell.* Eds. C. Argente del Castillo, et al. Granada: Universidad de Granada, 1989. 431–42.

—— and Ana Domínguez Rodríguez, eds. *El Scriptorium alfonsí: de los Libros de Astrología a las 'Cantigas de Santa María'.* Madrid: Editorial Complutense, 1999.

Morgan, David. 'Persian Perceptions of Mongols and Europeans'. *Implicit Understandings.* Ed. Stuart Schwartz. Cambridge: Cambridge University Press, 1994. 201–17.

Mottahedeh, Roy. *Loyalty and Leadership in an Early Islamic Society.* Princeton: Princeton University Press, 1980.

Mu'id Khan, M. A. 'As-Sahib Ibn-`Abbad as a Writer and Poet'. *Islamic Culture* 17 (1943): 176–205.

Murray, Stephen and Will Roscoe, eds. *Islamic Homosexualities: Culture, History, and Literature.* New York: New York University Press, 1997.

Al-Musawi, Muhsin (Muḥsin al-Mūsawī). 'Abbasid Popular Narrative: The Formation of Readership and Cultural Production'. *Journal of Arabic Literature* 38 (2007): 261–92.

Naaman, Erez. *Literature and the Islamic Court: Cultural Life under al-Ṣāḥib Ibn ʿAbbād.* London and New York: Routledge, 2016.

Neuwirth, Angelika. 'A Quarreling Couple in Court'. *Fī miḥrāb al-maʿrifa: dirāsāt muhdāh ilā iḥsān ʿabbās.* Ed. Ibrāhīm Saʿāfin. Beirut: Dār al-Gharb al-Islāmī, 1997.

Nicholson, Reynold Alleyne. *A Literary History of the Arabs.* New York: C. Scribner's Sons, 1907.

Nicolle, David. *The Crusades.* Oxford: Osprey Publishing, 2001.

Niederehe, Hans-J. *Alfonso X el Sabio y la lingüística de su tiempo.* Trans. Carlos Melches. Madrid: Sociedad General Española de Librería, 1987.

——. 'Lenguas peninsulares en tiempos de Alfonso X'. *Boletín de la Sociedad Española de la Historiagrafía Lingüística* 6 (2008): 13–28.

Nieto Soria, José Manuel. *Las relaciones monarquía-episcopado castellano como sistema de poder, 1252–1312.* 2 vols. Madrid: Universidad Complutense de Madrid, 1983.

——. *Iglesia y poder real en Castilla: el espiscopado, 1250–1350.* Madrid: Universidad Complutense de Madrid, 1988.

Nirenberg, David. *Communities of Violence: Persecution of Minorities in the Middle Ages.* Princeton: Princeton University Press, 1996.

——. 'Conversion, Sex, and Segregation: Jews and Christians in Medieval Spain'. *The American Historical Review* 107.4 (2002): 1,065–93.

Nodar Manso, Francisco. 'El carácter dramático-narrativo del escarnio y maldecir de Alfonso X'. *Revista Canadiense de Estudios Hispánicos* 9 (1985): 405–21.

——. 'La parodia de la literatura heroica y hagiográfica en las cantigas de escarnio y mal decir'. *DICENDA: Cuadernos de Filologia Hispánica* 9 (1990): 151–61.

——. *Teatro menor galaico-portugués (siglo XIII)*. Kassel: Universidad de La Coruña, Edition Reichenberger, 1990.

Noorani, Yaseen. 'Heterotopia and the Wine Poem in Early Islamic Culture'. *International Journal of Middle East Studies* 36.3 (2004): 345–66.

O'Callaghan, Joseph. *A History of Medieval Spain*. Ithaca: Cornell University Press, 1983.

——. *The Learned King: The Reign of Alfonso X of Castile*. Philadelphia: University of Pennsylvania Press, 1993. <http://www.questia.com/PM.qst?a=o&d=27831626>.

——. *Alfonso X and the* Cantigas de Santa Maria*: A Poetic Biography*. Leiden: Brill, 1998.

——. *Reconquest and Crusade in Medieval Spain*. Philadelphia: University of Pennsylvania Press, 2003.

——. *The Gibraltar Crusade: Castile and the Battle for the Strait*. Philadelphia: University of Pennsylvania Press, 2011.

Ortiz de la Rosa, Mariana. 'El personaje de Saladino en la literatura hispánica: los ejemplos XXV y L de *El Conde Lucanor* de Don Juan Manuel'. *Ensayos: Revista de la Facultad de Educación de Albacete* 13 (1998): 105–18.

O'Sullivan, Daniel and Shepard, Laurie, eds. *Shaping Courtliness in Medieval France: Essays in Honor of Matilda Tomaryn Bruckner*. Woodbridge: Boydell & Brewer, 2013. Ebook Library. Web. 7 October 2014.

Ouyang, Wen-chin. *Literary Criticism in Medieval Arabic-Islamic Culture: The Making of a Tradition*. Edinburgh: Edinburgh University Press, 1997.

Oxford English Dictionary, Second Edition. Ed. John Simpson. Oxford: Oxford University Press, 2009. <http://www.oed.com.ezproxy.library.wisc.edu> (last accessed 4 February 2017).

Paden, William. 'Chronology of Genres in Medieval Galician-Portuguese Lyric Poetry'. *La corónica* 26.1 (1997): 183–201.

——. 'Contrafacture between Occitan and Galician-Portuguese'. *La corónica* 26.2 (1998): 49–63.

——. 'Principles of Generic Classification in the Medieval European Lyric: The Case of Galician-Portuguese'. *Speculum* 81 (2006): 76–96.

Paredes, Juan [Juan Paredes Nuñez]. 'Representaciones del poder político en las *Cantigas de escarnio y maldecir* de Alfonso X'. *Cahiers d'études hispaniques médiévales* 27 (2004): 263–76.

——. 'Las cantigas de escarnio y las genealogías peninsulares: notas sobre algunos personajes del cancionero alfonsí'. *Revista de Filología Románica* 27 (2010): 131–42.

Paris, Gaston. *La légende de Saladin*. Paris: Imprimerie nationale, 1893.

Pedersen, Johannes. *Israel: Its Life and Culture*. 2 vols. London: Oxford University Press, 1964.

Peters, Rudolph, ed. *Proceedings of the Ninth Congress of the Union Européenne des Arabisants et Islamisants*. Leiden: Brill, 1981.

Petry, Carl. *Protectors or Praetorians? The Last Mamluk Sultans and Egypt's Waning as a Great Power*. Albany: State University of New York Press, 1994.

Philipp, Thomas and Ulrich Haarmann, eds. *The Mamluks in Egyptian Politics and Society*. Cambridge: Cambridge University Press, 1998.

Piscatori, James. 'The Turmoil Within: The Struggle for the Future of the Islamic World'. *Foreign Affairs* 81.3: 145–50.

Pomerantz, Maurice. 'Licit Magic and Divine Grace: The Life and Letters of al-Ṣāḥib Ibn ᶜAbbād'. Dissertation. University of Chicago, 2010.

Prado-Vilar, Francisco. 'The Parchment of the Sky: *Poeiesis* of a Gothic Universe'. *Las Cantigas de Santa María: Códice Rico, Ms. T-I-1*. Eds Laura Fernández Fernández and Juan Carlos Ruiz Souza. Madrid: Patrimonio Nacional: Testimonio Compañía Editorial, 2011. 474–520.

Presilla, Maricel. 'The Image of Death in the *Cantigas de Santa Maria* of Alfonso X (1252–84): The Politics of Death and Salvation'. Dissertation. New York University, 1989.

Procter, Evelyn. *Alfonso X of Castile*. Oxford: Oxford University Press, 1951.

Pucci, Pietro. *The Song of the Sirens: Essays on Homer*. Lanham: Rowman & Littlefield, 1998.

al-Qāḍī, Fārūq. *Āfāq al-tamarrud*. Beirut: Al-Mu'assasa al-ᶜArabiyya li-l-Dirāsāt wa-l-Nashr, 2004.

al-Qayrawānī, Abū ᶜAlī ibn Rashīq: see *Ibn Rashīq*.

Qudāma ibn Jaᶜfar. *Naqd al-shiᶜr: The Kitāb Naqd Al-Šiᶜr of Qudāma B. Ǧaᶜfar Al-Kātib Al-Baġdādī*. Ed. Seger Adrianus Bonebakker. Leiden: Brill, 1956.

Quṭb, Sayyid. *Al-Naqd al-adabī*. Cairo: Dār al-Shurūq, 1980.

Recueil des historiens des croisades. Historiens Occidentaux. 5 vols. Paris: Académie des inscriptions et belles-lettres, 1844–95.

Remensnyder, Amy. *La Conquistadora: The Virgin Mary at War and Peace in the Old and New Worlds*. Oxford: Oxford University Press, 2014.

Rescher, Oskar. *Alphabetischer Index zur Jetîmâ ed-Dahr des Taʿâlibî [Damaskus 1304].* Istanbul and Constantinople: Nefasset, 1914.

Reynolds, Dwight. *Interpreting the Self.* Berkeley: University of California Press, 2001.

Reynolds, Gabriel. *A Muslim Theologian in a Sectarian Milieu.* Leiden: Brill, 2004.

Riffaterre, Michael. 'Describing Poetic Structures: Two Approaches to Baudelaire's *les Chats*'. *Yale French Studies* 36/37 (1966): 200–42.

Riley-Smith, Jonathan, ed. *The Oxford History of the Crusades.* Oxford: Oxford University Press, 1999.

——. 'Islam and the Crusades in History and Imagination, 8 November 1898–11 September 2001'. *Crusades* 2 (2003): 151–67.

Riquer, Martín de. *Història de la literatura catalana.* 4 vols. Barcelona: Edicions Ariel, 1964–72.

Rodríguez de la Peña, Manuel Alejandro. 'Los reyes bibliófilos: bibliotecas, cultura escrita y poder en el Occidente medieval'. *En la España Medieval* 33 (2010): 9–42.

Rodríguez-Velasco, Jesús D. *Castigos para celosos, consejos para juglares.* Madrid: Gredos, 1999.

——. *Ciudadanía, soberanía monárquica y caballería: poética del orden de caballería.* Madrid: Akal, 2009.

——. *Order and Chivalry: Knighthood and Citizenship in Late Medieval Castile.* Philadelphia: University of Pennsylvania Press, 2010.

Roest, Bert and H. L. J. Vanstiphout. *Aspects of Genre and Type in Pre-Modern Literary Cultures.* Groningen: Styx, 1999.

Rogers, Donna. '*Cantigas de Santa Maria* 2–25 and their Castilian Prose Versions'. *Estudios alfonsinos y otros escritos.* Ed. Nicolás Toscano. New York: National Hispanic Foundation for the Humanities, 1991.

Rosenstein, Roy. 'The Voiced and the Voiceless in the *Cancioneiros*: The Muslim, the Jew, and the Sexual Heretic as *Exclusus Amator*'. *La corónica* 26.2 (Spring 1998): 65–75.

Rowson, Everett K. 'Religion and Politics in the Career of Badi` al-Zaman al-Hamadhani'. *Journal of the American Oriental Society* 107 (1987): 653–73.

——. 'The Categorization of Gender and Sexual Irregularity in Medieval Arabic Vice Lists'. *Body Guards: The Cultural Politics of Gender Ambiguity.* Eds Julia Epstein and Kristina Straub. London and New York: Routledge, 1991. 50–79.

al-Saʿāfīn, Ibrāhīm, ed. *Fī miḥrāb al-maʿrifa.* Beirut: Dār al-gharb al-islāmī, 1997.

Sadān, Yūsuf (Joseph Sadan). 'The Division of the Day and Programme of Work of the Caliph al-Manṣūr'. *Studia Orientalia Memoriae D. H. Baneth Dedicata.* Eds Joshua Blau, et al. Jerusalem: Magnes Press, 1979. 255–73.

——. *Maṣdar jadīd min al-fatra al-būwayhiyya.* Tel Aviv: Tel Aviv University, 1980.

——. *Al-adab al-^{c}arabī al-hāzil wa-nawādir al-thuqalā'.* Tel Aviv: Tel Aviv University, 1983.

——. *Nuṣūṣ min al-nathr al-^{c}abbāsī*: Tel Aviv: Tel Aviv University, 1983.

Sadeghi, Behnam, Asad Ahmed, et al., eds. *Islamic Cultures, Islamic Contexts: Essays in Honor of Professor Patricia Crone.* Leiden: Brill, 2015.

Said, Edward. *Culture and Imperialism.* New York: Random House, 1993.

——. *Orientalism.* New York: Vintage Books, 1994.

——. 'Impossible Histories: Why the Many Islams Cannot be Simplified'. *Harper's* 67 (2002): 69–74.

——. 'Living in Arabic'. *Al-Ahram Weekly* 677 (2004): 37 pars. < http://weekly.ahram.org.eg/2004/677/cu15.htm> (last accessed 20 January 2010).

Sales, Roger. *English Literature in History 1780–1830.* London: Hutchinson, 1983.

Salisbury, Joyce E. *Medieval Sexuality: A Research Guide.* New York and London: Garland Publishing, 1990.

Sallām, Muḥammad Zaghlūl. *Al-Adab fī l-^{c}aṣr al-ayyūbī.* Alexandria: Munsha'at al-ma^{c}ārif, 1990.

Salvador Martínez, H. *Alfonso X, el Sabio: una biografía.* Madrid: Polifemo, 2003.

Samir, Khalil and Jørgen Nielsen, eds. *Christian Arabic Apologetics during the Abbasid Period, 750–1258.* Leiden: Brill, 1994.

Samsó, Julio. 'Alfonso X'. *The Biographical Encyclopedia of Astronomers.* Eds Thomas Hockey, et al. New York: Springer, 2007.

Sánchez-Prieto Borja, Pedro. 'El castellano escrito en torno a Sancho IV'. *La literatura en la época de Sancho IV.* Eds Carlos Alvar and José Manuel Lucía Megías. Alcalá de Henares: Universidad de Alcalá, 1996. 257–86.

Sancho de Sopranis, Hipólito. *Juegos de toros y cañas en Jerez de la Frontera.* Jerez: Centro de Estudios Jerezanos, 1960.

Sanders, Paula. *Ritual, Politics, and the City in Fatimid Egypt.* Albany: State University of New York Press, 1994.

Santangelo, Salvatore. *Dante e i trovatori provenzali.* Catania: Università di Catania, 1959.

Satō, Tsugitaka. *State and Rural Society in Medieval Islam.* Leiden: Brill, 1997.

Saunders, J. J. (John Joseph). *A History of Medieval Islam.* London and New York: Routledge and Kegan Paul, 1965.

Savant, Sarah Bowen. *The New Muslims of Post-Conquest Iran: Tradition, Memory, and Conversion*. Cambridge: Cambridge University Press, 2013.

Al-Sayyid-Marsot, Afaf Lutfi, ed. *Society and the Sexes in Medieval Islam*. Malibu: Undena Publications, 1979.

Scarborough, Connie L. *Women in Thirteenth-Century Spain as Portrayed in Alfonso X's* Cantigas de Santa Maria. Lewiston, NY: E. Mellen Press, 1993.

——. 'Las voces de las mujeres en las *Cantigas de Santa María* de Alfonso X'. *Asociación internacional de hispanistas: Actas Irvine 92: La mujer y su representación en las literaturas hispánicas*. Ed. Juan Villegas Morales. Irvine: University of California Irvine, 1994. 16–24.

——. *A Holy Alliance: Alfonso X's Political Use of Marian Poetry*. Newark, DE: Juan de la Cuesta, 2009.

Schaffer, Martha E. 'The Galician-Portuguese Tradition and the Romance *Kharjas*'. *Portuguese Studies* 3 (1987): 1–20.

Schaus, Margaret, ed. *Women and Gender in Medieval Europe: An Encyclopedia*. New York and Oxford: Taylor & Francis, 2006.

Schimmel, Annemarie. *Islamic Names*. Edinburgh: Edinburgh University Press, 1997.

Schmitt, Arno. *Bio-Bibliography of Male-Male Sexuality and Eroticism in Muslim Societies*. Berlin: Verlag Rosa Winkel, 1995.

Scholberg, Kenneth. *Sátira e invectiva en la España medieval*. Madrid: Gredos, 1971.

Setton, Kenneth, M.W. Baldwin, Harry Hazard et al., eds. *A History of the Crusades*. 6 vols. Madison: University of Wisconsin Press, 1969–89.

Al-Shaar, Nuha. *Ethics in Islam: Friendship in the Political Thought of Al-Tawḥīdī and His Contemporaries*. London and New York: Routledge, 2014.

Shagrir, Iris. 'The Parable of the Three Rings: A Revision of its History'. *Journal of Medieval History* 23.2 (1997): 163–77.

Shahîd, Irfan. 'Review Articles: Arabic Literature to the End of the Umayyad Period'. *Journal of the American Oriental Society* 106.3 (1986): 529–38.

Sharlet, Jocelyn. *Patronage and Poetry in the Islamic World*. London: I. B. Tauris, 2011.

Shatzmiller, Maya, ed. *Crusaders and Muslims in Twelfth-Century Syria*. Leiden: Brill, 1993.

Shklovsky, Viktor. *Theory of Prose*. Trans. Benjamin Sher. Elmwood Park, IL: Dalkey Archive Press, 1990.

Smith, J. Mark, ed. *Time in Time*. Montreal: McGill-Queen's University Press, 2013.

Smoor, Pieter. *Wazāra: The Killer of Many Husbands*. Cairo: Institut Français d'Archéologie Orientale (IFAO), 2007.

Snow, Joseph T. 'Poetic Self-Awareness in Alfonso X's *Cantiga* 110'. *Kentucky Romance Quarterly* 26.4 (1979): 421–32.

——. 'The Central Rôle of the Troubadour *Persona* of Alfonso X in the *Cantigas de Santa Maria*'. *Bulletin of Hispanic Studies* 56 (1979): 305–16.

——. 'Alfonso X: sus Cantigas ... Apuntes para su (auto) biografía literaria'. *Josep María Solá-Solé: homage, homenaje, homenatge*. Ed. Antonio Torres-Alcalá. Barcelona: Puvill, 1984. 79–90.

Socarrás, Cayetano J. *Alfonso X of Castile: A Study on Imperialistic Frustration*. Barcelona: Hispam, 1975.

Soifer, Maya. 'Beyond *convivencia*: Critical Reflections on the Historiography of Interfaith Relations in Christian Spain'. *Journal of Medieval Iberian Studies* 1 (2009): 19–35.

Sourdel, Dominique. *Le vizirat abbaside de 749 à 936 (132 à 324 de l'hégire)*. 2 vols. Damascus: Institut français de Damas, 1959–60.

Spellberg, Denise A. 'Nizam al-Mulk's Manipulation of Tradition'. *Muslim World* 78/2 (1988): 111–17.

Sperl, Stefan. 'Islamic Kingship and Arabic Panegyric Poetry in the Early 9th Century'. *Journal of Arabic Literature* 8 (1977): 20–35.

——. *Mannerism in Arabic Poetry*. Cambridge: Cambridge University Press, 1989.

—— and Christopher Shackle, eds. *Qasida Poetry in Islamic Asia and Africa*. 2 vols. Leiden: Brill, 1996.

Spivak, Gayatri Chakravorty. 'Can the Subaltern Speak?' *Marxism and the Interpretation of Culture*. Eds Cary Nelson and Lawrence Grossbert. Urbana: University of Illinois Press, 1988. 271–313.

Stallybrass, Peter and Allon White. *The Politics and Poetics of Transgression*. Ithaca: Cornell University Press, 1986.

Stanesco, Michel. *Jeux d'errance du chevalier médiéval: aspects ludiques de la fonction*. Leiden: Brill, 1988.

Steiner, Peter. *Russian Formalism: A Metapoetics*. Ithaca: Cornell University Press, 1984.

Stern, Gertrude. *Marriage in Early Islam*. London: Royal Asiatic Society, 1939.

Stetkevych, Jaroslav. *Muḥammad and the Golden Bough*. Bloomington: Indiana University Press, 1996.

Stetkevych, Suzanne. *Abū Tammām and the Poetics of the ʿAbbāsid Age*. Leiden: Brill, 1991.

——. *The Mute Immortals Speak: Pre-Islamic Poetry and the Poetics of Ritual.* Ithaca: Cornell University Press, 1993.

——. *The Poetics of Islamic Legitimacy*. Bloomington: Indiana University Press, 2002.

——. 'From *Jāhiliyyah* to *Badīʿiyyah*: Orality, Literacy, and the Transformations of Rhetoric in Arabic Poetry'. *Oral Tradition* 25.1 (2010): 211–30.

Stewart, Susan. *Poetry and the Fate of the Senses.* Chicago: University of Chicago Press, 2002.

——. 'What Praise Poems Are For'. *PMLA* 120.1 (2005): 235–45.Stone, Marilyn. *Marriage and Friendship in Medieval Spain: Social Relations According to the Fourth Partida of Alfonso X.* New York: P. Lang, 1990.

Surdich, Luigi. *La Cornice di Amore.* Pisa: ETS Editrice, 1987.

Swartz, David. *Culture & Power*. Chicago: University of Chicago Press, 1997.

Szombathy, Zoltán. *Mujūn: Libertinism in Medieval Muslim Society and Literature.* Cambridge: E. J. W. Gibb Memorial Trust, 2013.

Ṭabāna, Badawī Aḥmad. *Al-Ṣāḥib Ibn ᶜAbbād: al-wazīr al-adīb al-ᶜālim.* Cairo: Al-Mu'assasa al-Miṣrīya al-ᶜĀmma li-l-Ta'līf wa-l-Tarjama wa-l-Ṭibāᶜa wa-l-Nashr, 1963.

Talib, Adam, Marle Hammond, and Arie Schippers, eds. *The Rude, the Bad and the Bawdy: Essays in Honour of Professor Geert Jan van Gelder*. Cambridge: E. J. W. Gibb Memorial Trust, 2014.

Tavani, Giuseppe. *A poesía lírica galego-portuguesa.* Trans Rosario Álvarez Blanco and Henrique Monteagudo. Vigo: Galaxia, 1986.

al-Tawātī, Muṣṭafā. *Al-Muthaqqafūn wa-l-sulṭa fī l-ḥaḍāra al-ᶜarabiyya: al-dawla al-buwayhiyya namūdhajan.* 2 vols. Tunis: Manshūrāt al-Maᶜhad al-ᶜĀlī li-Lughāt, 1999.

Thompson, Augustine. *Francis of Assisi: A New Biography*. Ithaca: Cornell University Press, 2012.

Tolan, John. 'Salâh al-Dîn in the Medieval European Imagination'. *Images of the Other: Europe and the Muslim World before 1700.* Ed. David Blanks. Cairo: American University in Cairo Press, 1996. 7–38.

——. *Saint Francis and the Sultan*. Oxford: Oxford University Press, 2009.

Torres Fontes, Juan. 'La cultura murciana en el reinado de Alfonso X'. *Murgetana* 14 (1960): 57–89.

Touati, Houari. *Islam and Travel in the Middle Ages.* Trans. Lydia Cochrane. Chicago: University of Chicago Press, 2010.

Touber, Anton, ed. *Le rayonnement des troubadours*. Amsterdam and Atlanta: Rodopi, 1998.

Touma, Habib Hasan. 'Indications of the Arabian Musical Influence on the Iberian Peninsula from the 8th to the 13th Century'. *Symposium Alfonso X el Sabio y la música*. Ed. unknown. Madrid: Sociedad Española de Musicología, 1987. 137–50.

Tsafrir, Nurit. 'The Beginnings of the Ḥanafī School in Iṣfahān'. *Islamic Law and Society* 5.1 (1998): 1–21.

Tyerman, Christopher. *God's War: A New History of the Crusades*. Cambridge, MA: Harvard University Press, 2006.

University of St Andrews. *Occasional Papers of the School of Abbasid Studies, 2*. St Andrews: Scottish Academic Press, 1990.

ᶜUwaiḍa, Kāmil Muḥammad Muḥammad. *Al-Ṣāḥib Ibn-ᶜAbbād: al-wazīr al-adīb*. Beirut: Dār al-Kutub al-ᶜIlmiyya, 1994.

Vadet, Jean-Claude. *L'Esprit courtois en Orient dans les cinq premiers siècles de l'Hégire*. Paris: G.-P. Maisonneuve et Larose, 1968.

van Gelder: see Gelder.

Velasco y Mèra, Alberto de. *XVI cantares de amor e mal-dizer*. Lisbon: G. M. Sequeira, 1935.

Villalon, L. J. Andrew and Donald Kagay, eds. *Crusaders, Condottieri, and Cannon*. Leiden: Brill, 2003.

Villares, Ramón. 'Castillos frente a castros: La edad media en la identidad nacional gallega'. *Historia Social* 69 (2011): 3–24.

Vleck, Amelia Van. *Memory and Re-Creation in Troubadour Lyric*. Berkeley: University of California Press, 1990.

Wacks, David. *Framing Iberia*. Leiden: Brill, 2007.

Waldman, Peter. 'A Historian's Take on Islam Steers U.S. in Terrorism Fight'. *The Wall Street Journal* 3 February 2004. <http://online.wsj.com/news/articles/SB107576070484918411> (last accessed 12 June 2014).

Watt, W. Montgomery. *The Influence of Islam on Medieval Europe*. Edinburgh: Edinburgh University Press, 1972.

Weaver, Elissa, ed. *The* Decameron *First Day in Perspective*. Toronto: University of Toronto Press, 2004.

Weiss, Julian. *The 'Mester De Clerecía': Intellectuals and Ideologies in Thirteenth-Century Castile*. Woodbridge: Tamesis, 2006.

Westermarck, Edward. *The History of Human Marriage*. New York: Allerton Book Co., 1922.

Westerman, William. 'Epistemology, the Sociology of Knowledge, and the *Wikipedia* Userbox Controversy'. *Folklore and the Internet: Vernacular Expression in a Digital World*. Ed. Trevor J. Blank. Logan: Utah State University Press, 2009.

White, Hayden V. *Tropics of Discourse: Essays in Cultural Criticism*. Baltimore: Johns Hopkins University Press, 1986.

Wiet, Gaston. *Baghdad: Metropolis of the Abbasid Caliphate*. Trans. Seymour Feiler. Norman: University of Oklahoma Press, 1971.

William of Newburgh. *The History of English Affairs*. Ed. and trans. P. G. Walsh and M. J. Kennedy. 2 vols. Warminster: Aris & Phillips, 1988.

Williams, Raymond. *Keywords*. Oxford and New York: Oxford University Press, 1985.

Wilson, Rob and Christopher Connery, eds. *The Worlding Project: Doing Cultural Studies in the Era of Globalization*. Berkeley: North Atlantic Books, 2007.

Winterling, Aloys, ed. *Zwischen 'Haus' und 'Staat': Antike Höfe im Vergleich*. Munich: Oldenbourg, 1997.

Wright, J. W., Jr and Everett K. Rowson, eds. *Homoeroticism in Classical Arabic Literature*. New York: Columbia University Press, 1997.

Yaren, Özgür. 'Interview with Martin Jay on Violence, Fundamentalism and Free Speech'. *Ilef* 2.1 (2015): 139–50.

al-Zuhayrī, Maḥmūd. *Al-Adab fī ẓill banī buwayh*. Cairo: Maṭbaᶜat al-Amāna, 1949.

Index

ᶜAbbāsid Empire, 13–14, 184
  and Hussein, 178–9
  ideology, 15, 30–1
  literary contests, 2, 5, 15, 24–66
ᶜAbd al-Wāḥid, 180
Abu Bakr, 81, 83
Abū l-Faḍl ibn al-ᶜAmīd, 24, 25, 28, 122
  cultural primacy of, 41–2, 60
  poetry, 34, 35–6, 48
  prose/*kitāba*, 32, 37–41, 46
  slander against, 29
  as teacher, 42–3
Abū Nuwās, poetry, 27–8, 32, 46, 56
Abū Tammām, 90
Abū Uthmān al-Jāhiz, 13
adab, 27, 60, 73, 98
  of Crusades-era, 67, 74, 86–9
  defined, 33
al-ᶜĀḍid li-Dīn Allāh, 76, 77, 83, 85
ᶜAḍud al-Dawla, 28, 30
agenda-driven dialogue, 160
Akbari, Suzanne Conklin, 8, 9
al-Andalus, 152
al-Aqsa, 90, 91, 94
Albigensian Crusade, 18–19
Aleppo, 89, 94
Alexander the Great, 38, 157
Alfonso X, 105–40, 167
  as combative poet, 1–2, 5–6, 15–16, 19, 133–4, 136
  and diplomacy, 116, 117, 123, 134
  historiography, Saladin, 143–4
  Holy Roman Emperor campaign, 109, 123, 124–7
  laws (*Partidas*), 109–10, 121, 123, 133, 134–5
  military campaigns, 116, 127–8, 134
  as multiculturalist, 105, 178
  political goals of, 107, 108–9, 110
  political/economic discourse, 16, 120–7
  profane songs (CEM), 118–36
  sacred verse (CSM), 106–9, 111–18, 134, 135
  and the Virgin, 118
  will and testament, 105–6
Ali ibn Abi Talib, 83
Althusser, Louis, 169
Antiquity, figures of, 155, 170
apostasy, 55
Arab history, versions of, 52
Arabic, Classical, 25–6
  literature, 30, 33, 37
Arabic, dialects, 147
Arabic hegemony, 14, 20
Aristotle, 37–8, 121, 164
ᶜArqala, Ḥassān ibn Numayr, 75–8, 79, 81, 98
Arthur, King, 181
assassination *see* execution motif
Averroes, 155
Avicenna, 155
L'avventuroso ciciliano, 142, 160–2, 170
Ayyūbid literature, *ifranj*, 92–8
Ayyūbids, 68, 73, 87, 90; *see also* Saladin

Baath Party, 20, 181, 184
Babylon International Festival, 177–8
Baghdad, 14, 30, 42–3, 91
  construction, 25, 26
  and rise of Iranian courts, 31
Barbarossa, Frederick, 165, 166
Barmakids, 26–8, 32, 48
Basra, poetry at, 12–13, 179
Baybars, 116
Bedouins, 13, 52
belles-lettres, 3
Berque, Jacques, 180
Bible, 108

biography, 29
blasphemy, 55
Boccaccio, Giovanni, 142, 155, 159
  Decameron, 160, 162–9
Bondoudar (sultan), 114–15
Bourdieu, Pierre, 84
Burroughs, Charles, 5
Būyids, 24–41, 67
  and Barmakids, 27, 48
  gain Abbāsid legitimacy, 14, 19
  as patron-poets, 32–3, 55, 59
  poetry, 31–2
  promote Persian traditions, 14–15
  as Shīʿī, 30
Byzantines (*rūm*), 30, 93–4
Byzantium, 68

Cahen, Claude, 71
Cairo, 90, 91, 143
  Saladin's court in, 81–5
caliphs, 27, 83, 90
  and jihad, 84
  as patrons, 26, 32, 33, 35
  weakness of, 59, 82
cardinals, in CEM 33, 126
Castile, 11, 117, 121
Castro, Américo, 7, 143, 146
CEM, Alfonso's, 118–36
chancery prose, 3, 5, 14–15, 25, 79, 84
  viziers and, 31, 33
  see also Kitāba
Chanson de Roland, La, 18
chivalric narratives, 2, 17–18, 141–76
chivalry, 98, 135, 150–2
  desecration/violence to, 132, 168
  ideal of, 148–9
  and modern fascism, 181
  and order/violence, 182
  and power, 166–8
  roots of, 157
Christendom
  and land acquisition, 146
  medieval ideal of, 109
Christianity, conversion to, 157, 158
clergy, Spanish, and Alfonso, 123
clerics, criticism of, 159
clothes motif, 126–7
Cobb, Paul, 95
Commedia, La (Dante), 154–8, 170
comparative studies, 6, 20–1
competition, literary, 182–3, 184–6
  as creating order, 5
  ethos of, 2–3
  and viziers, 26
competition motif, 6, 89
conflict, negotiation of, 96–7
conjunctures, 169–70
Conti di antichi cavalieri, 158–9
conversion, 141, 157, 158
convivencia ('living together'), 7–8
Cortés García, Manuela, 178
courtly conduct, Alfonso on, 109
courtly interactions, rules of, 167
courtly reasoning, 156
courts, medieval
  as multicultural, 8–9
  power of, 7, 181
critical literature, on Arabic poetry, 49
Crusader identity, 93; *see also ifranj*
Crusades, 15–20, 67–99
  Alfonsine literature on, 111–40
  Christian European narratives of, 141–76, 185
  failures of, 159, 171, 185
  ideology, 18, 19, 70
  Islamic literature on, 67–104
  and jihad, 83–4
  Levantine, 116
  literary communities and, 18–19
  Orientalist theories on, 71–2
  Third, 98
CSM, Alfonso's, 106–9, 111–18, 134, 135
cultural transfer, 105

al-Ḍabbī, Abū Abbās, 4
Damascus, 91, 92, 95, 149
Dante, Alighieri, 142, 169–70, 185
  La Commedia, 154–8, 170
Decameron (Boccaccio), 160, 162–9
delegation, 84–5, 88
dining and food, 95–7
diplomacy, 80, 88, 116, 117, 123, 125, 151
diplomacy, Alfonso's, 108–9
Ḍiyā al-Dīn, 86, 87
Domingas Eanes, 128–33
drinking parties, 43–6

East–West, binary opposition, 8, 9
Egypt
  Alfonso and, 116
  courts of, 34
  Fatimids in, 67, 93, 98
  halal food, 96–7

and literary prizes, 183–4
Saladin and, 70, 75, 77, 163–4, 168
see also Cairo
elegies, 27, 184
elision, 40
eloquence, 10, 41
emirs, and viziers, 82; *see also* princes
empire, geopolitical work of, 168
entertainment literature, 33
epigrams, 14–15
epistles, 26, 31, 39, 42
eschatology, 94
Eschenbach, Wolfram von, 18
ethics, 162; *see also* hospitality
ethnic diversity, 93
ethnicity, 60
non-Arab, 51–2
execution motif, 74–81
Exodus, 164

fables, 6, 18, 142, 147
fascism, 177, 181–2
Fatima (daughter of the Prophet), 76
Fatimids, 67, 70, 74, 75, 76–7, 98
diplomacy of, 80
legacy, under Saladin, 93
literature of, 82–5
feminine lyric figure, 128–33
Fernando III, 117–18, 120
food and dining, 95–7, 119–22
Foucault, Michel, 9
France, 98, 143
Franks, 68, 71
free will, 57
French chivalric literature, 141, 143–5, 158–9
friendship motif, 156, 164–5, 167

Galician-Portuguese (language), 110–11, 114, 117, 125–6
GCU (*gran conquista de Ultramar, La*), 143–5, 147
generosity, 88, 141, 145
genetes, 116, 127, 128, 129–32, 135, 152, 153
Gibraltar, 6, 20, 111, 143
gift-giving, 116, 141, 153, 156, 164, 165, 166, 168
Glick, Thomas, 7–8
Goitein, Shelomo, 7
Golden Age, 27, 35
Granada, 1, 112, 117, 127
Grass, Günter, 183
Greek philosophy, translations, 37–8; *see also* translations
Gulf War (1991), 179
Gully, Adrian, 39, 41

Haidu, Peter, 169
halal food, 96–7
Hārūn al-Rashīd, 26, 27, 35
Hattin, Battle of, 89, 98
hijā, 12, 13, 47, 48–50, 53, 57, 58, 60
ᶜArqala's, 75–8, 79, 81, 98
Himmler, Heinrich, 181
history, Islamic versions, 11, 52; *see also* Crusades
Holy Roman Empire, Alfonso's campaign for, 109, 123, 124–7
homiletics *see* sermons
homoeroticism, 45, 46–7; *see also* sodomy
hospitality, 10, 121, 149, 166–7
hosting, 165–7, 169
humour, 52, 59, 120
Hussein, Saddam, 177–82, 184

Iberia
culture of, 7–8, 19, 113, 143, 146–7, 152
languages of, 110, 126
wars, 111–12, 113, 116, 142, 146
see also Alfonso X
Ibn ᶜAbbād, al-Sahib, 3–4, 24–5, 28, 29, 32, 41–2
literary attacks on, 47–8
literary education of, 42–7
poetry/works, 31, 42, 44–6, 47–60
provincial court, Arabophones in, 30
Ibn al-Rabīᶜ 27
Ibn al-Zakī family, 89, 91, 92
Ibn Baqiyya, 28
Ibn Bullakā, 39, 41
Ibn Mattawayh, 53–7
Ibn ᶜAbbād, al-Sahib, 111
Ibrahim, Sonallah, 183–4
identity categories, 6–7
ideology, 51, 52, 106
of conquest, 185
Hussein's cult of personality, 181
of *mujūn*, 49
Persian and Arab, 30–1
Saladin as symbol of, 70, 72–3
of taxation, 121
see also Christendom

ifranj, 68, 73, 78–9, 92–8
ᶜImād al-Dīn, 78–81, 86–8, 128
imams, 89–92
incest, 50
instructional prose, 96–7
insult, politics of, 58–9
intertextuality, 142
invective, 54, 68; *see also hijā*
Iran, 3, 31, 67
Iranians *see* Būyids
Iran-Iraq War, 179–80, 181
Iraq, 5, 11, 67
  literary contests, 2
Iraq, modern, 20, 177–82
Irwin, Robert, 69–70
Isfahan, 3, 4
Italian chivalric narratives, 141–3, 154–76
Italy, 2, 80, 149

Jaᶜfar al-Barmakī, 27
al-Jāḥiẓ, 38, 39
Jāsim, Laṭīf Nuṣayyif, 178
Jerusalem, 111, 112, 149
  feminised, 80–1
  as Islamic, 106
  Saladin conquers, 89–90, 94, 106
  sermons in, 89–92
Jew, literary portrayal of, 163–5
jihad, 83–4, 95
Jījān, ᶜAbbās, 184
Juan Manuel, Don, 16, 142
  Lucanor, 145–54, 156, 158, 160–1, 162, 165, 166, 168, 170–1
Judaism, 159, 164
Judas Maccabeus, 108
judiciary, 91–2

khamriyya (wine poem), 44–6
al-Khwārizmı, Abū Bakr, 3–4
kings, as patrons, 33; *see also* princes
Kinoshita, Sharon, 9, 168
Kitāba, 31–2, 36–41, 42, 46
knighthood, 171
  and modern military regimes, 177
knights, 114, 121, 125–6, 145
  and Alfonso, 123
  education of, 150–1
  and failure at chivalry, 131, 132, 133, 135, 148
  literary discourse on, 17–18
  and *palanciano*, 1
  see also chivalry
Kraemer, Joel L., 59
Kurdish Ayyūbids, 15

laws (*Partidas*), Alfonsine, 109–10, 121, 123, 133, 134–5
legal school, Saladin's, 91
letter-writing, 39–41; *see also* epistles
Levantine wars, 67–8, 111, 113, 171
Lewis, Bernard, 71–2
Limbo, 154–7, 170
Liu, Benjamin, 134
loans/gifts, 164–5
love/sex motifs, 56–7, 152–3
Lucanor see Juan Manuel, Don

Machiavelli, Niccolò, 169–70
madḥ, 76
majlis, 42, 43–6
Mamluk regime, 70
mannerist poetry, 53
marketplaces, poetry at, 12, 13
marriage, 168, 169
  violation of norms, 50–1
martial poems, 85, 88, 110, 112, 114–15, 133
Mary, Virgin, 106, 108, 111, 113, 114–15, 116, 117–18, 134
masculinity, 50–1, 53, 133, 148–9
Mecca, 81
media, on Islamic history, 73
medicine, Ibn ᶜAbbād's treatise on, 31
medieval identity categories, 6–7
medieval poetry, two-party model of, 122
Medieval Studies, 8, 10
Mediterranean Studies, 8
Menocal, Maria Rosa, 8
mentor-pupil dialectic, 150
Middle Ages
  and Islam, historians on, 71–2, 105
  and Rome, 109
  and Said's binary theory, 8
  specificity of, 9
Middle Eastern Studies, 71–2
migration, forced, 18–19
miracles, 115
Mirbad, Umayyad poets at, 12–13
Mirbad Poetry Festival, 178–82, 183
Morocco, 111, 112, 117, 127
mosques, 94, 118
Mosul, 85–9
al-Muhallabī, Abū Muḥammad
  drinking parties of, 43–6

poetry, 46–7
seeks literary retribution, 34–5
Muhammad, the Prophet, 14, 76, 81
Muḥyī l-Dīn ibn Yaḥyā, 89–92, 94
Muᶜizz al-Dawla, 46, 47
mujūn, 47–9, 55
multiculturalism, 6, 7–9, 105, 143, 164, 178
Muslim culture, Frankish interest in, 96–7
Muslims/Moors
depictions of, 18, 153
excluded from Alfonso's court, 135
Romance texts on, 142
see also genetes
al-Mutanabbī, Abū l-Ṭayyib
employed by Abū l-Faḍl, 34, 36, 38, 55
literary attacks of, 34–5, 55
Muᶜtazila, 57–8

narrative framing, 142, 185
al-Nāṣir li-Dīn Allāh, 90
nation-states, and cultural citizens, 183–4
nobility, 16, 121, 123, 128
women, 131
see also knights
North Africa, 171
North Africans *see genetes*
Novellino, 142, 160, 161, 162, 163, 170

occasional poems, 48, 49
odes, long-form, 11–12, 26; *see also qaṣīda*
Orientalism, 8, 9, 71, 71–2, 105, 177

Pae Gómez Charinho, 16, 119–24, 126, 167
palanciano, 1
panegyrics, 11–12, 15, 34, 38, 78–80, 99
on Hussein, 178–82, 184
on Saladin, 68, 69
parody, 122–3
Partidas see laws (*Partidas*)
patrons, patronage, 25, 28, 32–4, 57, 95, 97, 121
Dante on, 185
ethics of, 122–3
poets vie with, 31
performance, 39–40
Persian (language), 69, 70
Persian literary traditions, 14–15
Persians, 14, 50, 51, 52, 59, 68
phallic signifier, 118
pilgrimages, 111, 116, 159

plagiarism, 86, 87
plague, 162–3
poetry contests, Alfonsine, 1–2, 5–6, 15–16, 19, 133–4, 136
political/economic discourse, 25, 32–3, 120–7; *see also* laws (*Partidas*)
popes, 18, 123, 124–7, 171
power, discourse on, 9
praise works, 32, 52, 77, 87, 111, 117
and political power, 73, 74
see also panegyrics
princes, 3, 14, 28, 30, 46, 57
and viziers, 31, 35–6, 40–1, 47, 53, 59
profane songs (CEM), 118–36
propaganda, 52, 113, 114–15, 116, 128
prophecy, 56, 90
prose, Arabic, 28–9, 36–41, 69, 82–5, 90, 95–8
prostitution, 128–9, 132–3
Provençal poetry, 118–19

Qābūs ibn Wushmagīr, 53
al-Qāḍī l-Fāḍil, 82–5, 87, 90, 94–5
qaṣīda, 48, 49, 52, 79, 90, 181
as invective, 12
as panegyric, 11–12, 26
qiṭᶜa, 48, 49, 50–1, 55–6, 79
Qur'an, 54–6, 57, 81, 94, 115

Ray, 28, 36, 42
Remensnyder, Amy, 116
Renaissance, European, 72, 105, 169
replacement motif, 82
Richard the Lionheart, 147, 153
risāla see epistles
Rome, Ancient, 108, 109
Roman-Jewish Treaty, 108
royalty, ambivalence towards, 36; *see also* caliphs; princes
Rukn al-Dawla, 39, 40, 46
rūm, 93–4

Saddam Hussein, 177–82, 184
Said, Edward, 8, 37, 40
Saladin, 5, 60, 67–104, 168
adopts ᶜAbbāsid courtly models, 67, 93
Arabic portrayals of, 68, 69, 70, 73, 81, 92, 98–9
capture of, 151
chivalry/generosity of, 145, 153, 155–6, 164, 169
as combative poet, 141

Saladin (*cont.*)
contests for writers/poets, 86–7
diplomacy of, 80
ethics and, 162
failure in sensual matters, 153
legend of, 16, 18, 20
love of poetry, 69–70, 85–6
in Mosul, 85–9
politics of, 70
religious identity of, 145, 157, 158–9, 162
revision of, 153–4
Christian European narratives of, 6, 141–76
as Sunni monarch, 99
Syrian campaigns, 89, 94, 98
as vizier-sultan, 82–4, 94–5
Saljūq regime, 88
Ṣamṣām al-Dawla, 30
Santiago de Compostela, 111
scholar-warriors, in jihad, 84
secretarial arts
and poetry, 25, 183
see also Kitāba
self/other binary, 7, 8, 9
sermons, 37, 89–92, 94, 95
Seville, 117, 118
sex, sexuality
illicit, 50–1, 53–7, 128–9, 131, 132–3
and military metaphor, 80–1
and the Virgin, 132
Shāwar, Abū Shujā^c 75, 77, 78–80, 81, 93
Shī^cism, 30, 74, 82, 83, 93
Shīrkūh (emir), 75, 76, 77, 78–9
Shu^cūbiyya, 51, 52, 58
singers and dancers, 128
slander, 1, 28, 29, 32, 53, 106, 111, 125
songs of (CEM), 118–36, 134
see also mujūn
sodomy, 55, 56–7
solitude, Saladin's, 155, 156
songbooks, Alfonso's *see* Alfonso X
Spain, 17, 18–19; *see also* Alfonso X; Iberia
Spanish chivalric narratives *see* Juan Manuel, Don
state ritual *see taqlid*
status, 35–6, 41, 45, 51
Saladin's, 70
viziers', 33
Stetkevych, Suzanne, 56
Subaltern Studies school, 9
Sunni, 30, 74, 77, 82, 83, 93, 99
Syria, 11, 70, 75, 114–15
Ayyūbids conquest in, 89
courts of, 34, 91
Saladin's campaigns in, 89, 94, 98
Shī^cism, 93

al-Tanūkhī, al-Muḥassin, 27
taqlīd, 82–5, 87, 90, 94–5
Tartus, 114–15
al-Tawḥīdī, Abū Ḥyyān
literary attacks of, 47–8, 49, 58, 59, 122
prose, 28–9, 47
taxation, 16, 98, 117, 120–2, 126, 171
Templar Knights, 114
Teutonic Knights, 181
al-Tha^cālibī, 31, 38, 49, 50
'Three Rings, The', 159–69
time, passage of, and wars, 94, 95, 97–8
Toledo, 116
translations, 37–8, 105, 124, 143–4, 152
travel motif, 149, 156
troubadours, 1–2, 5–6, 18–19, 111, 113, 119, 122, 130–1

Ultramar, 150, 151, 153
Umayyad poets, 11–13
universities, Western, 72
Usāma ibn Munqidh, 10, 85
Book of Contemplation, 95–8

van Gelder, Geert, 49
Vatican, 171
vergüença, 148–9, 154, 163
violence, and chivalry, 151
violence, social, 167
Virgil, 155
viziers
culture of, 24–66, 183
and emirs, 82

Wacks, David, 152, 153
Western Europeans *see ifranj*
Western scholarship, on Arabs *see* Orientalism
William of Tyre, *Historia*, 143–5
wine poems, 44–6, 56, 57, 58

youth, 45

Zangī dynasty, 79, 93

EU representative:
Easy Access System Europe
Mustamäe tee 50, 10621 Tallinn, Estonia
Gpsr.requests@easproject.com

www.ingramcontent.com/pod-product-compliance
Lightning Source LLC
Chambersburg PA
CBHW051115230426
43667CB00014B/2591
* 9 7 8 1 4 7 4 4 2 5 2 3 0 *